Spencer Tracy
Fox Film Actor

SPENCER TRACY FOX FILM ACTOR

The Pre-Code Legacy of a Hollywood Legend

Edited with Foreword by Brenda Loew
Introduction by James Fisher

New England Vintage Film Society, Inc.
Newton, Massachusetts

Copyright © 2008 by New England Vintage Film Society, Inc.

First Edition

Library of Congress Control Number: 2008904173
ISBN: Hardcover 978-1-4363-4138-7
Softcover 978-1-4363-4137-0

All rights reserved. No part of this book may be reproduced or transmitted in any form or by any means, electronic or mechanical, including photocopying, recording, or by any information storage and retrieval system, without permission in writing from the copyright owner.

Copyright Acknowledgments:

Excerpt from *Twinkle, Twinkle Little Star (but don't have sex or take the car)* (Harper & Row, NY. 1984.) Used with the permission of the author, Dick Moore, "once known as famous child star Dickie Moore" who appeared with Spencer Tracy in *Disorderly Conduct* and *Man's Castle*.

Excerpt from Harvard Film Archive Calendar Pre-Code Series. Haden Guest, Director. Used with Permission.

This book was printed in the United States of America.

To order additional copies of this book, contact:
Xlibris Corporation
1-888-795-4274
www.Xlibris.com
Orders@Xlibris.com
47406

Contents

Photo Credits 11
Foreword 15
Acknowledgments 19
The Films of Spencer Tracy 23
Introduction 27

Spencer Tracy at Fox: The Pre-Code Context 33
Up the River—Prison is Paradise 40
Up the River: Making Good in Comedy Prison 45
Quick Millions Message to the Masses:
    The American Dream Can Be Dangerous 53
Quick Millions: Unions and the Class Divide 58
Goldie: The Migration of the American Male 63
Goldie: A Black Mark for Relations Between the Sexes 68
Me and My Gal and Everyone Else:
    How a Comedy of Prohibition and Depression
    Puts Us All on the Same Level 73
Me and My Gal: Fanfare for the Everyday Hero 79
Countryside Blues: How the City Saves the Day in *Face in the Sky* ... 86
The Power and the Glory: Citizen Garner 92
The Power and the Glory: The Depression Never Looked So Good 97
"The power and the glory, what they can do to a man":
    Preston Sturges' Dark Vision of Success 103
Looking for Trouble and Finding Contentment: The Exciting Life of a
    Telephone Trouble Shooter 128
Bottoms Up:
    Spencer Tracy Comes Out on Top as a Hollywood Hero 135
Bottoms Up to Hollywood:
    Anyone Can Beat This Racket 142
Now I'll Tell: Crime Pays, At Least for the Story Rights 149
Cultural & Racial Stereotyping in *Marie Galante* 155
The International Perspective of *Marie Galante*:
    As Long as You Speak Our Language 159

It's a Small World After All:
   City Folk Run Smack-Dab Into Americana 165
Dante's Inferno: Pre-Code Decadence Falls to the Flames 172
Dante's Inferno: Tracy's Trial By Fire 179
Spencer Tracy: King of the Underworld 185
Spencer Tracy . . . Comedian?!? 201
Contributors 227

DEDICATION

To Spencer Tracy and his great film legacy and all those who love Spencer Tracy's films.

"When Spencer Tracy looked at you in a scene, you felt riveted. There was no place to hide."—Dick Moore

Photo Credits

Society Girl (1932) Spencer Tracy. Fox Film Corporation/Photofest.............. 2

Disorderly Conduct (1932) From left: Spencer Tracy, Dickie Moore. Fox Film Corporation/Photofest. 8

The Hard Guy (1930) Short. From left: Spencer Tracy, Valli Roberts, Katharine Alexander. Warner Bros. Pictures/Photofest. 21

Spencer Tracy (1931) Exclusive Portrait for Fox Film Corporation by Hal Phyfe. From a Private Collection © Fox Film Corporation. 26

The Power and The Glory (1933) Ad Mat. From a Private Collection © Fox Film Corporation..................................... 31

Up The River (1930) Humphrey Bogart, Spencer Tracy. From a Private Collection © Fox Film Corporation..................................... 38

Up The River (1930) From left, seated: Warren Hymer, Spencer Tracy. From left, standing: William Collier, Sr., Humphrey Bogart. From a Private Collection © Fox Film Corporation..................................... 44

Quick Millions (1931) From left: Spencer Tracy, George Raft. Fox Film Corporation/Photofest. 51

Quick Millions (1931) In foreground, from left: George Raft, Spencer Tracy. Fox Film Corporation/Photofest. 57

Goldie (1931) Jean Harlow, Spencer Tracy. Fox Film Corporation/Photofest. 61

Goldie (1931) Jean Harlow, Spencer Tracy.
From a Private Collection © Fox Film Corporation....................................67

Me and My Gal (1932) Spencer Tracy, Joan Bennett.
From a Private Collection © Fox Film Corporation....................................71

Me and My Gal (1932) Spencer Tracy, Joan Bennett.
Fox Film Corporation/Photofest. 78

Face in the Sky (1933) Spencer Tracy, Marian Nixon.
From a Private Collection © Fox Film Corporation....................................84

The Power and The Glory (1933) Colleen Moore, Spencer Tracy.
From a Private Collection © Fox Film Corporation....................................90

The Power and The Glory (1933) Helen Vinson, Spencer Tracy.
From a Private Collection © Fox Film Corporation....................................96

The Power and The Glory (1933) From left: Spencer Tracy,
Ralph Morgan. From a Private Collection © Fox Film Corporation. 102

Looking for Trouble (1934) From left: Jack Oakie, Spencer Tracy.
From a Private Collection © Fox Film Corporation.................................. 126

Bottoms Up (1934) Spencer Tracy, Pat Paterson.
Fox Film Corporation/Photofest. 133

Bottoms Up (1934) Original Herald.
From a Private Collection © Fox Film Corporation.................................. 141

Now I'll Tell (1934) From left: Spencer Tracy, Shirley Temple,
Alice Calhoun, Ronnie Cosby, Henry O'Neill.
From a Private Collection © Fox Film Corporation.................................. 147

Marie Galante (1934) Ketti Gallian, Spencer Tracy.
From a Private Collection © Fox Film Corporation.................................. 153

Marie Galante (1934) From left: Spencer Tracy, Leslie Fenton,
Robert Loraine. From a Private Collection © Fox Film Corporation....... 158

It's a Small World (1935) Wendy Barrie, Spencer Tracy, Raymond
Walburn. From a Private Collection © Fox Film Corporation. 163

Dante's Inferno (1935) Spencer Tracy (in tuxedo).
Fox Film Corporation/Photofest. 170

Dante's Inferno (1935) From left: Spencer Tracy,
Director Harry Lachman, Captain Jules Strasser (technical
consultant), L.B. MacDonald (ex-*Morro Castle* engineer), William
Clay (MacDonald's friend). From a Private Collection © Fox Film
Corporation. 178

20,000 Years in Sing Sing (1932) Spencer Tracy, Bette Davis.
From a Private Collection © First National Pictures. 184, 191

Me and My Gal (1932) Original Herald.
From a Private Collection © Fox Film Corporation. 200

Up The River (1930) Original Herald.
From a Private Collection © Fox Film Corporation. 225

Bottoms Up (1934) Original Herald.
From a Private Collection © Fox Film Corporation. 230

Foreword

"... A new and remarkable energy animated the American cinema between the coming of sound at the end of the 1920s and the strict enforcement of the 1934 Production Code censoring "unwholesome" onscreen behavior.... The twilight of the Jazz Age and the Great Depression encouraged directors and screenwriters to seriously examine the moral and sociopolitical underpinnings of the changing nation through frank and, quite often, extremely graphic stories designed to titillate and shock. Encouraged by the box office, Hollywood produced startling depictions of infidelity, prostitution, drug use, crime, homosexuality and miscegenation. The injustices of corporate capitalism and the sexual experimentation of the period, particularly by women, were also newly exploited as fitting subjects for the screen..."
—Harvard Film Archive Calendar Pre-Code Series

The New England Vintage Film Society, Incorporated (NEVFS)—a charitable, tax-exempt, non-profit, 501 (c) (3) public corporation as defined by the laws of the Commonwealth of Massachusetts and the Internal Revenue Service (IRS)—is committed to the preservation, restoration and presentation of classic and vintage American films to enlighten, enrich, educate and entertain.

We invite you to share in our mission extolling Hollywood's Golden Age and America's feature films of that era—evaluating our interpretations, findings, discoveries and viewpoints in view of the state of contemporary American society and world affairs.

Motion pictures created for mass audiences throughout the United States from the 1930s through the 1960s serve as important historical records documenting and reflecting America's prevailing social, cultural, economic, political, religious and moral attitudes of those decades.

By sponsoring special projects, activities and events, including but not limited to, publications, lectures, film series and film festivals, private screenings, acquiring and exhibiting memorabilia, selling merchandise and soliciting members, donors and grants—the New England Vintage Film Society, Inc. raises funds: 1) to affirm the significance of these films by actor, director, studio, genre, theme, etc.; and, 2) to preserve and restore Golden Age films at risk of loss.

One of our organization's goals towards fulfilling our mission is to preserve and restore legendary film actor Spencer Tracy's little known screen performances in his early 1930s films, most of which are from Fox's pre-Code era. Our effort is being realized, in the short term, by publishing this book of essays and images celebrating a selection of Mr. Tracy's essentially forgotten and "lost" Fox masterpieces, including:

Up the River (1930)
Quick Millions (1931)
Goldie (1931)
Me and My Gal (1932)
The Face in the Sky (1933)
The Power and the Glory (1933)
Looking for Trouble (1934)
Bottoms Up (1934)
Now I'll Tell ((1934)
Marie Galante (1934)
It's a Small World (1935)
Dante's Inferno (1935)

All materials in this book were provided by academicians, private collectors, vintage film aficionados and Tracy admirers with the intention that the general public will discover and appreciate Spencer Tracy's early motion picture career, especially in pre-Code Fox films. Each essay evaluates Tracy's characterization and the picture's storyline and provides an unfiltered window to the Depression-era presented in the movie connected to our world today. The films in this compilation represent a fraction of Mr. Tracy's 1930s pre-Code film performances.

Other pre-Code films Spencer Tracy appeared in are:

Six Cylinder Love (Fox, 1931)
She Wanted A Millionaire (Fox, 1932)
Sky Devils (United Artists, 1932)
Disorderly Conduct (Fox, 1932)

Young America (Fox, 1932)
Society Girl (Fox, 1932)
The Painted Woman (Fox, 1932)
20,000 Years in Sing Sing (Warner Bros.-First National, 1933)
Shanghai Madness (Fox, 1933)
The Mad Game (Fox, 1933)
Man's Castle (Columbia, 1933)
The Show-Off (MGM, 1934)

In 1904, Fox Film Corp. movie mogul William Fox opened his first entertainment venue, a nickelodeon, in Brooklyn. Today, Fox is owned by Rupert Murdoch's News Corp. Yet nearly all of Spencer Tracy's 1930s Fox films are forgotten. Time and neglect are dissolving these celluloid artworks. Most have yet to be fully preserved, restored and commercially distributed. However, from time to time unusual circumstances do prevail such as a rare screening of a 16mm collector's print; programming on Turner Classic Movies (TCM) or the Fox Movie Channel; and inclusion in a Film Forum (NYC) series, i.e. "Fox Before the Code," which, in December 2006, promoted:

Young Spencer Tracy

Years before he even heard of Katharine Hepburn and before prematurely becoming MGM's elder statesman, straight-from-Broadway Spencer Tracy was signed by Fox and became the studio's answer to James Cagney: a cocky, brash, wisecracking Irish-American, creating on-screen fireworks with such leading ladies as Joan Bennett, Jean Harlow and Alice Faye. Tracy stars in the following films in the series:

December 1/2: *ME AND MY GAL*
December 3: *GOLDIE*
December 6/7: *BOTTOMS UP*
December 9: *NOW I'LL TELL*
December 15: *LOOKING FOR TROUBLE*
December 15: *THE PAINTED WOMAN*
December 15: *QUICK MILLIONS*
December 20: *SHE WANTED A MILLIONAIRE*

Clearly, these films still hold up on re-screenings today!

True, Spencer Tracy's "nothing parts" in Fox's "nothing pictures"—as he called them—are not what we remember him for. Nor is he remembered for his outstanding dramatic pre-Code performance opposite Loretta Young in *Man's Castle* (Columbia, 1933), directed by Frank Borzage, in which we witness free lovers Tracy and Young swimming nude together, living together, in bed together and, subsequently, her unwed pregnancy. Nor do we visualize his magnificent pre-Code performance as Tom Connors in *20,000 Years in Sing Sing*, the only film he appeared in with Bette Davis—an intense, emotional gangster film about love, murder, guilt, innocence and the death penalty!

Tracy's genius and star quality as a young up-and-coming film actor is obvious in each and every one of his 1930s Fox films. The early screen images of Tracy honing his art and craft are truly inspirational and we can learn much from them even now. In 1935, at the end of the pre-Code era, Tracy left Fox, and, under contract to MGM, became 1938s biggest box-office attraction for his role as Manuel in *Captains Courageous*. In 1939, Tracy became the first actor to win a second consecutive Best Actor Oscar for his performance as Father Flanagan in MGM's *Boys Town*. His career is legendary: the stuff that dreams were made of during Hollywood's Golden Age. As Humphrey Bogart once remarked, "Spence is the best we have because you don't see the mechanism at work . . ."

The publication of this book comes 108 years after Spencer Tracy's birth on April 5, 1900 and 41 years following his death on June 10, 1967—two days before the United States Supreme Court declared in *Loving v. Virginia* all U.S. state laws prohibiting interracial marriage to be unconstitutional—and six months before the Christmastime release of *Guess Who's Coming to Dinner*, his final film with Katharine Hepburn, on the fitting subject of racial intermarriage.

The New England Vintage Film Society, Inc. is proud to keep before the public legendary film actor Spencer Tracy's outstandingly energetic legacy of lost performances in Fox's lively 1930s Depression-era pre-Code films—a rare selection of Americana from Hollywood's Golden Age that must be rediscovered, seen, heard, thought about, discussed and learned from today.

Brenda Loew
President
New England Vintage Film Society, Inc.

Acknowledgments

On behalf of the Board of Directors of the New England Vintage Film Society, Inc., I want to express my gratitude and thanks to the following individuals and institutions for their support and encouragement, guidance, expert assistance and patience with this book as it journeyed from being a thought, an idea and inspiration, to this final, finished product:

James Fisher, Professor and Head, Dept. of Theatre, U of North Carolina at Greensboro; Linda Harris Mehr, Director, Margaret Herrick Library, Los Angeles; William Russo, Coordinator, Professor, English, Curry College, Milton, MA; Haden Guest, Director, Harvard Film Archive, Harvard University; Cyndi Tracy; Judy Lewis; Mike Merrill; Tom Sturges; Dick Moore and Helaine Feldman, Dick Moore and Associates, NYC; Thomas Doherty, Professor of American Studies, Brandeis University; Rob Stone, Todd Weiner, C. Allen Giles and Mark Quigley, UCLA Film & Television Archive; Julie Graham, UCLA Arts Library Special Collections; Schawn Belston and Deborah Marriott, Fox Corp.; Anthony Labbate, George Eastman House, Rochester, NY; Eliot Stein, Village Voice, NYC; Barbara Hall, Greg Walsh and Brian Meacham, Academy of Motion Picture Arts and Sciences, Los Angeles; Doug McKeown, S. Victor Burgos and Buddy, Photofest, NYC; Elaine Gottlieb and Barbara Mende, Boston Chapter, National Writers Union; Ruth Van Stee, Grand Rapids MI Public Library; Brian Bengtson, Wisconsin Historical Society Press, Madison, WI; Gene Stavis, School of Visual Arts, NYC; Steve Leggett, National Film Preservation Board, Library of Congress, Washington, DC; Larry Smith, Cinerama Preservation Society, Inc. and Nitrate Film Specialist, Library of Congress; Jennifer Paxson, Reviewer, Cinefest, Cinevent, Cinesation; Christine Arnold Schroeder, American Academy of Dramatic Arts, NYC; Colleen Simpson, Technicolor Film Preservation, N. Hollywood, CA; David Wells, National Film Preservation Foundation, San Francisco; Christine Karatnytsky, Scripts Librarian, The Billy Rose Theatre

Collection, The New York Public Library for the Performing Arts; Katie Kramer and Yadirs Pizarro, PARS International Corp, NYC; Tracy Duggan, Boston Public Library; Paula Ogier and Jenna Moskowitz, Cambridge Center for Adult Education, Harvard Square, Cambridge, MA; Theo Gluck, Director of Film Library Restoration, Walt Disney Company; Rhea Gay Villacarlos, Xlibris Publishing, Philadelphia, PA; George Bragdon, Coolidge Corner Theatre, Brookline, MA; Mick Lasalle; Amy Hillgren Peterson; Judy Samelson; Eric and Lisa Sigman; Chris Dingman; Ray Delgado; Neal Godfrey; Jeremy Bond; Shelly Brisbin; Sean Connell; Cinzi Lavin; Charles Morrow; Paul Sherman; Eric Shoag.

The Films of Spencer Tracy

The Strong Arm (1930, Short, Vitaphone)
Taxi Talks (1930, Short, Vitaphone)
The Hard Guy (1930, Short, Warner Bros. Pictures, Inc./Vitaphone)
Up the River (1930, Fox)
Quick Millions (1931, Fox)
Six Cylinder Love (1931, Fox)
Goldie (1931, Fox)
She Wanted a Millionaire (1932, Fox)
Sky Devils (1932, Caddo-United Artists)
Disorderly Conduct (1932, Fox)
Young America (1932, Fox)
Society Girl (1932, Fox)
Painted Woman (1932, Fox)
Me and My Gal (1932, Fox)
20,000 Years in Sing Sing (1932, Fox)
The Face in the Sky (1933, Fox)
Shanghai Madness (1933, Fox)
The Power and the Glory (1933, Fox)
Man's Castle (1933, Columbia)
The Mad Game (1933, Fox)
Looking for Trouble (1934, 20th Century-United Artists)
The Show-Off (1934, MGM)
Bottoms Up (1934, Fox)
Now I'll Tell (1934, Fox)
Marie Galante (1934, Fox)
It's a Small World (1935, Fox)
The Murder Man (1935, MGM)
Dante's Inferno (1935, Fox)
Whipsaw (1935, MGM)

Riffraff (1936, MGM)
Fury (1936, MGM)
San Francisco (1936, MGM)
Libeled Lady (1936, MGM)
They Gave Him a Gun (1937, MGM)
Captains Courageous (1937, MGM)
Big City (1937, MGM)
Mannequin (1938, MGM)
Test Pilot (1938, MGM)
Boys Town (1938, MGM)
Stanley and Livingstone (1939, 20th Century-Fox)
I Take This Woman (1940, MGM)
Northwest Passage (1940, MGM)
Edison, the Man (1940, MGM)
Boom Town (1940, MGM)
Dr. Jekyll and Mr. Hyde (1941, MGM)
Men of Boys Town (1941, MGM)
Woman of the Year (1942, MGM)
Tortilla Flat (1942, MGM)
Keeper of the Flame (1942, MGM)
A Guy Named Joe (1943, MGM)
Thirty Seconds Over Tokyo (1944, MGM)
The Seventh Cross (1944, MGM)
Without Love (1945, MGM)
Cass Timberlane (1947, MGM)
The Sea of Grass (1947, MGM)
State of the Union (1948, MGM)
Edward, My Son (1949, MGM)
Adam's Rib (1949, MGM)
Malaya (1950, MGM)
Father of the Bride (1950, MGM)
Father's Little Dividend (1951, MGM)
The People Against O'Hara (1951, MGM)
Pat and Mike (1952, MGM)
Plymouth Adventure (1952, MGM)
The Actress (1953, MGM)
Broken Lance (1954, 20th Century-Fox)
Bad Day at Black Rock (1955, MGM)
The Mountain (1956, Paramount)
Desk Set (1957, 20th Century-Fox)
The Last Hurrah (1958, Columbia)

The Old Man and the Sea (1958, Warner Bros.)
Inherit the Wind (1960, United Artists)
The Devil at 4 O'Clock (1961, Columbia)
Judgment at Nuremberg (1961, United Artists)
How the West Was Won (1961, MGM)
It's a Mad, Mad, Mad, Mad World (1963, United Artists)
Guess Who's Coming to Dinner (1967, Columbia)

Introduction

The cinematic achievements of the iconic, indelible screen stars of the Golden Age of Hollywood—Greta Garbo, Clark Gable, Katharine Hepburn, Bette Davis, James Cagney, Humphrey Bogart, Joan Crawford, Fred Astaire, John Wayne, Judy Garland—are, thanks to art house cinemas, television, and DVD, there to be seen and seen again by film lovers despite the passage of the years. Contemporary society moves further and further away from the worlds depicted in their films, yet audiences in the first decade of the Third Millennium become increasingly interested in these appealing shadows of the silver screen. Many of them developed into fine actors, while others were merely "movie stars" with screen personas that were extensions of their own personalities. The Hollywood studio system tended to keep its stars in screen vehicles that exploited the characteristics audiences liked and many of the stars were comfortable with their images. Others resisted "type-casting" and fought for diversity in their work, seeking new challenges in varied characters and movie genres. Those stars with the skill and ambition to reach beyond their well-honed iconic persona tended to have more enduring careers, although those stars seem to have less-frequently inspired the "cult" followings acquired by some.

To a great extent, this has been the fate of Spencer Tracy, perhaps the finest and most versatile actor of that Golden Age generation of movie stars. His acting talent was such that he effortlessly entered any screen genre or character with ease, in fact with such ease that he seems not to act at all—he becomes the character with astonishing completeness. He effortlessly played the lightest comedy or the darkest drama with a simplicity and humanity that drew viewers close to the character and obscured the process of the actor at work. He acted with distinction in thoughtful dramas of social significance (*Fury, Bad Day at Black Rock, Judgment at Nuremberg*), romantic comedies (*Man's Castle, Woman of the Year, Adam's Rib, Pat and Mike*), screwball farces

(*Libeled Lady, It's a Mad, Mad, Mad, Mad World*), adventure epics (*Captains Courageous, Northwest Passage, The Mountain, The Devil at Four O'Clock*), gangster melodramas (*Quick Millions, 20,000 Years in Sing Sing, Now I'll Tell*), drawing room dramas (*Keeper of the Flame, Edward, My Son*), biopics (*Stanley and Livingstone, Boys Town, Edison, the Man*), courtroom dramas (*Inherit the Wind*), westerns (*Sea of Grass, Broken Lance*), film noir (*The People Against O'Hara*), horror (*Dr. Jekyll and Mr. Hyde*), and even a musical (*Bottoms Up*). Among Tracy's contemporaries, only James Cagney and Bette Davis challenged his dominance in virtually every screen genre. Unlike them, however, Tracy is not remembered for any particular set of mannerisms nor is he associated with a particular kind of character. Cagney's pugnacious and electric vitality in gangster films or the occasional musical and the intensely neurotic, eye-popping, cigarette puffing, sashaying anti-heroines played by Davis in melodramas have insured their iconic status, but Tracy's only mannerism seems to be the lack of any, while at the same time there is no particular character he is most associated with in the audience's memory, although some might argue that across a variety of films he presented an image of the typical American male of the lower and middle classes, a profoundly decent and modest man of strength and integrity. These qualities are certainly evident in many films, but Tracy's lexicon of screen characters included as many evil and misguided men as lovable lugs and mugs, understanding fathers and priests, and wise, socially-committed leaders. While Cagney and Davis—and other screen legends of the 1930s—provided imitators and comedians with vivid and consistent characteristics, Tracy defies imitation. While Marlon Brando, James Dean, and Montgomery Clift are credited with bringing greater realism and naturalness to screen acting in the 1950s, Tracy was already doing what they did in the early 1930s.

The lack of mannerisms in Tracy's acting is only part of his cinematic legacy and it is certainly less significant than the depth and humanity of his acting. It may seem banal to state it so directly, but Tracy's characters—good and bad, tragic or comic (and he deftly combined seriousness with humor in virtually all of his characterizations)—are real people grappling with real life and, as such, he is among the most "approachable" of Hollywood stars. Tracy was simply so good that his mastery of the craft of acting permitted him to consistently deliver pure essences of the human experience, devoid of mannerism or artifice unless a particular character demanded such embellishment. The viewer does not see the actor at work—or a vivid star personality overwhelming a role—the image is of a human being thinking and behaving in a life situation. Tracy is also a great inter-actor and reactor, frequently achieving his strongest effects interacting with his fellow players, responding to their impulses with a spontaneity that is natural and affecting.

Had Tracy come to the screen in the 1910s or 1920s, he would have been a great silent film star since frequently his finest moments come not when he is speaking, but when he is listening. An obvious case in point can be found in *Father of the Bride* (1950), in which most of his performance is involved in playing off the other characters and the increasingly surreal events surrounding the wedding of his daughter (played by Elizabeth Taylor). Tracy's performance in this small comic gem of a film is difficult to describe—the viewer creates the comedy through him, by sensing what he is thinking through the slightest of reactions in his face and body language. Even for this most "natural" of actors, Tracy's performance in *Father of the Bride* offers a mastery of screen acting so total that there is no technique in evidence.

Admiration of Tracy's acting is reflected in the ways in which generations of his fellow actors, critics, and audiences think about his achievements. Over eighty films in thirty-seven years, but the first five years of his screen career—Tracy's years under contract to the Fox Studio (with occasional loan-outs to Warner Bros. and Columbia)—are almost unknown even to the most educated film fan. His reputation for versatility and naturalness are based on the twenty years (1935-1955) he acted at Metro-Goldwyn-Mayer and for the subsequent dozen years (1955-1967) when he was an independent actor. Yet the nearly twenty-five films he made prior to his move to M-G-M are remarkable in that they impressively demonstrate the range and diversity of characters he would consistently deliver throughout his post-Fox career (and which would earn him two Academy Awards and a total of nine nominations).

The essays in this wide-ranging volume focused on Tracy's early career offer guidance and bring to rich life not only Tracy's artistry, but also the dawn of sound films and pre-production code era during which they were made, as well as the cultural values, fears and deprivations, and vast social changes inherent in the Great Depression. Many of the movie titles featured will be unknown to most cinema lovers; such forgotten features as *Looking for Trouble, Bottoms Up, Goldie, Face in the Sky, Dante's Inferno*, and *It's a Small World*, among others, may rate attention merely for the presence of Tracy, an entertaining plot, or one or more of his co-stars or director, usually at the beginning of careers that would eventually provide finer achievements, while other essays focus on little-known films deserving more prominent placement among classic and near-classic films, including *Up the River, Quick Millions, Me and My Gal, Man's Castle, Marie Galante, 20,000 Years in Sing Sing*, and *The Power and the Glory*. An impressive and diverse array of contributors bring to life the finest and the weakest of these films, all of which are enriched by Tracy's acting and all of which demonstrate that the versatility and naturalness of his acting was in ample evidence from the very beginning of his long and illustrious career.

The intentions of this collection of varied essays on Tracy's films from the Fox era include a desire to introduce (or more aptly, reintroduce) these films to Tracy's admirers and cinephiles in general, expand and enhance knowledge of Tracy's cinematic achievement, and return these obscure or under-appreciated works to movie and television screens—and to encourage their restoration (and availability in digitized commercial formats). Spencer Tracy, cinemactor par-excellence, deserves nothing less—his unchallenged reputation as the finest of American screen actors stands with or without these early films, but the good news is that with them the rich tapestry of his artistry takes on new colors—and the roots of his art in all its variety and nuance are preserved within them for all to see.

James Fisher
2008

...AND THIS PICTURE IS *TOO BIG* TO JUDGE BY ORDINARY STANDARDS

That's why an entirely new method of screen production had to be devised to tell it. Drama so amazingly unusual, so powerful that present day methods were inadequate to bring it to the screen. Presented in NARRATAGE — talking pictures' newest wonder — forever revolutionizing screen entertainment. Marking the biggest step forward since the introduction of sound and another great triumph for FOX FILM. Watch for your theatre's announcement of this sensational picture.

THE POWER AND THE GLORY

SPENCER TRACY • COLLEEN MOORE
RALPH MORGAN • HELEN VINSON
A JESSE L. LASKY PRODUCTION
Directed by William K. Howard   Story by Preston Sturges

Spencer Tracy at Fox: The Pre-Code Context

Thomas Doherty

The career of Spencer Tracy at Fox dovetails neatly with one of the most notorious—and beloved—periods in American motion picture history: the outbreak of sex, immorality, and insurrection known as pre-Code Hollywood cinema. Though Tracy was never as saucy as Mae West, as lecherous as Groucho Marx, or as caddish as Warren William, the rookie film actor took on a variety of roles that gave full expression to the unbridled eroticism, soaring liberation, and dark cynicism unleashed on the American screen in the early 1930s. By the time Tracy donned a priest's collar for MGM in *San Francisco* (1936), both the outlines of his screen persona and the fabric of Hollywood cinema had been cut to a fashion more stiff-necked, button-down, and, frankly, Catholic.

To film programmers, buffs, and historians, pre-Code Hollywood shines as the marquee name for a privileged zone of relative screen freedom that dates from (roughly) 1930 to (precisely) July 15, 1934, a time when trigger-happy gangsters, wisecracking dames, and subversive rebels ran wild through the lawless territory of American cinema. To survey the titles is to take the temperature of the type: *Red Headed Woman* (1932) and *Baby Face* (1933), where shameless hussies trade horizontal favors for vertical mobility; *Skyscraper Souls* (1932) and *Employee's Entrance* (1933), where ruthless capitalists violate business ethics and female chastity at will; and *I Am A Fugitive from a Chain Gang* (1932) and *Wild Boys of the Road* (1933), where the forces of law and order are the true criminals in a bleak Depression landscape.

It was fun while it lasted. In 1934, capitulating to outraged moralists and government coercion, Hollywood empowered an in-house agency known as the Production Code Administration (PCA) to actually enforce the document the major studios had pledged to abide by in 1930: the Production Code, a set of commandments mandating a strict moral universe on screen. The PCA would snip and scrub studio system cinema until 1968, when the regime was replaced by the alphabet ratings system we know today.

Hollywood submitted to the rigorous oversight of the PCA because the alternatives to "censorship at the source" were far worse. After all, motion picture censorship had been a fact of creative and commercial life from the very birth of the medium. By common consent, motion pictures—an entertainment accessible to all levels of society and degrees of moral temperament, including unassimilated immigrants, impressionable juveniles, and other menacing types—required editorial supervision from more mature, pious, and usually Protestant sensibilities. Keeping pace with the rise of the new medium, city and state censor boards proliferated to examine, shred, and ban the unruly, uppity and increasingly popular art that (so ruled the Supreme Court in 1915) was "a business pure and simple" and therefore not protected by the First Amendment.

In 1922, beset by a spate of sensational scandals that seemed to validate Hollywood's reputation as a Sodom on the Pacific, the studio chieftains (already dubbed "moguls") formed a protective consortium by way of defensive perimeter, the Motion Picture Producers and Distributors of America (the MPPDA; after 1945, the Motion Picture Association of America, the MPAA), and appointed as its president Will H. Hays, the former Postmaster General in the administration of Warren G. Harding and a tee-totaling elder of the Presbyterian Church. In June 1927, in his most reassuring public relations gesture, Hays promulgated a prim list of cautionary injunctions for motion picture content called "the Don'ts and Be Carefuls" and appointed his assistant, Col. Jason S. Joy, to command a watchful supervisory agency, the Studio Relations Committee (SRC).

By the close of the Jazz Age, however, the sound revolution rung in by *The Jazz Singer* (1927) was inciting a renewed chorus of howls over Hollywood immorality: the gestures and mimed insinuation of the silent screen now burst forth audibly in sinister wisecracks and sex-drenched sweet talk. To placate the resurgent opposition, the MPPDA promised to abide by a set of guidelines more extensive and restrictive than the simple nostrums enshrined in the "Don'ts and Be Carefuls." The document that articulated the new commitment to screen morality was the Production Code. Written in 1929 by Martin J. Quigley, an influential editor and publisher of motion picture trade periodicals, and Rev. Daniel A. Lord, S.J., a multitalented Jesuit who first lent his spiritual expertise to Hollywood as the Catholic advisor to Cecil B. DeMille's biblical epic *The King of Kings* (1927), the Production Code was the template for a theological takeover of American cinema. As devout Catholics, both men viewed the movies not merely as a business opportunity but as a missionary duty.

The document crafted by Quigley and Lord expressed an overarching philosophy ("no picture should lower the moral standards of those who see it"); provided specific instructions on "details of plot, episodes, and treatment;" and set down precise guidelines on flash points such as blasphemy, obscenity, vulgarity, costuming, and national and ethnic sensitivities. Though the Code was a deeply Catholic document in tone and temper, the Jesuit theology was concealed for tactical reasons under a broader, Judeo-Christian blanket. On March 31, 1930, the MPPDA formally ratified the Code—whereupon, almost immediately, the studio signatories brazenly defied its letter and spirit.

Obedience to the Code was undercut by a more urgent consideration: economic survival. In the darkest days of the Great Depression, with box office returns plummeting and more than one studio on the brink of ruin, Hollywood was willing to risk opprobrium and tussle with state censors in order to lure back a depleting audience with tommy-gun-toting gangsters and hip-swinging vixens. Wily producers readily outfoxed the watchmen charged with implementing the Code because, however noble its sentiments, the document lacked an effective enforcement mechanism; it depended on the good faith and willing obedience of the ostensibly regulated. First under Colonel Joy and later under former New York state censor Dr. James Wingate (1932-34), the Code was little heeded or obeyed. Frantic for patrons, every studio—Fox included—risked a raid from the vice squad to lure moviegoers whose spending was no longer discretionary, who were sometimes choosing between food and film.

Though later lauded for its frank sexuality and bared skin, pre-Code Hollywood was driven as much by economics as erotics. Scarred by the beaten-down quality of the harshest years of the Great Depression, the films careen through a universe cut loose from sure moorings and friendly ports, adrift and unanchored. Where the silent screen of the 1920s reveled in tweaking Victorian decorum with the antics of wild youth and dancing daughters, the pre-Code screen bespeaks more than a generational spat over manners and morals, bobbed hair and bathtub gin. In its most radical guise, pre-Code Hollywood denied the bedrock verities of American culture, knocking down the pillars of Christian justice, capitalist progress, and constitutional democracy. While the world outside the theaters twisted in convulsions, the world inside spun its own topsy-turvy tales. Consider, for example, Tracy's role as Tom Garner, the rapacious tycoon in William K. Howard's *The Power and the Glory* (1933), a kind of precursor to *Citizen Kane* (1941) scripted by Preston Sturges. With the nation's economy in free fall, businessmen made ripe targets for pre-Code brickbats.

Needless to say, Hollywood's defiant commandment breaking put bluenoses from coast to coast seriously out of joint. In 1934, livid that the moguls who had gone to confession in 1930 had refused to do sincere penance, American Catholics formed the National Legion of Decency to boycott the vile products rolling off the studio assembly line. Catholics of a certain age may remember reciting the "Legion pledge" in parochial school or at Sunday mass. "I condemn absolutely those debauching motion pictures which, with other degrading agencies, are corrupting public morals and promoting a sex mania in our land," affirmed the pledger. "Considering these evils, I hereby promise to remain away from all motion pictures except those which do not offend decency and Christian morality." To encourage compliance, priests stood vigil outside neighborhood theaters, eyeing parishioners contemplating a matinee with Mae West.

The campaign to convert Hollywood was joined by a powerful ally, a man ever mindful of the importance of Catholics to his New Deal coalition: Franklin Delano Roosevelt, lately elected on a program of activist government and regulatory reform. FDR sent out word that unless Hollywood censored itself Washington would do the job for it. Not without reason, the moguls feared that FDR's brain trust would seek to regulate motion picture content with the same vigor that the Blue Eagle was auditing industry finances.

Desperate to forestall government censorship and stop the crippling boycotts by the Legion of Decency, the MPPDA re-committed itself to the Production Code and created a new agency with the teeth to enforce its edicts, the Production Code Administration, the name signaling the centrality of the document. Adherence to the principles of the Code would be certified by a Code Seal printed on the title card of each Hollywood film, an emblem that would be the motion picture equivalent of the imprimatur the Vatican stamped on approved books. Thus, throughout the vaunted Golden Age of Hollywood and on through the less glimmering sunset of the studio system, the PCA vetted, censored, and sealed virtually every Hollywood movie released in the American marketplace. In its own glory days, the in-house censorship regime (motion picture executives always preferred the term "self regulation") was as essential to the smooth operation of the studio machinery as the soundstages, stars, and 35mm film stock.

The sheriff recruited to clean up the town was a prominent Catholic layman named Joseph I. Breen. Born in Philadelphia in 1888, the Jesuit educated Breen embodied the stern Irish Victorian cast of his tribe and time. From July 15, 1934, the day he set up shop, until his retirement in 1954, he held American cinema to the Code's stern catechism of thou-shalt-nots. "The vulgar, the cheap, and the tawdry is out!" Breen promised moviegoers in a special newsreel appearance ballyhooing the creation of the PCA. "There is no room on the screen at any time for pictures which offend against common decency—and these the industry will not allow." He vetted story lines, blue-penciled dialogue, and exercised the moral equivalent of final cut over hundreds of motion pictures per year—expensive "A" caliber feature films, low-budget B-unit ephemera, short subjects, previews of coming attractions, even cartoons. The "pre-Code Hollywood" label is thus something of a misnomer; a more accurate term would be "pre-Production Code enforcement" or better, "pre-Breen."

As fellow "made men" in Hollywood's informal Irish Mafia, Joe Breen and Spencer Tracy inevitably crossed paths at St Patrick's Day dinners, the Church of the Good Shepherd at Beverly Hills, and the occasional Hollywood premiere. In more professional terms, the work of the PCA chief also intersected with the credit list of the actor in a pair of emblematic confrontations. The risibly titled Fox musical *Bottoms Up* (1934) provided an early test case for Breen's power before the official establishment of the PCA. Breen frowned upon certain lyrics and revealing costumes, but the old Studio Relations Committee overruled his objections. Nonetheless, producer B. G. "Buddy" DeSylva—sensing a future downside to crossing Breen—deleted the offending sequences anyway. Later, with the full authority of the PCA behind him, Breen personally choreographed the boxing match-ups between Tracy's Father Tim Mullin and Gable's Blackie Norton in *San Francisco*. Of course, the congenial, but two-fisted padres that Tracy embodied in *San Francisco*, *Boys Town* (1938) and *Men of Boys Town* (1941) could only make the eyes of the Irish censor smile.

Today, few moviegoers lament the passing of the Production Code Administration, the most draconian mechanism for the censorship of American cinema ever devised. But before the steel curtain came down, some of the most innovative, insurrectionist, and just plain whacked-out films in Hollywood history managed to jump through the four-year window of opportunity. Tracy's pre-Code interlude is a reminder of what an alternative motion picture universe might have looked like—a Hollywood Golden Age untarnished by the censor's hands.

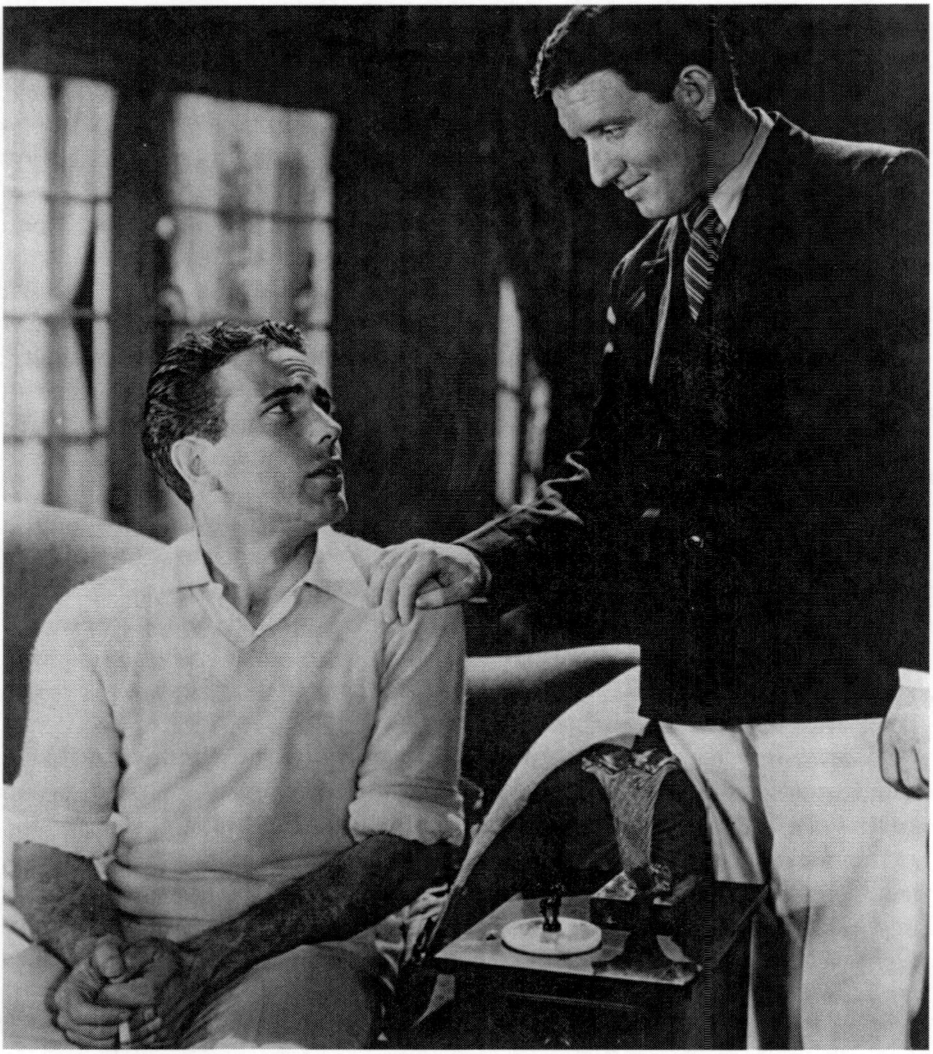

UP THE RIVER

John Ford, Director
William Fox, Producer
Maurine Dallas Watkins, Story & Screenplay
Joseph H. August, Cinematographer
Production Company: Fox Film Corporation
Distributed by Fox Film Corporation
Released October 10, 1930
92 min

Cast
Spencer Tracy . . . Saint Louis
Claire Luce . . . Judy
Warren Hymer . . . Dannemora Dan
Humphrey Bogart . . . Steve
William Collier, Sr . . . . Pop
Joan Marie Lawes . . . Jean
George MacFarlane . . . Jessup
Robert Emmett O'Connor . . . Warden
Steve Pendleton . . . Morris
Sharon Lynn . . . Edith LaVerne
Noel Francis . . . Sophie
Goodee Montgomery . . . Kit
Robert (Bob) Burns . . . Slim
John Swor . . . Clem
Louise Mackintosh . . . Mrs. Massey

And other cast

Up the River—
Prison is Paradise

Jeremy Bond

Spencer Tracy's feature film debut in a comic prison role might have been the first sign that he was going to be a different kind of screen actor. Hollywood released a wave of prison dramas in the late 1920s and early 1930s that portrayed incarceration as Hell on Earth and the prisoners as sympathetic, if not innocent. *Up the River* was different the prisoners were likable, all right, but their situation wasn't dire. They practically looked like they were having a good time.

Farces such as *Up the River* weren't the kind that would earn the director, John Ford, an unprecedented four Academy Awards. But the appeal of this film was the way the actors seem to have the run of the movie, giving the illusion of spontaneity only the best directors can pull off. In this way, it was a perfect introduction to Tracy for film audiences. He often acted from the gut, as if he weren't taking direction but simply acting as any ordinary guy would act in a similar situation.

So with *Up the River* we have not only Tracy's film debut but also his debut as Everyman. The prisoners weren't hardened criminals, but guys like us. Their fate might have been the result of bad decisions, but their incarceration wasn't a mark on their characters. They were still loyal Americans who played baseball and who loved their mothers.

The Characters: Morality and Values

The film is more interested in characterization than plot. Tracy is "Saint Louis," a wiseacre who, despite being a prisoner, believes his charm entitles him to his own rules. His buddy, "Dannemora Dan" (played by Warren Hymer), is the prison idiot whose fluid moral compass points toward whomever he's with at the time—and that's usually Saint Louis. Steve (Humphrey Bogart, in his own film debut) is the handsome prisoner who is released early in the film. On the outside, Steve gets swindled, and Saint Louis and Dan escape from the prison to help him out. The reasons these men are in prison are not made entirely clear; focusing on any sociopathic behavior would turn them into criminals and not the ordinary guys the audience was meant to see them as.

The fact that this film has a cynical perspective on morality is clear near the beginning, when Dan makes a speech at a "Brotherhood of Hope" march. He intends to atone for his past sins and begins a pep talk for others who are ready to seek the light. But this high-mindedness crumbles rapidly when Saint Louis shows up to mock him.

Then we have Saint Louis himself, a chronic prison escapee who insists that prison administrators should trust him because he is a man who keeps his word. He is a gentleman, so he promises to tell them when he "plans to leave" (notwithstanding his lack of parole). He may have deceived them the last time, but he creates a persona of honesty that he says should override past behavior. If he is a man who keeps his word—and he is because he says he is—then how could he deceive them *again*? The audience sees through that, but the joke's on us: Saint Louis does escape again, but after he helps Steve, he returns to the prison voluntarily. He told us so.

The Characters: Race

There is one African American woman inmate who has a fairly prominent role and is portrayed as just as intelligent and three-dimensional as the other characters. The token African American man doesn't fare as well. He is a member of the audience during the prison talent show, and we never hear him speak; we see him only with mouth gaping open and applauding wildly.

One of the scenes at which he's applauding is a blackface routine almost too dumb to be offensive; it's practically a parody out of *Blazing Saddles*. Stereotypes are unchallenged in this film.

The Characters: Gender

Women play an unusually prominent role for prison films of this period (except for a small handful of films that focused exclusively on women's prisons). In *Up the River*, the female social worker brags that the female inmates are "good-looking girls, not a humble one among them."

Are the women treated any better than the men? Their femaleness might have initially been an advantage: one of the inmates sighs that "the only ones that were acquitted were the ones who were smart enough to cross their legs during the trial." But once they are incarcerated, there is notably less sympathy for them than for the men.

While the women are as tough as the men, there is a gender bias against them for being so. A female welfare worker turns up their nose at them. When asked if she is afraid of the male prisoners, however, she dismisses the question. "They're just like little children to me," she says. In other words: they may be criminals, but boys will be boys. Girls, however, aren't supposed to be that way.

One of the older male prisoners, nicknamed "Pop," bemoans the newest crop of male prisoners as not being man enough. It used to be different: "There was men in those days with real needles in their chests." The bad guys have become nothing more than boys who got in some trouble.

As if to drive home the impression that these men are really overgrown children, they get teary during a prison talent show when somebody sings a song about mothers.

The American Ethic

Indeed, motherhood is the root of innocence. A visit to Steve's mother's house is a door into childhood and purity. (The worst thing that his mother ever caught Steve doing was "smoking corn silk" as a child.) Steve's sister, a grown woman, is told she has to go to bed. Steve, a grown man, is asked, "Aren't you going to say good-night to Mother?" It is a place where nothing changes.

Steve is from "New England." No state or town is identified; "New England" is enough to represent wholesomeness. Even in 1930, when the film was released, New England was a diverse place. Stamford, Connecticut, probably meant something very different than Woodstock, Vermont. But the mother, who lives in New England, treats it as one whole: "No one in the country can cook like our New Englanders do."

Steve tells his girl that upon her release from prison, New England was where they would start over "at the bottom of the ladder." (Presumably that's not an insult to New England.) When Saint Louis and Dan return to the prison and see Steve's girl, they tell her how wonderful it will be for her to live in New England with Steve. Dan tries to describe how "the birds are singing, the flowers . . ."—he isn't articulate enough to finish his thought. But at the very least, this demonstrates how New England has an aura about it for the characters who aren't from there. The character's name of "Saint Louis" may not be arbitrary; it identifies him as from somewhere other than New England. (Middle America is its own source of Americana, however.)

Finally, the other American tradition the characters cherish beyond motherhood and apple pie is baseball. It is the most important thing of all to "Pop," and even to the prison administrators, who bemoan Saint Louis's escape most of all because of the effect on the baseball team.

The Prison Genre

Up the River was released soon after hard-bitten prison dramas such as *Condemned*, *Thunderbolt* and *The Big House*, and was soon followed by *The Last Mile*, *Hell's Highway*, and the famous *I Am a Fugitive from a Chain Gang*. Before *Up the River*, Tracy had played the leading role in a stage version of *The Last Mile*, a dark anti-death penalty treatise.

Up the River seems to date less than these films do because melodrama appears to age more than comedy does. The elements that hold up the best in the prison dramas are the light-hearted moments, such as those provided by Wallace Beery in *The Big House*. But *Up the River*, which took nothing seriously, is a uniquely comic contribution to the genre.

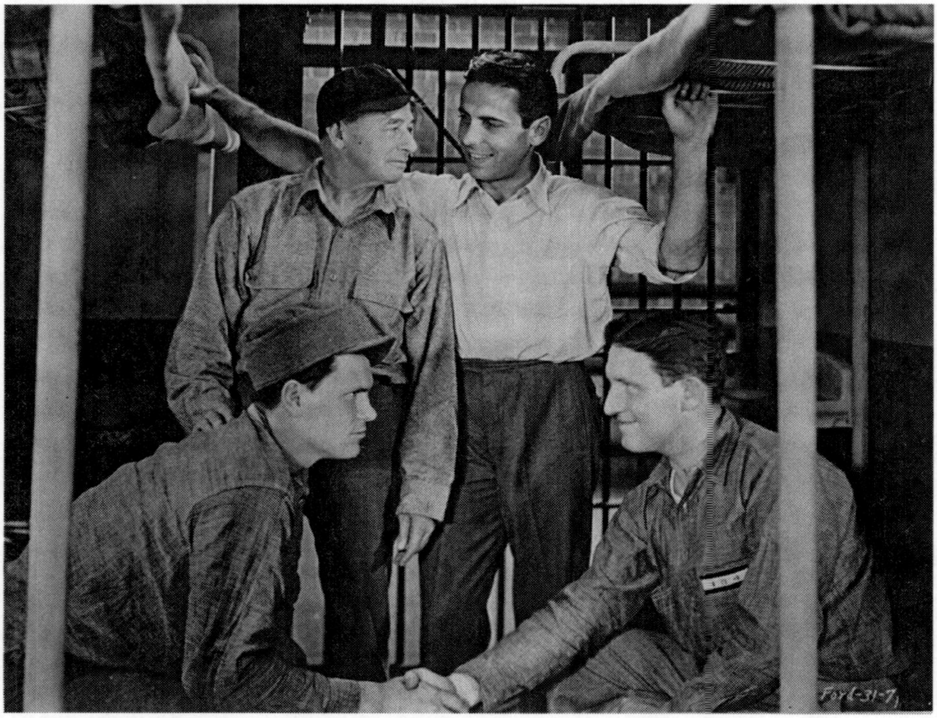

Up the River: Making Good in Comedy Prison

Shelly Brisbin

In the summer of 1930, Fox Studios had a problem. The studio was planning a prison picture, based loosely on the Auburn prison riot in New York. John Ford was set to direct, and a screenplay based on Maureen Dallas Watkins' story was already complete. Ford had even found an actor he wanted for the leading role, and another for an important supporting part. But in June, MGM's *The Big House*, a tense prison drama starring Robert Montgomery, Wallace Beery, and Chester Morris, caused Fox Studio head Winfield Sheehan to rethink his project, even considering scrapping it completely. *The Big House* was just too daunting a genre success, and Fox was in no position to match MGM's critically and popularly acclaimed effort, not to mention its star power.

In an era where the movie industry thrives on sequels and formulas, Fox's pause about shooting a prison drama so soon after MGM's success is a little hard to imagine. But even in 1930, MGM was a powerhouse, and a second-rank studio like Fox was forced to take note of the bigger company's success. John Ford wanted to salvage the picture, and struck on the idea of turning the prison *drama* into a prison *comedy*. And in saving *Up the River*, which turned out to be a hit for Fox, Ford also gave life to the film career of its star, who had previously made unsuccessful screen tests at four studios, including Fox, and been told that he was too ugly to be a leading man, not ugly enough to be a villain. Spencer Tracy was 30 years old.

John Ford, an experienced contract director at Fox, didn't rely on an old screen test to cast his movie. Before *Up the River's* retooling, Fox sent him to New York to see five Broadway shows, each featuring actors who might be right for the film. On the first night, Ford saw *The Last Mile*, a drama about a murderer on death row. Tracy was the star. By most accounts, especially Ford's, the young actor was riveting as the brutal Killer Mears. Instead of using his other theatre tickets, Ford returned to see *The Last Mile* on each of the following four nights, and offered Tracy the lead in *Up the River* as his week of scouting ended. Ford did manage to squeeze in a matinee of a second play, where he saw another actor with a legendary career ahead of him, Humphrey Bogart.

When Tracy arrived in California in the summer of 1930 for work on *Up the River*, he did not expect to remain for long: he had a one-picture contract with Fox, and had taken six weeks' leave from *The Last Mile*, in which he was obligated to appear for several more months when he returned to New York. And whatever John Ford had seen in him, the four failed screen tests didn't bode well for a career in the movies. Tracy's wife and son remained on the East coast.

Up the River was still planned as a drama when Tracy left New York. On his arrival in LA, Ford came to see him, and told the actor that the film was now to be a comedy, with Tracy as star, and Bogart in a supporting role. When the screenplay emerged from rewrites, Tracy's character was a swaggering, serial prison breakout artist who, as it transpired, had a heart of gold. Bogie was a naïve rich kid who had stumbled onto the wrong side of the law.

Tracy, though an experienced light comedian in the theatre, was apprehensive, having prepared himself for a serious drama. It was Ford who successfully reassured and soothed him.

Tracy Goes to Jail

Up the River tells the story of a state penitentiary run by a firm-but-fair warden, and the men (and women, surprisingly) who call the place home. Rounding out the population are the warden's young daughter and the welfare workers who come to the penitentiary regularly to do volunteer work with the prisoners.

Tracy plays Saint Louis, an inmate whose crimes are never listed, but who shows all the signs of being a skilled con man, perhaps one with well-publicized felonies to his credit. He's also more clever than most of his fellow inmates. No stranger to the penitentiary, Saint Louis makes a grand entrance as he returns to prison after an escape that opens the film. He's greeted not only by the inmates' marching band, but newsreel cameras too, chronicling what he plays as his triumphant return to the lock-up.

We next see Saint Louis confidently entering the warden's office (after he's passed through a gauntlet of swooning female prisoners), good-naturedly listing his demands for creature comforts while forced to live on the inside. The scene with the warden, though not his first in *Up the River*, serves as an introduction to Tracy's character. It's no accident that this scene is the one most often shown in film clip retrospectives representing his early career. It exemplifies his easy acting style.

In it, Tracy is physically and verbally the center of attention, both as he enters the room swinging his walking stick, and when he takes a seat across the desk from the warden. As in so many great Tracy scenes, he controls the room at his ease. In this case, his tools are his still relatively lean body, which he drapes on the desk, then in a chair, his jauntily perched hat (shades of many future Tracy performances) and his dialogue, which is light and casual. It is striking, in a filmmaking era still only a couple of years removed from silent film, and in which many actors were stiff and spoke in stilted, mannered language, to see Tracy, in his first outing, give so relaxed and natural a performance.

My Buddy

When Tracy became a star at MGM, he could always expect top billing—except when teamed with the only male star who outranked him at the studio, Clark Gable. In the four films he made with Gable, Tracy played second banana; following in the wake of the dominant Gable, cleaning up his messes, socking him in the jaw when he needed it, and sometimes even surrendering the girl to The King by the end of the picture. In the early 30s, though, it was Tracy who dominated a series of buddy pictures for Fox, beginning with *Up the River*.

In the lockup, Saint Louis is reunited with Dannemora Dan (played by Warren Hymer) who Saint Louis ditched during the previous prison break that opens the film, and whose subsequent attempt to go straight Tracy thwarts. Hymer, who appeared with Tracy in five films, will never come out on the winning side of a scheme hatched by Tracy. His character is not the sharpest tool in the shed, and can't quite manage either to get even with, or get rid of, his partner. Dan strings along with Saint Louis, serving as a foil, and providing the extra muscle needed to carry out his plans.

Unlike the later Gable-Tracy films, the Fox buddy pictures, with Hymer and other hapless partners including Stuart Erwin and Jack Oakie, belonged solely to the star. In a Gable-Tracy film, the shorter, less easy-on-the-eyes second lead got to take the hero down a few pegs, and even saved Gable's characters from making irreparable mistakes. In *Test Pilot*, Tracy even got a film-stealing death scene. Tracy's own sidekicks, including Hymer's befuddled Dannemora Dan, were usually left to take orders, or to ask the hero what his plans were, as a means of narrating the story for the audience.

While it is certainly true that by the time Tracy played second banana in the Gable pictures at MGM, he was the beneficiary not only of better scripts, but the power that comes with a stellar career as a leading man in his own right, the role of Tracy's own talent can't be under-estimated. At Fox, his easy-going brashness lent itself perfectly to the buddy picture model, especially when the buddies were down-and-outers, or even running some sort of scam. At MGM, Gable did his share of buddy pictures with weaker partners. With Tracy on the bill, the second lead role could be turned into a better part, and used to take some of the edge off Gable's dominating, and often one-dimensional screen performances.

A Cast of Characters

The other inhabitants of *Up the River's* penitentiary include an old-timer whose main interest is in fielding an inmate baseball team (Saint Louis is an ace pitcher), and the young man of high New England birth (Steve) played by Bogart, working much closer to his real roots than he ever did in the gangster roles that would later make him famous. There's a would-be tough guy, too (who Saint Louis will later tame), and a black inmate who makes with the wisecracks.

Across the prison yard is the women's section, populated by its own set of "types." While fraternization is supposedly not allowed, there are chances for men and women to see one another and, in Steve's case, fall in love. The object of his affection is Judy, a young con woman played by Claire Luce, who Steve correctly guesses isn't quite as hard-bitten as she pretends to be when they meet in the prison office where he works. Judy is assigned to tutor to the warden's daughter. The little girl, in scenes that would shock 21st century sensibilities, is sort of a mascot for the prisoners, and performs cartwheels in the yard for the entertainment of the male inmates

In comedy prison, the welfare ladies, who are dotty, stout, and well meaning, bring treats for the confined, and seem to be helping the women learn trades they can use on the outside. The welfare ladies are easily tricked. They believe the best of the prisoners, who play on their sympathies. One becomes an unwitting carrier pigeon, when the women inmates slip a message for Steve onto her person, which his friends skillfully remove as Mrs. Massey leaves the prison for the day.

The central plot revolves around Steve and Judy, who have fallen in love. Steve is due to be released soon, and promises to write to Judy, and to marry her when her term is up. Unfortunately, she makes the mistake of telling her no-good ex-boyfriend and con man accomplice not only that she's moved on to someone new, but his name, too. No-good ex proceeds to the bucolic New England town where Steve has returned after prison, and attempts to blackmail him, since his wealthy mother knows nothing of Steve's imprisonment.

Saint Louis and a reluctant Dan hatch a plot to break out of jail, help Steve shake off the blackmailer, and bring the lovebirds together. To make their break they create a diversion at the prison talent show, a long sequence featuring a tuxedo-clad MC introducing a series of inmate vaudeville acts, including Saint Louis, throwing knives at the hapless Dan.

After some scenes of domestic bliss in small-town New England, Saint Louis and Dan do thwart the blackmailer and make things right for Steve and Judy. Saint Louis and Dan return to prison under their own steam, just in time to play in the big jailhouse baseball game.

Depression Context

Though John Ford steered as far as he could from *The Big House* with his prison comedy, *Up the River* certainly represented a fad in 1930. Prison pictures, and crime films in general, were high on the list for most studios, especially the grittier ones like Fox and Warner Brothers. They offered working class stories and characters, and a scruffier set of leading players than the high-toned MGM.

As the genre developed throughout the Depression, more politically tinged stories were added, with characters fighting to sustain themselves against pressure from banks, rich employers, and the generally bad state of urban life. But *Up the River*, released less than a year after the stock market crash of 1929, wore its Depression-era setting lightly. A Salvation Army parade evokes the down-and-outers whose misery is more the result of sin than hard economic times—the US had been through a revivalist religion phase in the 20s. And the prison welfare ladies, and even Steve's wealthy mother, are benevolently depicted. Con men and opportunistic prisoners dupe both, but the movie's take on them is sympathetic, rather than cynical or angry, and the wealthy are most definitely not shown as the oppressors of those who entered lives of crime. By contrast, rich people in later Depression-era films often took the brunt of working-class outrage, or were portrayed as the villains, in stories where their poorer cousins ended up behind bars, or on bread lines.

What *Up the River* illustrates that those later films in the Depression era did not, was hope. The sweethearts, strayed into their crimes, and are imprisoned for relatively short terms. They will bear few scars. *Up the River* is a diversion, not a film intended to make you think, or come anywhere near what it might have been like to be in jail in 1930.

The Start of Something Big

If 1930 signaled the first full year of economic depression in the US, it meant the opposite to Spencer Tracy. He had been struggling as a theatre actor for seven years rising from bit parts and stock company tours to the point where he was offered leads on Broadway. *The Last Mile*, which ended up becoming his big break in film, might well have signaled the beginning of a stellar Broadway career, had he elected to stay in New York. But if he had, the financial rewards would not have come close to those he could obtain if he became a star in Hollywood, or even got a nice multi-year contract.

But these were only possibilities when Tracy took a six-week leave from *The Last Mile* to make *Up the River*. It was common for studios to sign one-picture deals with untried film actors, and Tracy had no reason to feel confident that he was about to leave the struggles of a New York acting life behind. Fortunately for him, *Up the River* was a hit, and his performance was correctly seen as an important reason for the film's success.

Winfield Sheehan soon offered Tracy a five-year contract at Fox. Though the coming years would be difficult for the actor, both personally and professionally, he amassed a collection of early performances that consistently outshone the films in which he was cast. The actor who joined MGM as a star five years later was both respected and thoroughly versed in the art and craft of film acting. And he made it look easy.

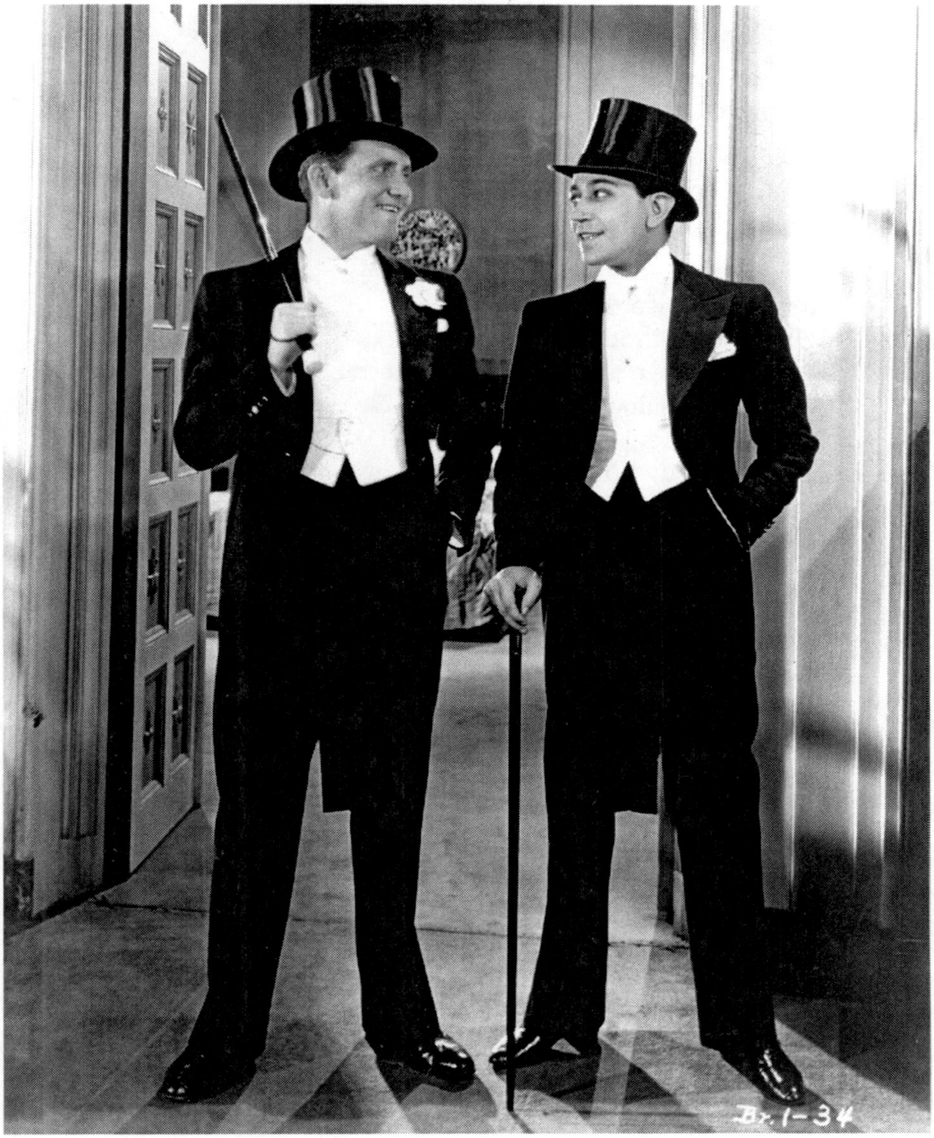
Br. 1-34

QUICK MILLIONS

Rowland Brown, Director
William Fox, Producer
Rowland Brown and Courtney Perrett, Story & Screenplay
Additional Dialogue, John Wray
Joseph H. August, Cinematographer
Distributed by Fox Film Corporation
Released 1931
72 min.

Cast
Spencer Tracy . . . Daniel Raymond
Marguerite Churchill . . . Dorothy Stone
Sally Eilers . . . Daisy De Lisle
Bob Burns . . . Arkansas Smith
George Raft . . . Jimmy Kirk
Leon Ames . . . Hood
Ward Bond . . . cop (uncredited)

And other cast

Quick Millions Message to the Masses: The American Dream Can Be Dangerous

Jeremy Bond

Spencer Tracy's second feature film arrived amidst an explosion of gangster crime dramas in early 1930s Hollywood. While the most famous films in the genre revolved around Prohibition—in Prohibition's final years, when it had become clear that it was causing more societal problems than it was solving—*Quick Millions* told the story of a racketeer. To modern audiences, all of these films could be classified as "message" films about the horrors of organized crime. But to Depression-era audiences, *Quick Millions*' focus on the criminals' wealth was probably meant to sting.

Tracy's character of "Bugs" Raymond in *Quick Millions*, like James Cagney's character of Tom Powers of *The Public Enemy* the same year, were ill-fated gangsters who were almost likeable. This was perhaps an unexpected problem for directors claiming that they were condemning crime and not exploiting it for entertainment. The message might be that crime doesn't pay, because the protagonists end up being killed, but by that point the films have somewhat desensitized the viewers to murder.

The Message

While *The Public Enemy* and other crime films begin with a text narrative to rail against criminals, *Quick Millions* uses several supporting characters to get its point across in distinctly American ways. A radio commentator, a precursor of the modern talk radio host, intones that "it is the duty of every citizen of these United States to lend himself." He reminds his audience of the similarities between Prohibition-related crimes and fraudulent business dealings: the racketeer, he says, is a "direct byproduct of the bootlegger." (This radio "loudspeaker," incidentally, gets shot dead, so the movie doesn't spare the virtuous any more than the criminal.)

Then there is the American-style uprising of the common people. At a meeting of indignant citizens, an older woman complains that Americans would soon "no longer have a republic. We'll have a gangster-governing kingdom." Her voice has the quintessential quavering of the righteous, God-fearing American, almost to the point of cliché. At the same meeting, the district attorney is even more melodramatic, warning that "we're becoming a race of underdogs, tearing at the entrails of society."

The district attorney's speech most directly reflects the American penchant for passing the buck. He blames dishonest and weak judges. He acknowledges that his office hasn't adequately prosecuted the racketeers, but then turns the tables on the audience of businessmen. "You're all guilty," he says, because they refuse to testify against the racketeers. Sure, testifying could get them killed, their businesses ruined or their families harmed, but "that's the risk you take when you perform your duty as citizens." We, the movie audience, watch the speech from the same level as the audience within the movie, so perhaps the message is for us as well. Movie viewers were suffering from the Depression and might have seen collaboration with racketeers as an easy way out.

But it's also possible that the filmmakers were cynical and shared our frustration with public figures who want us to do their job for them. After all, shouldn't John Q. Public work hardest at keeping his business stable and his family safe?

The American Ethic

The D.A. makes some other telling judgments of 1931 American society. He complains that the "younger generation" has grown contemptuous, citing his daughter's remark that "we have the best judges money can buy." Her generation apparently thinks that to "spend the night in jail is a lark." It would seem that the cynicism of American youth has a long history.

The D.A. blames the racketeering on America's preoccupation with wealth. The film has a cynical view of the American dream: that the goal is to get as much money as possible, and that this breeds a society of corruption. Even a standard-bearer of Americana—the corner newsboy shouting "EXtree, EXtree!"—is linked to con-artistry.

If the American dream is financial success, then Bugs is simply trying to live the American dream. His stint as a truck driver and a brief jail sentence leave him broke, so he sees racketeering as the most viable option. He justifies it as just "getting what the other guys got, in a nice way." He's willing to do whatever is the most lucrative at the time, and for a while, he's a (somewhat) legitimate businessman.

Once Bugs enters the real business world—"that's the dream of every racketeer, gentlemen, to have a legitimate racket"—he courts the daughter of a developer he railroaded into making his business partner. "It's too bad you never had the same chance that other boys have," she tells Bugs. He lights up when Dorothy talks about her grandfather, who "educated himself" and "drove a team of mules." Bugs' history isn't so different from the history of these high society folks after all.

Humble beginnings are not only considered quaint, but are a type of excuse for achieving the American dream by any means possible. "Nails" Markey, Bugs' partner in crime, hosts an appreciation dinner for "prominent citizens," and reveals their histories. One used to be the delegate to the bricklayers union. Another "helped himself" to the fruit out of Nails' first produce stand. Reminders of these humble beginnings are greeted with chuckles, and we realize that the public officials could have just as easily become hoodlums. We quickly discover that both are collaborating in criminal activity.

American law is treated with sarcasm. The D.A. warns Bugs to choose the law he is going to live by, "the law of the citizen or the law of the hoodlum." What difference does it make, Bugs replies, "whether they're [laws] made by lawyers for other lawyers to break," or laws made by hoodlums for hoodlums. In the film's only veiled reference to religion, the D.A. replies, "There are other laws that are not manmade laws, Bugs." In a sense, the film itself is having this same debate. The viewing public eschews hooliganism just as it shares Bugs' contempt for wrongdoing by the powerful.

Class Distinctions

Persons in power have not earned the public's respect. A Newsreel technician rolls his eyes during a dedication speech praising a developer for building "another titan stretching into the blue." The camera is placed high above the dedication ceremony, as if to look down on these supposed pillars of the community. Director Rowland Brown affords the public officials as much deference as Charlie Chaplin does the same year in *City Lights*, in which a speech is replaced by hilarious gibberish.

Bugs marvels at his quick rise, constantly reminding himself that he was so recently a truck driver in "over-halls." Certain activities are reserved for people with money—billiards, the opera—and undertaking these activities automatically gives a person prestige (or, as Bugs calls it, "PRESStidge").

Wealth and personal value are considered one and the same. Bugs' girl, Daisy, loses interest in him at the beginning of the film because he doesn't have any money. Bugs in turn loses interest in her once he makes his millions and starts going to the opera.

Gender Distinctions

As if to emphasize the coarse materialism of America, Bugs pays Daisy off so she'll go to Europe. "You can pick up a lot of, whatchamacallit, class," he says. He's not the only one to see women as objects that can be shipped. A businessman, pressured by the D.A.'s speech, announces that he'll send *his* wife and daughters to Europe so he can clean up a mess caused by his tolerance of corruption.

Women are largely passive to the action, and they are told to stick to their place. Bugs complains to Daisy that she's not "ladylike" enough after she sits on his desk. The film also finds humor in challenging the notions of ladylike activity. "Baby, what do you do in your spare moments?" Bugs' bodyguard asks a secretary. "I like to go to wrestling matches," she replies.

The Gangster Genre

The hoodlum was a very temporary persona for Tracy, while *Little Caesar*, *The Public Enemy* and *Smart Money* assured that James Cagney and Edward G. Robinson would be forever associated with the Prohibition-era gangster film. Brown, who directed only three movies, also had an affinity for crime stories; he had already written about corruption in high places in a story that became the prison film *The Doorway to Hell*, released the previous year.

Because *Quick Millions* is about racketeering instead of bootlegging, its message remains relevant (and arguably still resonates in an era of corporate scandals). And many Depression-era viewers undoubtedly resented the racketeers for having $12,000 at the drop of a hat to spring for a square-cut diamond. By placing criminal conduct in the larger context of government ineffectiveness or corruption, *Quick Millions* suggests that the "public enemy" extends beyond the gangster himself.

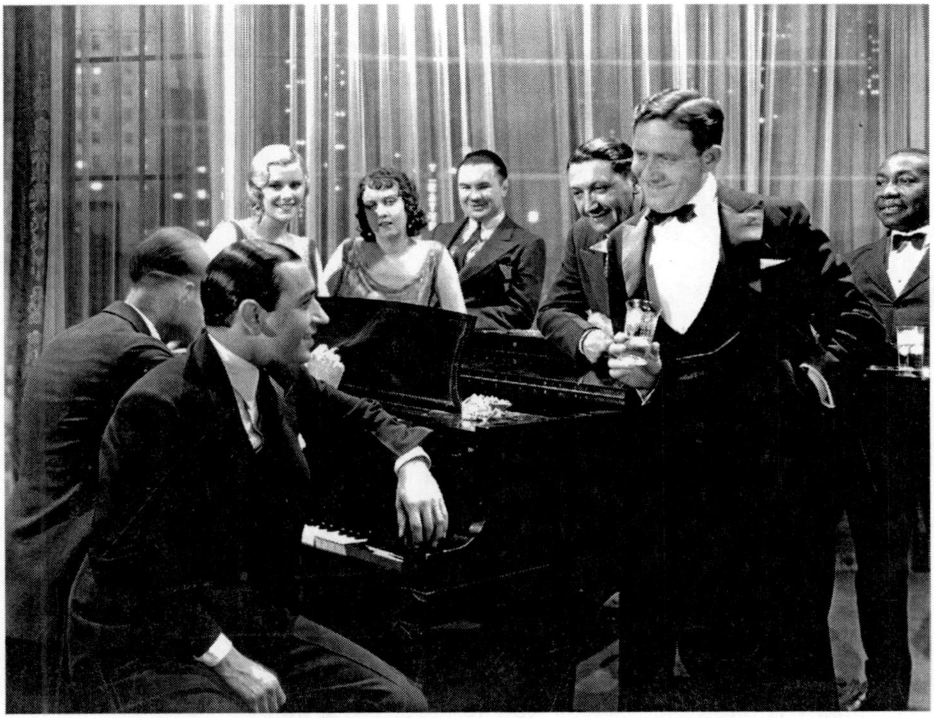

Quick Millions: Unions and the Class Divide

Sean Connell

Quick Millions takes place between 1925-1931. The storyline is simple and comparable to other gangster films of that era such as *Little Caesar*. However, the pacing and structure of this cautionary tale is less overtly violent and far more intelligent and cerebral. As such, the lessons drawn from it are somewhat more complex than simply "crime doesn't pay," and coupled with the complications of Spencer Tracy's evolving character, "Bugs" Raymond, make the movie stand out from others of that era. *Quick Millions* provides two important insights into the lawlessness of the 1920s and 1930s when racketeers committed crimes for their own profit.

Tracy's character, "Bugs", is a hoodlum "too nervous to steal and too lazy to work" looking for an angle to get rich. Bugs' early illegal actions include vandalizing and torching cars parked on the street at night to drum up business for garage owners and orchestrating the armed robbery of prominent citizens. Criticizing his racketeering accomplice, "Nails" Markey (played by Warner Richmond), Bugs refuses to threaten food suppliers or engage in personal blackmail. The main money-making machine for Tracy and his cohorts is the trucking strike and organizing the trucking companies. Tracy realizes that truck drivers are the ones who literally make things move in the city, and that without them everything comes to a halt, especially construction work on New York City's skyscrapers. Tracy's protection racket is an extortion scheme and his gang coerces Kenneth Stone (played by John Wray), a wealthy New

York City real estate developer, to purchase his organization's "protection" services against a work slowdown by the construction truck drivers.

This puts anyone who can control the trucks into a very powerful position, something that was also realized by the real-life Teamsters. What separates Tracy's gang from the Teamsters is that Bugs was motivated by personal profit rather than concern for his fellow workers. The movie does not address why the truck drivers would agree to strike in the first place if they weren't getting some benefit in return. Bugs, forever aspiring to higher things, elevates himself from a working class truck driver in overalls to a spit and polished opera-goer and country club golfer, leaving the truck drivers and gangsters behind.

Labor unions were still struggling to gain official recognition. The resemblance of the tactics of organized labor with those of organized crime is quite obvious, and one that was commonly recognized at the time. *Quick Millions*, released in 1931, four years before the Wagner Act legalized collective bargaining, is essentially how Tracy accomplishes his ends. The manner in which Tracy deals with the prime real estate financier, Stone, is reminiscent of meetings between labor representatives and big business. To be fair, many methods used by the unions in those days weren't entirely above board and there were good reasons to fear them. Violence often accompanied strikes on both sides of the labor divide, further widening the divide between those trying to improve their working conditions (or simply their pay) and those they viewed as "fat cats" getting rich off of their efforts. There were also concerns about the personal ethics of some labor leaders and questions about just whose interests they were truly representing.

The "Us vs. Them" dimension between labor and capital leads to the movie's other theme—class divide—and Bugs' own downfall. As Tracy makes his transformation from work shirts to top hats and decides to marry a high society girl, he transcends his working class roots. The 1930s are still very much a time when there are only two classes: the working class and the upper class. There is a continuum in the working class between white and blue collar workers, but these gradations are dwarfed by the overall gap between workers and the wealthy. Neither side trusts the other. Despite Stone's wealth, there is total disdain for Tracy amongst the more well-heeled he attempts to hob-nob with while in pursuit of Stone's socialite sister, Dorothy (played by Marguerite Churchill). And it is Tracy's desperate attempt (to the point of kidnapping) to marry into this upper crust that leads his fellow gangsters to distrust him enough to murder him.

The film's portrayal of this theme is accomplished, cinematically, via two devices: the trappings of wealth and the discarding of vestiges from the previous, poorer existence. Bugs goes to the opera and dresses up far beyond the means of Bugs the truck driver we first meet. He casts aside the old girlfriend, who has of course valiantly, or perhaps foolishly, stood by him while he makes his ill-gotten riches. Neither is terribly innovative, and it is to the credit of Spencer Tracy that he manages to put something more into his character and elevate the role beyond the inevitable stereotypes. When Bugs' own mob turns against him, one can almost see in Bugs someone who acts a precursor to Jimmy Hoffa, and who shares a similar end.

This is not a film that, aside from Tracy's own acting skills, is interested in exploring any of the complexities of the issues it (inadvertently) raises. Once Bugs elevates himself out of the cab of his truck, the audience is no longer presented with that street-level perspective. *Quick Millions* is a fascinating portrayal of how Bugs leaves behind not only his fellow gang members but also his fellow truck drivers to become the guys in the *other* car, the town car at the start of the film. Once on the other side of the divide, again little attempt is made to provide depth to the wealthier, high society characters Bugs interacts with. It simply isn't that kind of film, and therefore superficially skims the surface rather than delve for meaning. The film does take sides, of course, as this was not an era where gangsters (or union leaders) were glorified. There was a certain fascination with the criminal element but always within a strict moral code: in the end the criminals are not allowed to get away with it. And although audiences in 1931 were probably satisfied with that, looking back, one does wish that the filmmakers had tried to get away with a little more.

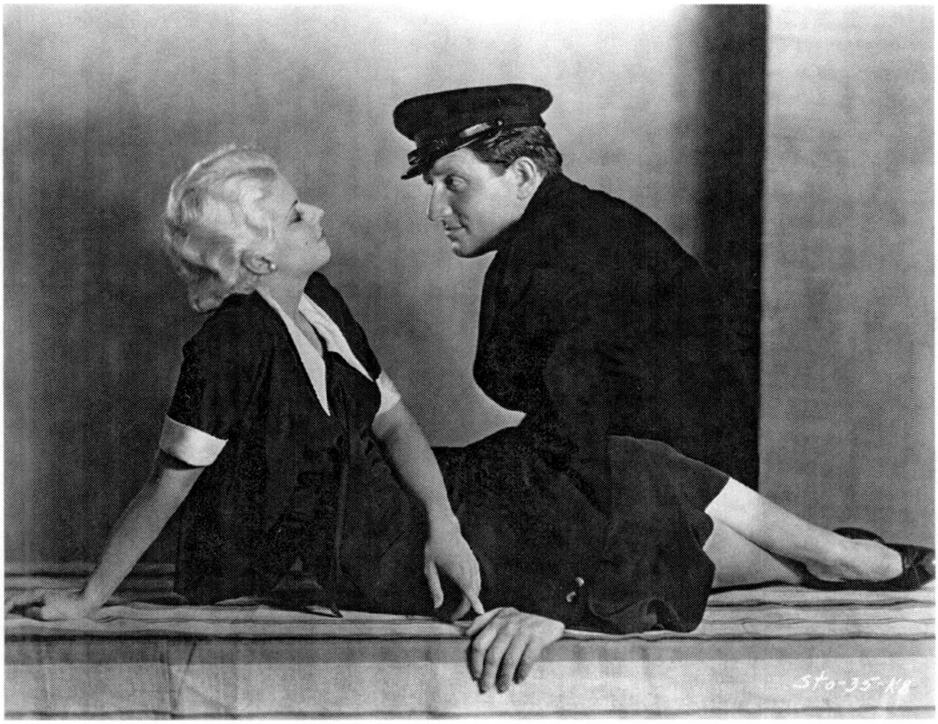

GOLDIE

Benjamin Stoloff, Director
William Fox, Producer
Written by Paul Perez & Gene Towne
Music by R.H. Bassett & Hugo Friedhofer
Ernest Palmer, Cinematographer
Distributed by Fox Film Corporation
Released June 28, 1931
68 min.

Cast
Spencer Tracy . . . Bill
Warren Hymer . . . Spike
Jean Harlow . . . Goldie
George Raft . . . pickpocket (uncredited)

And other cast

Goldie: The Migration of the American Male

Jeremy Bond

*G**oldie* takes a Spencer Tracy role overseas, where Americans swagger to distract themselves from the reality that they are fish out of water. It's not just the language that they don't understand and never bother to learn, but also the cultural norms that wouldn't be out of place in formal settings in the United States. The problem for America is that its ambassadors in *Goldie* are sailors who are particularly uncouth. It's unclear whether the film is stereotyping sailors or Americans in general, or whether the main characters reflect outside perceptions of Americans more than Americans themselves. Either way, Americans do not come off well.

That isn't really a problem, because this is a comedy and we're all expected to laugh at these characters. Bill (Tracy) is slick, Spike (Warren Hymer) is dumb—not unlike the team these actors made in *Up the River*. Their humorous chemistry elevates the film above *Goldie*'s silly script, adapted from the 1928 Fox silent *A Girl in Every Port*. Like the Marx Brothers' films, *Goldie* derives humor from dishonorable characters acting as embarrassing as possible in highfalutin' settings. The Marx Brothers were practically cartoon characters, however they didn't represent Americans any more than Groucho Marx represented an actual physician in *A Day at the Races*. By contrast, Bill and Spike are uncomfortably closer to home.

The Americans

Over the course of *Goldie*, Bill and Spike are in Odessa, Russia; Venice, Italy; Greece (no city is given); Rio de Janeiro; and Calais, France. Aside from the languages, these places are not presented any differently from one another.

Bill and Spike improbably keep bumping into each other in their travels. Spike is irritated that every girl he meets has a brand on her skin, made by another sailor, of an anchor inside a heart. Americans love marking their territory, and nothing says "I wuz here" like a tattoo. (The marks are actually from Bill's ring; unlike in *Quick Millions*, in which Spencer Tracy's assault of a woman is considered mean, Bill's knuckle sandwiches are treated as lighthearted trademarks.)

We are clued in that Spike is from Peoria, and you can't get more quintessential mid-America than that (it's why there are all those warnings about something that's "not going to play in Peoria.") But Hymer sounds much more Brooklyn than Midwest; as a Dumb Guy, he can't speak proper English and says "dis" instead of "this."

Spike is too stupid to know that he's breaking any norms. He attends a fashion show, where the applause is dainty and polite, and claps like a hyena. "Ain't she a beauty? Not a mark on her!" he says giddily to the proper older lady sitting next to him. (She begs his pardon, and he asks, "Why? You haven't done nothin'.") When he steps away, he says to her, "Watch that seat for me, will ya, pal?"

Even as outsiders, the Americans have a way of taking charge. A classy club in Rio becomes a free-for-all suggesting a saloon of the Old West. The Americans are invincible: the cops show up, and Bill tells Spike, "You take the little ones and I'll take the big ones." Apparently Americans win no matter how much they're outnumbered.

The third American, the title character, shows up after the film's halfway point. Goldie (Jean Harlow) has stuck around Calais long enough to learn French, but her speech is pure Coney Island. She is a high-diver at a carnival that is just like a good old American carnival, complete with a sword-swallower and competitive carnival barkers reminiscent of those portrayed in other 1930s Hollywood films such as *The Great Ziegfeld*. The setting is more American than French, just as the film's other settings do not reflect the countries in which they take place.

Spike and Goldie are relieved to meet another American, and Spike falls for her—unaware that she has Bill's stamp, too, from a Coney Island tryst. These Americans are now officially world travelers, but their tastes and interests apparently have not become more sophisticated. Spike dreams of settling down with Goldie at a chicken ranch.

The Characters: Gender

The film is full of gender commentary, mostly through Bill complaining about women. The two lead male characters are boisterous, but not all of the women they court are passive and innocent. When a woman holds Spike at a distance, he asks, "Whatsa matter, you're a widow, ain't you?" "Not till tonight," she replies.

Still, like many American films, *Goldie* shows sexy women who don't speak English fawning over brawny American men who don't understand what they're saying (and nobody seems to mind). The strongest woman in the film, least likely to fall under the men's sway, is the title character, an American who speaks English. She turns out to be cunning and deceitful, traits that Bill implies are typical of women. His own wily ways somehow don't extend to the entire population of men.

Bill uses a variety of slang names for women beyond the common 1930s use of the word "dame." The women are "squaws," "seagulls" (just like the birds they meet at every port, ready to pounce and steal), as well as "tomatoes" or "onions." The terms are all insults. The worst of all is "tramp," which Bill calls Goldie based on his experience with her.

Spike, despite his shallow way of finding women through his little black book, is a lot more respectful. When he meets Goldie, he tries to reassure her when she laments, "Men don't date carnival girls. They think we're all bad." He replies, "I know a lot of girls who makes (sic) an honest living doing their own thing." But, he adds, "not in a tank like a sea lion"—her diving routine demeans her, he says. She tells him that he understands women well, and he beams.

But Spike clearly views women as little innocents. He suggests to Goldie that she needs him for protection. In courting her, he promises to give up drinking and swearing—and he'd even take up chewing tobacco, just so he could give it up for her. But the viewer gets the impression that Goldie is just as likely to do these things herself.

Goldie is only after Spike's dough, and to convince him of that, Bill asks Spike to look at himself in the mirror. (Hymer then makes himself as ugly as possible, doing his best Moe Howard imitation.) While Bill is hinting that Goldie is shallow enough to be interested in only looks or money, his implication is that any woman or man isn't interested at all unless a person has good looks. Ultimately good looks trump good judgment, for after swearing off women for good, the men are immediately drawn back after seeing some sexy legs.

The Pre-Code Comedy

At the women's fashion show, Spike tells Bill not to clap so loud. "The more you clap," Bill says, "the more they take off."

There are a few suggestive moments in the script. It's probably no accident that Bill's middle finger gets misaligned whenever he punches somebody. Goldie kisses Bill and tries to seduce him while he's sleeping, and the sexual friction is palpable.

But some of the jokes evoke humor that didn't change appreciably after the enforcement of the Production Code in 1934. One scene calls Harpo Marx to mind: Bill and Spike whistle and use body movements to attract the attention of a guard, whom they subsequently push into a pool of water. Another scene calls Groucho to mind: Spike complains that a would-be dentist (a carpenter) extracted the wrong tooth, and Bill replies, "Let me be the first to congratulate you." (The only thing that distinguishes that quip from what Groucho might say is that Tracy didn't pronounce "first" like "foist.")

A handful of 1930s film adaptations explore the difference between grubby Americans and high-class foreigners. In the comedy *Ruggles of Red Gap*, a stately British butler endears himself to the rambunctious residents of a small town in Washington state, and the story doesn't judge one way of life or the other. *Goldie*, by contrast, treats its foreigners like props. Americans come off worse than they do, and yet Tracy's character, as the one semi-intelligent protagonist, is supposed to be the one we relate to because he is an American. It may not be pretty, but at least *Goldie* is among the earliest in a long line of Hollywood films to portray the lives of American sailors.

Sto-35-23

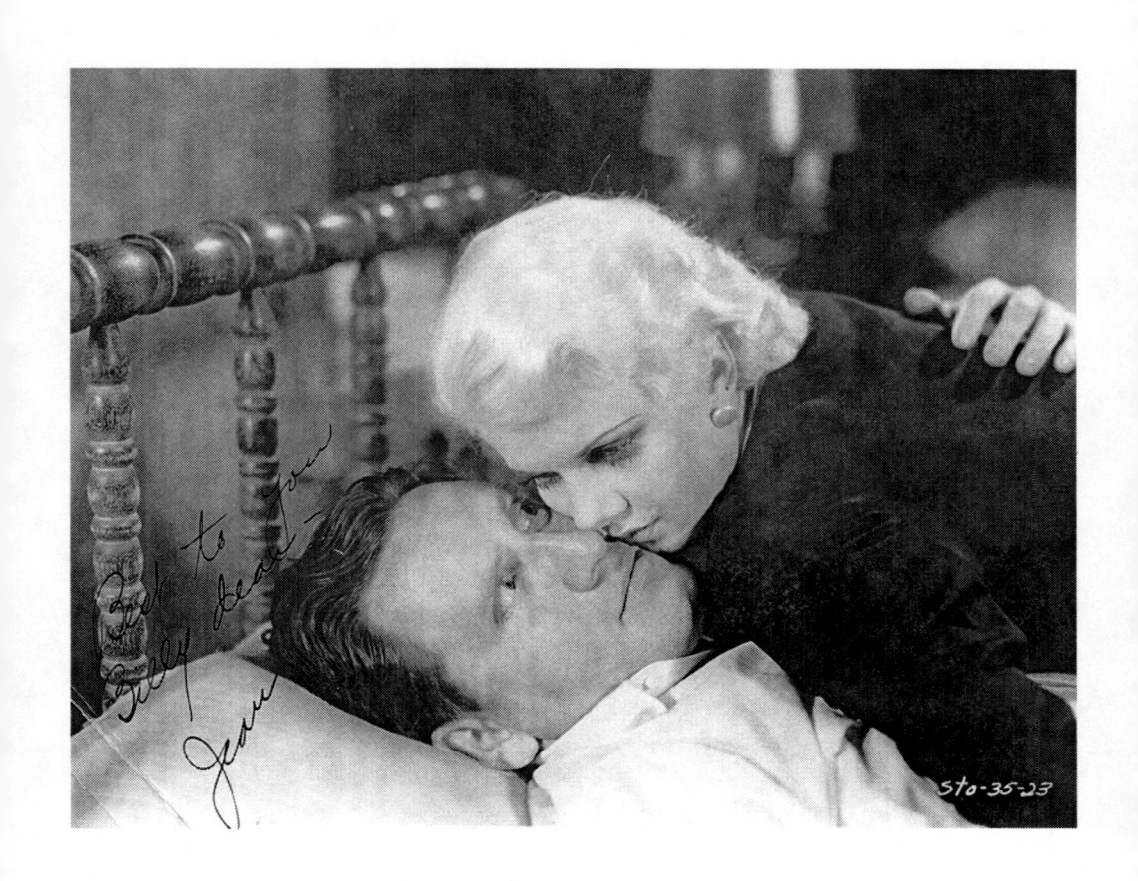

Goldie: A Black Mark for Relations Between the Sexes

Sean Connell

Fox's 1931 pre-Code film *Goldie* features a well-worn plot of two sailors who first squabble then bond over their pursuit of women. The first half of the film is comprised of throw-away sketches where the two sailors—one a nice guy who can't seem to catch a break with women (or his fellow sailors), the other a guy who drinks, chases women, and causes no end of trouble and heartbreak for the first. Eventually they both bond, and the second half of the film introduces the woman who tries to come between them. A few unlikely coincidences and cliché plot elements later, and the film ends with the two sailors best of friends again—and still competing over women.

Goldie stars Spencer Tracy and Jean Harlow, neither in the lead, and both either too early in their careers or not given enough to work with in the meager script. Harlow is at best a "femme fatale" in a pre-noir fashion, meaning no one dies (though not for lack of effort). Her role as a beautiful but treacherous platform diver is never given much depth, and it's obvious her only real value on screen is to drive what little there is to the plot forward. Tracy's character, Bill, is equally limited and again one that has been seen before. A boozer, a womanizer, something of a lout, yet, despite an early rivalry, a guy who eventually takes under his wing the main character of Spike, here played by Warren Hymer. Tracy steals every scene he's in, and there are glimmers of the actor to be.

Even as a pre-Code film, there isn't anything risqué enough to shock modern audiences. The exception is the most overt manner in which the film conveys its attitude towards women: the blatantly sexist and misogynous treatment of every woman in the picture. The extent to which this permeates the film goes way beyond even the standards of conduct between the sexes in the 1930s. There are plenty of other films that feature a more balanced (for the times) relationship between men and women. It does not appear to have caused any great scandal when it was released, though this may be a result of its lack of box office success more than anything else. It may also be a result of the predominately male-dominated studios and media of the time, which may not have given much thought to the film's overtones.

Bill (Tracy) accumulates and discards more sweethearts than James Bond, and then marks each of his conquests. In every port the two sailors visit, Spike (Hymer) seeks out a girl only to find that someone else has gotten there first. He knows this because each girl bears a distinctive tattoo. It isn't until shortly before Spike bonds with Bill that he and the audience learn that the mark comes from a ring Tracy wears.

(It would be interesting to find out whether this was in any way the inspiration for the similar method used by Lee Falk's comic creation, The Phantom, to mark both his enemies and his friends.)

Leaving aside the practical matter of how such a trick is accomplished, the act itself speaks volumes about the attitudes expressed in the film. Far from being upset at being branded like cattle (and treated just about as casually), each girl gets a dreamy look in her eye when Spike confronts them about the mark. Even Harlow's character, the titular Goldie, maintains a soft-spot for the man who marked her despite being revealed as a woman nothing short of crooked. There are obvious sexual connotations to the mark, and it is unlikely any audience—even in the 1930s—would be so naive to believe that Bill's interest in these women is limited to witty conversation. (A facet further bolstered by the stunning lack of such exchanges.)

The lack of comment about the mark is almost as notable as the mark itself. It is difficult to imagine that even audiences of the day would condone such a practice. At the least it would seem to symbolically mark Bill as a disreputable character. Such a turn to the script would have been far more welcome than the well-trod paths it does venture down, but alas it is not to be. In fact, Spencer Tracy plays Bill with such charm—in stark contrast to the other characters—that despite reprehensible behavior you end up liking him anyway. Instead of revealing psychologically complex motivations, the tattooing of his women is treated as little more than a quirk and never delved into. Even when it becomes apparent that Bill has been doing this for a while, and possibly even before he became a sailor, little else is said about it.

This is a film where even the male leads are one-dimensional characters, so it is too much to expect a nuanced female role. Still, the lack of any positive female role is almost as stark as the tattoo. Aside from the lackadaisical, even romantic attitude the marked women display toward their "branding," not one of them has an occupation or a role of substance. They are models—swimsuit models no less—or women of leisure who have nothing better to do than plan a picnic in anticipation of meeting a man. It's the 1930s, so modern audiences should not be expecting career women. On the other hand, even Goldie is little more than a plot device, something that could have been accomplished with an inanimate object just as easily as a woman. Greed for wealth drives many a movie partnership apart without the help of cardboard cutout women. The fact that women were chosen as this plot device speaks volumes about someone's attitudes somewhere, it's just not clear whose.

Whether the fault lies with the writer, the director, or some other source, the "love 'em and leave 'em" manner in which Tracy's character bounces from port to port and girl to girl is not undermined or questioned for a single moment in the film. The philosophy of the two sailors, paraphrased as "dames are trouble," is also never called into question. Neither is the idea that women are only good for a quick liaison, and nothing that would induce a sense of commitment once the boat pulls out of port. *Goldie* is at heart a loveless film, with one striking exception.

The only character to which Tracy maintains any sort of affection is for his fellow sailor. In modern times this might lead to the exploration of more complex issues, "Brokeback Merchant Marines" perhaps, or at least the unspoken overtones of the *Odd Couple*. But in *Goldie*, like all other complex issues the matter is left well alone, save for a scene of domestic bliss that is pointedly interrupted by a discussion of the merits of Harlow's character. To not read something more into the manner in which the two sailors go about setting the table and preparing their meals, coupled with the expressions of misery (heartbreak?) when Tracy walks out of the apartment . . . well, perhaps that requires a 1930s audience instead of a Twenty-First century one.

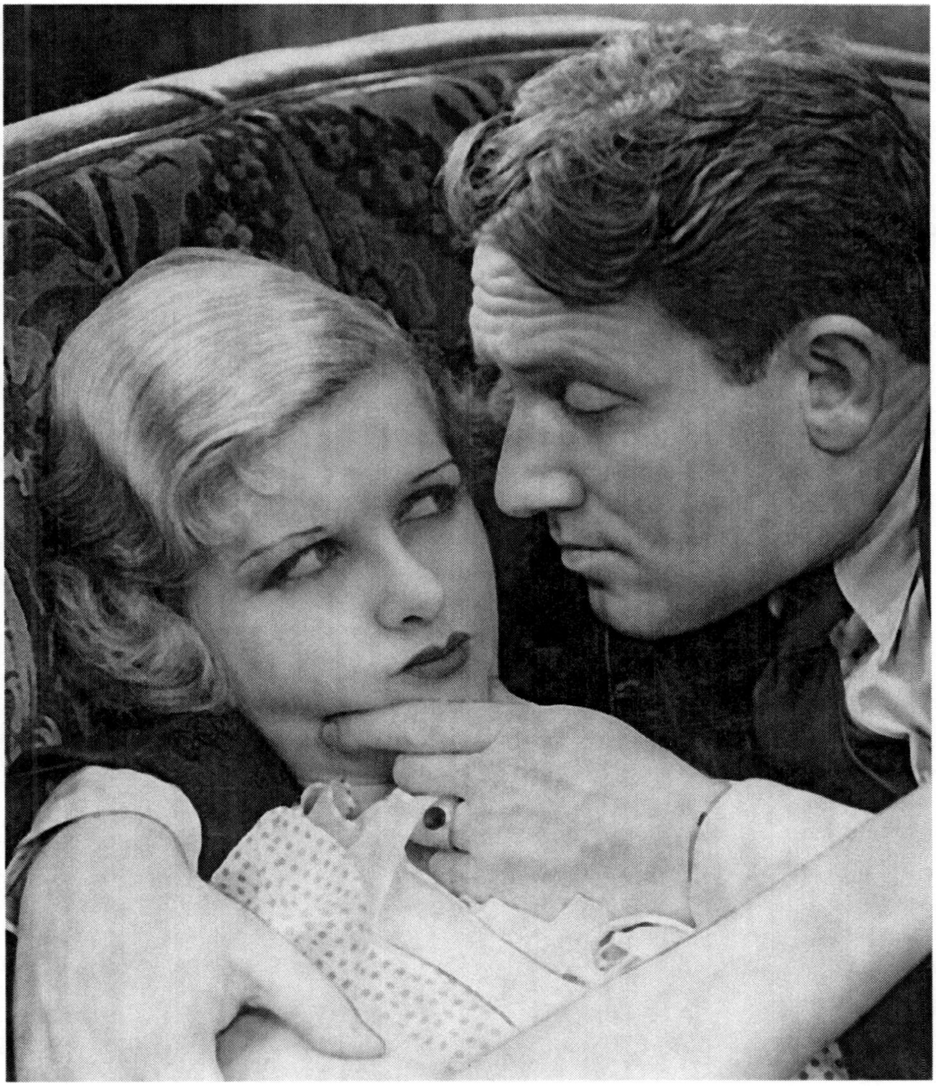

ME AND MY GAL

Raoul Walsh, Director
William Fox, Producer
Written by Arthur Kober
Story by Philip Klein & Barry Conners
Arthur C. Miller, Cinematographer
Released 1932
79 mins

Cast
Spencer Tracy . . . Danny Dolan
Joan Bennett . . . Helen Riley
Marion Burns . . . Kate Riley
George Walsh . . . Duke
J. Farrell MacDonald . . . Pop Riley
Noel Madison . . . Baby Face
Henry B. Walthall . . . Sarge
Bert Hanlon . . . Jake
Adrian Morris . . . Allen
George Chandler . . . Eddie Collins
Emmett Corrigan . . . Police Captain
Jesse De Vorska . . . Jake
Lemist Esler . . . Doctor
Hank Mann . . . Hank
Frank Moran . . . Drunk's Foil
Will Stanton . . . Drunk

And other cast

Me and My Gal and Everyone Else: How a Comedy of Prohibition and Depression Puts Us All on the Same Level

Jeremy Bond

Me and My Gal isn't the only film of its era to offer social commentary. But few comedies did so, and fewer still alluded to crime and politics without overtly trying to send a message. This 1932 film reflects the cynicism accompanying the end of Prohibition and the failure of the government to deal with the Depression. But *Me and My Gal* also is a comedy that is too good-natured to be angry about much of anything.

The film has gangsters, seemingly omnipresent in 1930s Hollywood films, and its heroes are decidedly low-key. Spencer Tracy is a cop—smart-mouthed but kind, a role that helped round him out after he played a few criminals. Another hero in the film is an elderly man, wounded in war, paralyzed and unable to speak. The film plays like a celebration of the accidental hero—quintessentially American—in contrast with the larger-than-life heroes of so many westerns. It's also a pre-Code example of characters who aren't heroes or villains and who don't get praised or punished. There is enough crookedness to go around. In the waning days of Prohibition, everybody's sin is nobody's sin.

Pre-Code Morality

If the film accurately portrays the end of Prohibition, people drank and walked around drunk right in front of the indifferent police. The film implies that this laxity extended to law enforcement in general.

Tracy's cop, Danny Dolan, catches a couple of boys who broke a window during a baseball game. The boys begin fighting. "Could you lick this guy?" Danny asks one of them. Sure, the kid says. "Are you sure about it? . . . Well, don't let me see you fightin'," the officer says, giving them the green light to do so—and turning around to see that they are.

The good and bad are so intertwined that a heist ends up falling in Danny's lap. He courts a chowder house cashier whose sister is protecting her gangster ex-boyfriend, even after her respectable marriage to someone else. The sharp contrast between the strapping former beau and the scrawny new husband is meant to show us why a decent girl would be taken in by a criminal in the first place. The only thing the film does to make the husband appealing is to make him the son of a war hero, a sergeant who was paralyzed in combat.

One scene has the son reading his father a letter from the War Department, promising that he would be given a pension "indefinitely" and that the government would pay for his proper treatment, even though a cure would be impossible. The son tries to cheer him up, assuring him that he would find a doctor who could cure him. Because the sergeant cannot move a muscle, we do not know his emotional reaction to the letter, so we are left to react for him. We might think, that sounds generous of the government, but is that all it can do for someone who sacrificed so much? The sergeant ends up being a quiet hero, alerting Tracy to a wanted mobster. That twist in the story is a recognition that nobody should be speaking down to a sergeant just because he lacks the ability to talk back. He is the moral center in a film in which morality for everyone else is decidedly relative.

This becomes especially clear at the end, when Danny skirts the truth about his heist to protect his girlfriend's sister and praises the sergeant for not alerting his son about his wife's dalliance with the gangster. It is the sort of moral ambiguity that would be resolved by the enforcement of the Production Code.

Danny at least warns the sister about her dalliance. "You oughtta remember that you're a married woman. And married women don't cheat—much."

Pre-Code Dialogue

The film makes light of not only adultery, but also premarital sex. Danny tries to seduce his girlfriend Helen, and her resistance is more of a tease than anything else.

They speak about it the next time they meet. Danny says it is hard for men because if they don't try to "neck," women will think they are too slow. If they do, they will think the men are "fresh." Helen acknowledges a parallel dilemma for women: If she lets someone "maul" her, he will think she's "no good"; if she doesn't, he'll think she's old-fashioned. But Danny claims that guys appreciate the kind of girls who resist: "that is, if he thinks something of her." It was when she "gave (him) the air" that he really began liking her, he tells Helen. This exchange demonstrates the sexual freedom that had expanded in the 1920s; discussing sex so freely was among those freedoms.

Rather than simply speaking in double entendres, the film's characters speak and move much more blatantly than they would in the Production Code era. There are three separate references in the film to a character threatening to kick another character where the sun don't shine. "I'm going to hide my foot in a minute," Danny tells a drunken man who continually shows up in the film. "You won't have to look for it. You'll know where it is." In another scene, Danny's girlfriend turns on the radio and the camera focuses on her backside as she shakes to the music.

Depression-Era Politics

In *Me and My Gal*, authority is scoffed at, and no one is "above" anyone else. Class distinctions are challenged from the start.

Frank, a scruffy guy who hangs around the docks, reads the newspaper for news about the Metropolitan Opera. Danny replies, "That reminds me, I think I'll go to a bur-lee-cue show tonight." Reading further, Frank says, "How do you like this? Mr. Brisbane says that the capitalistic Depression spasm is only a slight chill." Danny: "He does, huh? Aw, those politicians are all alike. They're all of 'em crooks." Frank: "Hey, here's a piece about social economy." Danny: "Social economy? Aw, nuts to social economy. What's on the sportin' page?"

In an America with significant class disparities, Frank is no less interested in these things than a person of high society would be. Danny is no more or less likely to be interested, too, and he isn't. Bored, Danny hands Frank a banana. Hank peels it, throws away the banana on the inside and begins chewing on the peel. The disparity between a man speaking intellectually and chewing on a banana peel is a source of humor.

Politics enters the picture when Danny is shopping in a hat store and the salesman offers him a hat he claims was worn by Alfred E. Smith (the 1928 Democratic nominee for president and former governor of New York, where this film takes place. He was defeated by Herbert Hoover.) Danny wonders out loud what good the hat is if it didn't help Smith to win the presidency. "You know," he says, "I was disappointed. I thought Smith was going to win." The salesman replies, "Me too. There's enough Smiths in the phone book to elect him." After a while, Danny says, "A Smith might not have made a bad president." The word "a" is barely audible, but it changes his meaning entirely—not that Alfred Smith would be a good president, but that a man named Smith, perhaps the most common American last name, would have been.

Me and My Gal was released in early December, 1932, so Hoover's tough reelection battle was likely under way during filming. By the time this film was released, Hoover had lost to Franklin D. Roosevelt. Both Hoover and Roosevelt came from prosperous families, while Smith was born to working-class parents in New York's Lower East Side and worked at a fish market possibly not unlike the one in this film. These characters could relate best to Smith, an everyman (and not to mention a favorite native son). The film also is filled with characters of Irish origin and/or people who like to drink; they probably would have appreciated a Smith in the White House in part because he was Catholic and anti-Prohibition. Historians have attributed Smith's defeat to anti-Catholic sentiment. The nod to Smith in the script was undoubtedly a little nudge to the audience, which was watching the film as an escape from the Depression—blamed, fairly or not, on Herbert Hoover.

The Characters: Stereotypes

Irish culture is most represented in the movie by the sisters' father, Pat Riley, a tugboat captain played by real-life Irishman J. Farrell MacDonald (a favorite of Irish director John Ford). At the end of his daughter's wedding ceremony, he kisses the bride before her new husband does. Riley's buddies are hard drinkers, and Riley himself is a party animal with a temper. The wedding reception has kegs of beer and men belching and eating like "sea lions." A song on the radio includes the word "gigolo," and when Riley is told what that means, he throws the radio out the window. Not even the Corleones threw a wedding like that.

While the portrayal of the Irish appears like benign stereotyping, a few fleeting references to national origin seem unnecessary. The participants in a fight are incorrectly called "Spaniards" or a "Chinaman"—another intended source of humor. Immigrant family members sit emotionless as thieves enter their home and drill a hole in their floor. Their passivity is perhaps explained away by the fact that they are immigrants who hold no power, but they are depicted as people with less life in them than everybody else.

The paralyzed sergeant represents a rare departure for old Hollywood's depiction of disability. He is not pitied. His mind is not compromised. The other characters come close to treating him something like less than human—a realization that "he's trying to tell us something!" is a little too reminiscent of the Lassie films—but that has more to say about the way people react to the disabled than about ignorance on the filmmakers' parts.

The Anti-Message Film

The open sexuality of the pre-Code era would reach a peak with Mae West and films like *Baby Face*, in which Barbara Stanwyck sleeps her way to the top (of a skyscraper). Raoul Walsh, who directed *Me and My Gal*, was a perfect fit for the era. His skepticism toward morality was evident in his 1928 film *Sadie Thompson*, in which a zealous religious "reformer" brainwashes a prostitute into repentance then is overcome by lust for her. At Fox, Walsh revealed more of his appreciation for the gritty with films such as *The Bowery*, which also featured a blustery Irishman and less-than-stellar sensitivity toward ethnic minorities. *Me and My Gal* only skims the surface.

A handful of "social conscious" dramas in the early 1930s allowed audiences to hear about the Depression rather than simply escape from it. *Heroes for Sale*, also released in 1932, tackled Communism and the mistreatment of veterans, among other things. *Me and My Gal* addressed the Depression but allowed people to escape from it by laughing about it. The film makes a point without having a point of view, apart from a general critique of people in charge. It is a 1930s dose of antiestablishment.

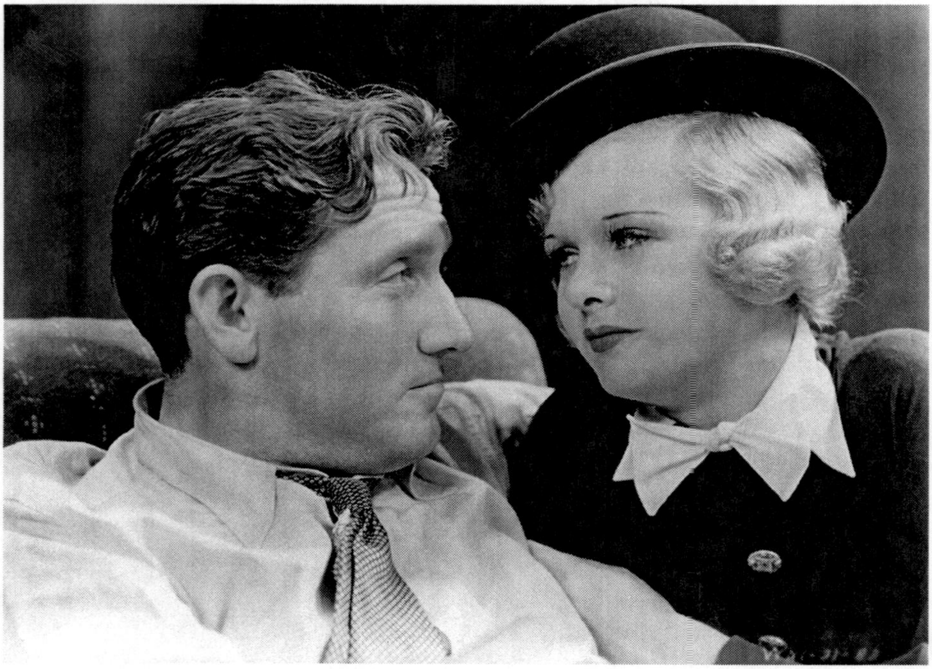

Me and My Gal: Fanfare for the Everyday Hero

Eric Shoag

Me and My Gal was made in 1932, at the height of the Depression, and it takes only moments to learn its attitude toward that harrowing time. The opening shot is of the hands of patrolman Danny Dolan (Spencer Tracy) gloved in immaculate white, brushing off his hat and setting off on his beat—the busy, bustling docks. Dolan is the picture of scrubbed cheerfulness as he greets Frank, a tough-as-nails character with an impossibly deep, gravelly voice, who is perusing the morning paper. Frank reads off some items of note disgustedly, and Dolan rattles off an instant wisecrack to each one. "I see where the Metropolitan Opera is gonna open the season with Pagliacci," spits Frank. "Yeah? That reminds me, I think I'll go to a burly-q show tonight," Dolan retorts. "How do ya like this?" Frank offers, "Mr. Brisbane says that the capitalistic depression spasm is only a slight chill." "He does, eh?" answers Dolan, warming to their act, "Ah, those politicians are all alike. They're all of 'em crooks!" No sooner are the words out of his mouth than he's swiped a couple bananas as a load is carried by, handing one to his pal. "Here, wrap your kisser around that." In a bit of bewildering surrealism, Frank throws the meat of the fruit away and chomps grimly on the peel.

In case there are any lingering doubts as to the picture's tone, Depression-era pathos then makes an appearance in the form of a sad old man and the dog he has brought along to drown. "You'll never miss another one," he wails, lamenting all the meals they haven't eaten together. Dolan quickly dispatches this bleak specter of despair, taking charge of the pet to the man's overwhelming disbelief and gratitude. The pooch stays in the picture, while his owner is pushed to the sidelines, there to stay with the rest of the degradation and horror that was the reality of the Depression for so many. For we are concerned here with Danny Dolan and his kind: The Working Man—plucky, resilient, and relentlessly positive, always ready with small talk and good humor, the grease that makes the hard hours go by faster, and, more importantly, makes for a life of activity and optimism. Instinctively he knows the value of clear thinking and quick action, of not being dragged down by hopelessness. He is the perfect hero for this wonderful piece of disposable entertainment, existing only in this simplified cartoon version of the Depression, and yet still resonating with us over seventy-five years later.

Simple, disposable entertainment is exactly what *Me and My Gal* is, the kind studios turned out by the dozens back then—uncomplicated pictures for the masses to get caught up in and forget their troubles for an hour and a half. In many ways we can understand why it has remained forgotten, that is to say unavailable on DVD or video, existing only in its original celluloid form to be seen exclusively (if at all) in darkened theaters. *Me and My Gal* is not at all glamorous and doesn't boast a particularly potent plot or riveting romance. It is not timeless, like many films from that era that stand up to repeated viewing today, but intimately connected to its time, and yet it sparkles nonetheless, offering a fascinating and rewarding glimpse at another kind of movie made in those days. A multitude of moods and characters are packed into its seventy-eight minutes, with director Raoul Walsh juggling the genres and elements deftly and maintaining a breezy pace. Writing in the *Village Voice*, Elliot Stein found it impossible to categorize simply, calling it " . . . arguably the quintessential gum-chewing fast-talking, Depression-Prohibition melodrama romance comedy of the period."

It is all of that and more: we get a suspenseful "film noir" type crime thriller with melodramatic trappings played out among the Irish working-class, with a strong sense of family and community, all wrapped up in the tough and funny romance between Tracy's Danny Dolan and his perfect match, one Helen Riley (Joan Bennett). Here is a simple, almost childlike picture of life and morality: work hard and remain upbeat, don't be tempted by crime or depravity, and with persistence and a little luck you will succeed. Dolan saves the life of a drunk and is instantly promoted to detective. Money matters are never addressed specifically, but the main characters are almost always at their jobs. The Depression exists on the fringes of the world of this movie, and we are made aware of the unfortunates out there again and again; families crammed into small apartments, the drunk and the destitute, dirty children brawling in the streets, but mostly they are played for laughs. Banks are frequently the butt of jokes, albeit bitterly, as when Dolan hears of a bank robbery and asks who they robbed now. "This time the bank was robbed," he is told. "Oh, they were double-crossed, huh? Gettin' a little dose of their own medicine!"

This good-natured wisecracking is at the core of what makes *Me and My Gal* so appealing, and the script by Arthur Kober (from a story by Phillip Klein and Barry Conners), while possessing no earth-shattering wit, is full of humorous banter that seems completely natural and spontaneous. Tracy, one of the great naturalistic actors, is perfectly at ease walking the fine line between innocent and jaded sensibilities, and his level-headedness and good nature anchors the film. Sure, you've got to work hard in this world, but the other, equally important message is to enjoy life to the fullest whenever possible. There is a remarkable sequence at the wedding of Helen's sister Kate, where after the ceremony the huge craggy head of old Pop Riley (J. Farrell MacDonald) approaches the camera, quickly filling the screen, as he addresses the audience itself: "Who'd like a drink, huh? Come on!" What follows is a frenzy of celebration, a montage showing food and drink being consumed at an astonishing rate. One heavily jowled guest pauses after gulping down his beverage, commenting aloud to no one in particular, "That's good beer," then letting out a thunderous belch.

One character who finds it difficult to share in this overflowing enjoyment of life is the bride Kate herself, played to brittle perfection by Marion Burns. It is she who opens the door to darkness and suspense, being tempted by a dashing and dangerous former lover, Duke Castenega (George Walsh, director Raoul's brother), who has just escaped from prison. Kate, a bank employee, is immediately approached by Castenega and his cronies, who need a key piece of information from her to plan their next job. She is vulnerable and weak, and becomes instantly distracted. Even on her wedding day she is led into dark rooms, and later into the attic of her apartment with its jagged shadows and sharp angles, appropriate settings for her betrayal. These sudden bursts of "noir" are photographed beautifully by Arthur Miller.

The darkness never takes over, though, as Kate repents her misdeeds after Castenega's capture, and is welcomed back into the bosom of her family. Indeed, for a "pre-Code" film, that is, one made before the Hays Code was enacted in 1934 to regulate the content of motion pictures, *Me and My Gal* is relatively tame, consistent with its "all-ages" message of family and morality. There are, however, some curious exceptions, the most obvious of which is the omnipresent drunkenness. This was, of course, the era of Prohibition, and the movie is constantly flaunting its alcohol consumption. From the recurring presence of the drunk whose life Dolan saves (Will Stanton, who has far too much screen time, his shenanigans being milked for laughs well beyond the point of humor), to Pop Riley encouraging the audience, booze is everywhere.

At one point, Duke Castenega and company wine and dine Kate, hoping to loosen her tongue a bit. As a result, she becomes completely sloshed, unsteady on her feet and slurring her speech, and then we learn she must now return to work, as this was her lunch break! Even Dolan takes it all in stride, investigating a disturbance at the Riley apartment during Kate's wedding party (Pop has thrown a bulky record player out the second story window, offended at the word "gigolo" being mentioned in a song). He and his partner Al are immediately offered a drink. "No, no," Dolan politely demurs, "I'm on duty." The final image of the film is Pop again striding up to the camera, laughing and repeating his exhortation to the crowd of moviegoers, as if inviting us to join him and his family in celebrating a satisfactory conclusion to their story.

One interesting presence in the film, and one that surely would not have been there once the Hays Code was enacted, is that of Kate's father-in-law Sarge (Henry B. Walthall), a paralyzed World War I veteran who can communicate only by blinking his eyes. Dependent on government support, veterans were among those hit hardest by the Depression, in addition to being a reminder of a recent past too horrible to contemplate. Sarge sits in Kate's apartment, alone and eerily silent, like a conscience to her sneaky subversions, and while she avoids him, Dolan shows no hesitation in making him feel included, still a vital part of the world.

But the most wonderful and satisfying, yet also the most subtle of pre-code sensibilities, is the romance between Danny Dolan and Helen Riley. Their attraction is plainly sensual, from her saucy strut to his eyes glaring at her in lust. There is nothing fancy here, no conflicts of class or interest, just like-minded people sparking that most ineffable and elusive of qualities: chemistry. Joan Bennett is a revelation as Helen, her relaxed self-assuredness a perfect contrast to her sister's panic and guilt. Seeing Kate's apprehension at her wedding, Helen tries her best to be encouraging. "Snap into it," she says, not knowing the real reason behind her sister's attitude. The earthy romance between Helen and Dolan plays out, as the whole movie does, in ordinary settings; in unremarkable apartments, on the docks, and in the coffee shop where Helen works as a cashier. In a marvelous bit of underacting, she sits behind the register, nose in a newspaper, chewing the piece of gum that is her constant companion, not looking up until Dolan addresses her. Their first exchange sets the tone for all that follows:

> "Hiya Red, here's half a buck."
> "Yeah I know what it is. My name isn't 'Red' and besides I'm a blonde."
> "Well, whatever you are it's very beautiful hair, where'd ya get it?"
> "Aw, go take a walk and feed your dog."
> "All right, baby, I'll see ya later."

That he does, and soon she takes to brazenly mocking him, throwing his own phrases back in his face in the manner of his partner Al (Adrien Morris), who repeats everything Dolan says. With Al, the result is oddly comical. "What's this, a brother act or something?" Pop asks in bewilderment. In the case of Helen, however, their lines laconically rub against each other in sensual, hypnotic repetition. "What're you tryin' to do, kid me?" Dolan asks her, puzzled. "Good old Sherlock," she replies, "you catch right on."

Dolan may be comfortable and confident, but he's got nothing on Helen, who slowly saunters through every scene, chewing gum, leaning against countertops, banisters and doorframes, completely at home in her skin and in the world. After their one spat, the two meet accidentally at the docks, where they each have come to visit the dog Dolan has made a home for there, and they slowly circle each other during the ensuing reconciliation, showing their gift for simple physicality as well as the pleasure they take in the whole process of falling in love. Their courtship is remarkably chaste by today's standards, in keeping with the "all-ages" theme; when they kiss for the first time, she thinks "I'm so thrilled. But I'll pretend I'm mad." But when Dolan at last bursts out with a proposal, after hours at the coffee shop, the two meet in a carnal kiss over the counter, with her grabbing his hair and he climbing up to meet her, his foot twitching in ecstasy.

And it is a breezy sort of ecstasy that characterizes *Me and My Gal*. Writing in the *Chicago Reader*, Jonathan Rosenbaum called it " . . . a simple picture, but in many ways an ecstatic one." For what we are left with ultimately is the ecstasy of Dolan and Helen's relationship. After all, there is nothing more timeless than the profundity of two people coming together and connecting amidst surrounding chaos and evil (or indifference, for that matter), building a life together and becoming a force for good. No, *Me and My Gal* doesn't address any "big" issues, it is only a momentary diversion, but in the end it is the little issues that really matter: how to keep going from day to day, how to enjoy existence to the best of our ability. Unlike many more popular and remembered films from the 1930s, *Me and My Gal* doesn't show an inaccessible world of luxury and decadence, but rather a simple one within the reach of its audience. In some strange way, it shows us an ideal world, where celebration is mandatory, where darkness is swept away, a flesh wound and fading memories of guilt the only price, and where hard work, the right attitude and a little luck can bring, if not prosperity, certainly happiness and fulfillment. This was no doubt a tonic for the masses in 1932, and it is still more than slightly relevant today.

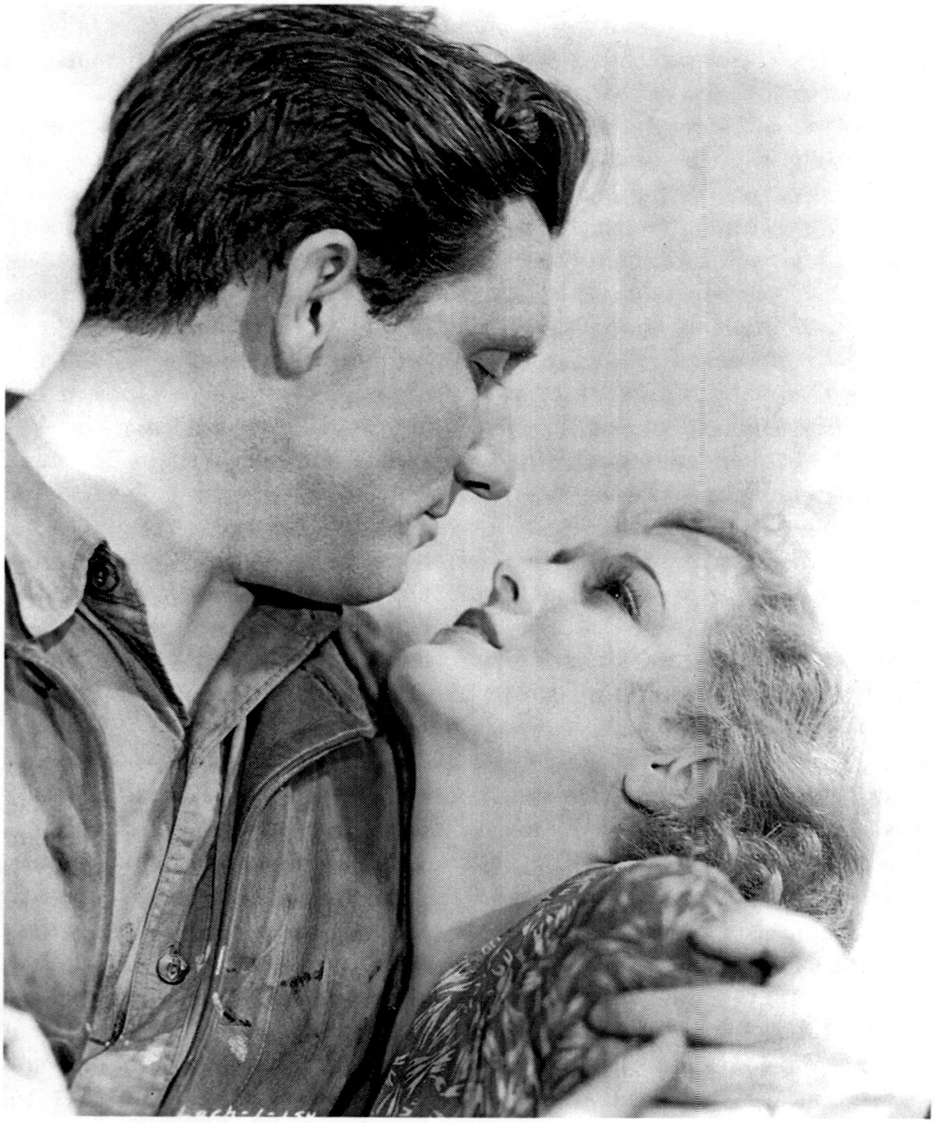

FACE IN THE SKY

Harry Lachman, Director
William Fox, Producer
Myles Connolly, Story
Humphrey Pearson, Writer
Lee Garmes, Cinematographer
Distributed by Fox Film Corporation
Released January 15, 1933
77 minutes

Cast
Spencer Tracy . . . Joe Buck
Marian Nixon . . . Madge
Stuart Erwin . . . Lucky
Sam Hardy . . . Triplet the Great
Sarah Padden . . . Ma Brown
Frank McGlynn Jr . . . . Jim Brown
Russell Simpson . . . Pa Brown
Billy Platt . . . Midget
Lila Lee . . . Sharon Hadley
Guy Usher . . . Albert Preston

And other cast

Countryside Blues: How the City Saves the Day in *Face in the Sky*

Jeremy Bond

Face in the Sky is a battle between rural and urban sensibilities, a reverse *Wizard of Oz*. Rural life is a dead end after all. No place is as bad as home, which lacks kindness and innovation. There really *is* a better life over the rainbow in a large, magical city that is mysterious and frightening. And strength for a young woman does not come from within, as it did for Dorothy, but through a man from that faraway city.

Spencer Tracy plays an advertising sign-painter from New York City named Joe Buck who describes his profession in glorified terms. His line of work is no more or less reputable than that of a farmer, but his urban roots are an asset in themselves. He is dreamy and kind-hearted while the farmers are thoughtless and callous.

With little effort on his part, Joe "rescues" a childlike farm girl from her Cinderella existence. The girl forever leaves a life of hard work behind for a life of commercialism and new clothes. This story would be a complete triumph for an urban existence except that Tracy's character prefers this farm girl over a wealthy celebrity. It would seem, then, that 1933 America favored men who aimed high in the business world and women who remained starry-eyed and innocent.

Breaking Free of the Country

Rural residents are represented through the Brown family, which share a surname with so many other fictionalized farm families. The Browns are less intelligent and less spirited than the urban dwellers in the film. Even their commitment to God, more associated with rural populations, is not reliable. A minister complains that he seems to see Pa Brown only at funerals, and Pa replies that he has too much work to go to church.

Joe Buck works for a big-time New York cosmetics company and is sent for moneymaking opportunities in the New England countryside with his dimwitted partner, Lucky. (Tracy was appealing enough without a dumb guy tagging alongside, but many of his Fox films burdened him with one nevertheless.) Neither Joe nor Lucky went to school, but Joe knows how to make himself sound erudite.

Joe's destination is the Brown farm, where he barely convinces Pa Brown to paint a giant face on the side of his barn advertising "Beauty Magic" cosmetics. He offers the farmer a free box of the product, but Pa wants money instead. Apparently Pa is no fool—until he agrees instead to a valueless watch. While the business is legitimate, the fact that Joe and Lucky use this little scam on everybody gives an impression that rural people can be had. Forty years later, the Depression-era film *Paper Moon* gives a similar impression.

Ma and Pa Brown are guardians to Madge, who falls for Joe from the start. She is so underexposed to the outside world that she never even gets to hear music. She has apparently read books or newspapers, because she's heard of the Ritz-Carlton Hotel (Joe fibs that he lives there). Joe brags that he would paint the biggest sign in New York City, and Madge sighs that she would never see it. Madge wears the only dress she owns.

Joe impresses upon Madge that anyone could be anything, claiming that he could have been president of the United States if only he hadn't "turned it down." She believes everything he says. He inadvertently gives her the courage to run away from home by hiding in his truck, but he had never suggested anything that she might be capable of accomplishing over the rainbow. He only brags about his own profession.

"I wouldn't trade jobs with anybody in the world," he says. "I mean, these guys they call the great captains of industry—why, they're a lot of buck privates. Why do you suppose this country built all the good roads? So people could look at the billboards.... I keep millions of clerks at work. I make the whistles toot and the factories smoke. And that makes us outdoor artists the greatest salesmen in the world."

"I didn't know it was so easy to be somebody," Madge says.

"With my system, it's a cinch.... Try it sometime. And don't get discouraged. I wasn't so much either when I started, and look at me now."

In the context of the Depression, which is largely absent from this movie, Joe's speech has a cynical edge. Having a job, any job, probably was the best thing anyone could hope for. But Joe is clearly intended to be seen as optimistic. And his homily is a reminder that the Little Guy without a job impacts much more than the Little Guy himself. At the same time, Joe seeks to be one of those "great captains of industry" and one day become president of the company. The message: Be happy with what you've got, but always aim higher.

The Characters: Gender

Although this talk apparently inspires Madge, little of it is relevant for her. She is a woman. It is Joe's sample makeup kit, which Madge shares with Ma Brown, that seems to liberate the women. When Ma Brown tries it on, Pa grumbles, "What's that stuff? You take it off! You want to make a fool of yourself?" Madge is so inexperienced that she globs it on as if she were five years old. The makeup, as well as the paint, colors these women's drab lives in the same way that color represented liberation in the 1990s fantasy "Pleasantville."

Yet the colors are simply products, and the women are simply being taken in by advertising. Joe is a salesman above all else.

The male-dominated Brown family keeps the womenfolk in their place. Ma Brown is so meek that she is practically scared of strangers. The men rough everybody up and have guns on hand. Then Joe Buck, the city dweller, arrives and protects a lady's honor from these authoritarians. "That's no work for a girl," he tells Madge as she prepares to carry slop buckets. Joe treats her nice, but she is too naïve to object that he doesn't treat her like an adult.

Madge acts terribly innocent. "I'm not supposed to speak to you," she tells Joe shyly upon meeting him. Later, she is offered an alcoholic beverage, but she asks for milk. She is no child, but Joe calls her a "great little kid." At one point, he sighs, "Gosh, bringing up a woman is a tough job."

Joe is threatened with charges for transporting an "underage" girl across state lines, although it isn't clear how old Madge is supposed to be. The actress, Marian Nixon, was in her late 20s at the time, just a few years younger than Tracy. One of her on-screen roles the previous year was Rebecca of Sunnybrook Farm.

At the beginning, Joe dreams of marrying a "delicate dame," particularly one whose old man owns a railroad. When he returns to the city, he is assigned to painting a celebrity who is, indeed, the daughter of a railroad magnate. She is seductive. In one of the film's rare pre-Code style exchanges, she suggests he take her home—then tells him not to bother when he says he would have to get up early the next morning. Come and see me tomorrow instead, she says, when she'll have "a few people over"—meaning just the two of them. But Joe ultimately rejects this woman for Madge. While Madge sought refuge in an urbanite, he seeks someone as pure as the country.

The Varied Landscape

The spread of visual advertising into the countryside threatened the charm of rural areas. Not only does Joe have no qualms about painting a brash billboard on a country barn, but he even imagines painting the moon. In New York City, of course, outdoor advertising is everywhere. *Face in the Sky* includes a strange sequence in which Madge imagines the people in the billboards coming to life and speaking to her. The consumer culture, as depicted in the film, is alive and well even in the midst of the Depression.

Carnivals, portrayed in this movie and in so many others, offer rural residents a taste of the outlandish world of urban life and its overindulgent consumerism. Joe tries to keep Madge away from a carnival con artist who is no more legitimate than Professor Marvel, the phony fortune teller who would become the Wizard of Oz of Dorothy's fantasy. The con artist, we discover, is from the city.

The film's juxtaposition of urban and rural residents is not exactly comparing apples to apples. The farm family is working class, while the urbanites hobnob with the rich. The Ritz-Carlton is featured, but not the working-class tenements shown in films such as King Vidor's 1931 *Street Scene*.

Face in the Sky does provide a brief scene of the seedy side of New York, though it would not be portrayed with significantly more realism until after the dissolution of the Production Code. In 1969, another Joe Buck would conquer New York: Jon Voight's male prostitute in *Midnight Cowboy*. In that film, New York is suffocating and Florida is over the rainbow. Film characters continue to roam from the city to the country or the country to the city—as long as it is wherever they aren't.

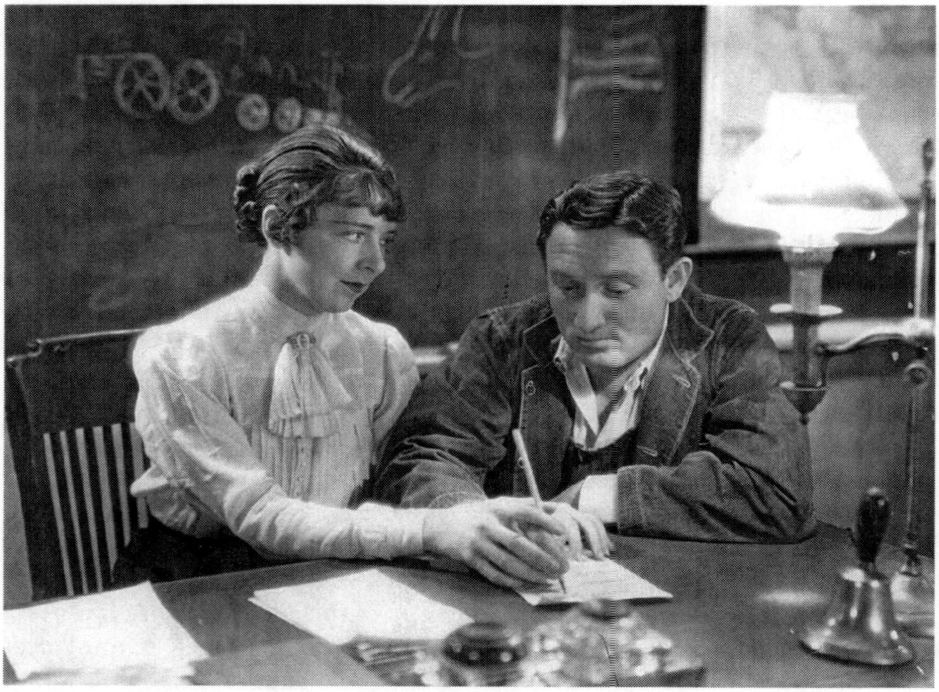

THE POWER AND THE GLORY

William K. Howard, Director
Jesse L. Lasky, Producer
Preston Sturges, Writer
James Wong Howe, Cinematographer
Distributed by Fox Film Corporation
Released 6 October 1933
76 minutes

Cast
Spencer Tracy . . . Tom Garner
Colleen Moore . . . Sally Garner
Ralph Morgan . . . Henry
Helen Vinson . . . Eve Borden
Clifford Jones . . . Tom Garner, Jr.
Henry Kolker . . . Mr. Borden
Sarah Padden . . . Henry's Wife
Billy O'Brien . . . Tom (younger)
Cullen Johnson . . . Henry (younger)
J. Farrell MacDonald . . . Mulligan

And other cast

The Power and the Glory: Citizen Garner

Paul Sherman

"Narratage" is the term Fox Films attached to Preston Sturges' script for *The Power and the Glory*, a movie which opens through non-linear flashbacks guided by a narrator who often describes the action being seen. "Narratage," it turned out, was not the popular innovation its marketers thought it would be. A flashback or non-linear structure has long ago ceased to be a novelty or a challenge to an audience, and even in 1933 it was not new (critics of the day delighted in pointing this out and mocking Fox for actually mounting a plaque in Manhattan's Gaiety Theater, the first New York picture palace to show their "narratage" film). But it was somewhat different, and such a structure—in which the high points and low points of the main character's life are weighed—epitomizes the ambivalence with which director William K. Howard's movie perceives its hero, Tom Garner.

Like most any memorable Spencer Tracy character, Garner is full of stubborn determination. He shares a physical toughness with Tracy's typical characters from the early 1930s, though instead of inhabiting a cellblock, a cop's beat or a sailor's sea routes, Garner's domain is a corporate boardroom, making *The Power and the Glory* a step up in prestige for the emerging actor. The movie allows Tracy to play the role from the age of 20 (a big leap of faith) to the mid-50s, for which he sports dyed grey hair (which actually looks more blond than the head of white hair the actor would eventually have himself years later).

A railroad tycoon whose funeral opens the movie, Garner is reviled by most but defended by his confidential secretary and oldest friend, Henry

(Ralph Morgan). We feel this conflict between others' perception and Henry's feelings for Garner before the flashbacks even start. Henry ducks out of Garner's funeral and returns to the offices of the Chicago & Southwestern Railway Company, where a watchman snarls "I'm glad he croaked" before Henry shuts him up. Henry's wife (Sarah Padden) is no fan of Garner, either, and the flashbacks begin after Henry gets home and tries to explain to her that the tycoon's suicide was not a result of guilt over the sorrow he brought to employees and relatives, but the result of something more sympathetic.

Much of what follows is pure Horatio Alger success story. Henry details his first meeting with Tom Garner at a swimming hole, where self-assured farm boy Tom taught him how to swim and protected him from bullies; he tells of how he was later responsible for Tom and wife Sally (silent-film star Colleen Moore) becoming so close, since Tom—who was too busy working on his father's farm to ever go to school—had to have her read a letter Henry wrote (Sally eventually schools 20-year-old Tom in the three R's in her spare time); he also tells of Tom's struggle, after marrying Sally, to complete his engineering studies and the drive that quickly brought him promotions on the railroad line for which he is initially employed as a track walker.

Tom Garner is an All-American hero in these biographical glimpses, with a Huck Finn sense of adventure in the boyhood scene and a desire to work hard and make a good life for his family in his early adult life. In keeping with the "narratage" marketing, though, these flashbacks from decades ago mingle with Henry's more recent recollections of how middle-aged Garner buys out a smaller rail line by sheer force of will, overpowering a skeptical board of directors to endorse his idea, and how he falls for Eve (Helen Vinson), the much-younger, divorced daughter of the purchased line's owner. Although there is almost always a hint of a dark side to the ferocity of Tom's alpha personality—in the swimming hole sequence, he hurts his hand after he dives off a high tree limb into the water—it's here that the rosy, even overeager portrayal of Tom's headstrong approach to life really gives way to something ominous. His refusal to negotiate with striking workers results in a violent walkout in which 400 die; his confession to wife Sally about falling for Eve causes his trusting partner to kill herself; and, once into his second marriage, his workaholic personality leads neglected Eve to seek solace from his grown son, Thomas, Jr. (Clifford Jones), who has lots of his dad's money but little of his ambition.

Written nearly a decade before he would become the king of 1940s comedy, Sturges' dramatic script casts a shadow on the American Dream. It was inspired by Sturges' second wife's tales about her grandfather, cereal magnate C.W. Post, a success whose life also ended in suicide. Despite Henry's defenses of his pal, Sturges' Tom Garner is not an admirable fellow.

The come-uppance he gets in his personal life is meant to be seen as a bit of karmic payoff for the way he's steamrolled over everyone else in his life, particularly in his professional life. The movie leaves us with mixed emotions about Garner, sympathetic to his pain but wary of his selfish personality, drawn to the charisma of Tracy's performance but repulsed by the callousness the actor brings to the tycoon.

The film negative of *The Power and the Glory* was destroyed in a fire and the movie thought lost for many decades. Despite still being obscure—the poor quality of existing prints makes one wonder if it ever will be released on home video—it's hard to call it true buried treasure, since its most interesting qualities are offscreen, not on. The "narratage" wasn't the only unusual thing about Sturges' script. At a time when screenplays were fashioned by a committee of studio staff writers, then-playwright Sturges wrote the movie on his own, received lone writing credit and negotiated a deal with Fox that granted him a share of the movie's gross receipts. The script was also shot just as Sturges wrote it, and the writer was even allowed to observe all of the filming. The arrangement outraged many in Hollywood, and Sturges, widely resented, endured a three-year drought before later becoming the prolific writer-director he would become.

But despite the "narratage" ballyhoo and the important role *The Power and the Glory* played in the careers of Tracy and Sturges, the movie itself is rather plodding. The overbearingly maudlin music of the opening sequence sets a heavy tone the movie never really sheds, save for a few comic sequences (especially the one in which Tom tries to muster the nerve to propose to Sally), and the "narratage" structure is not very conducive to character development. For instance, the wife played by Moore (returning to the screen after a four-year absence) pops up only whenever needed; at different junctures, she is a sweet schoolteacher, an ambitious wife pushing her husband to improve his lot in life and a middle-aged, overburdened rich man's wife. There's little sense of transition or the passage of time. One of the hallmarks of Sturges' script—having the narrator occasionally voice the dialogue mouthed by characters in the flashbacks—is also highly *un*cinematic, as any movie with as much narration as this can be. That Sturges' script tempers Garner's business success with personal failure, illustrating a downside to his ego-driven ambition, is notable. The decades when the movie was thought lost added legendary status to it. Even with its surprise ending as a pre-Code movie, it is difficult to imagine anything in it that would not have been permissible when the production code started being enforced more ardently in 1934.

There's both historical and entertainment value to the movie. *The Power and the Glory* was not the one and only story of a polarizing, headstrong, scandalous tycoon who dies at the beginning of the movie, and whose life and times are pieced together via flashbacks. *The Power and the Glory* reportedly was an influence on Orson Welles, who co-wrote, directed and starred in *Citizen Kane*. *Citizen Kane* may have brought a more expressive visual style to its "narratage" but before there was Charles Foster Kane, there was Tom Garner.

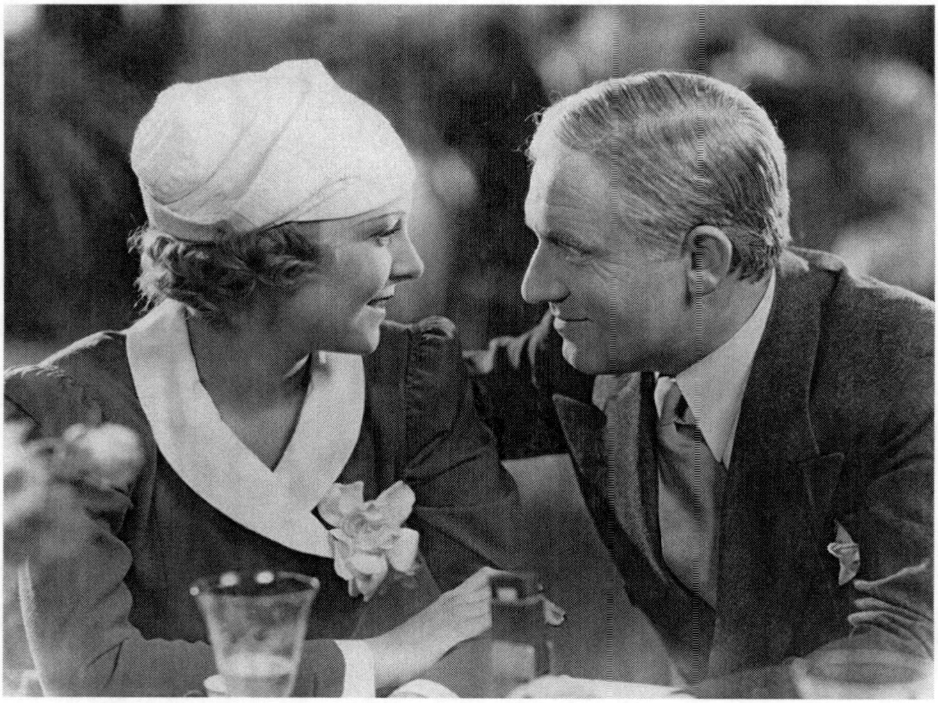

The Power and the Glory: The Depression Never Looked So Good

Jeremy Bond

The Power and the Glory pits small-town American humility against the American dream of success. A precursor to—and reportedly an inspiration for—*Citizen Kane*, this film implies that what a man has in the first place is better than what he winds up with. Spencer Tracy's Tom Garner is likable as an uneducated trackwalker, incorrigible as a railroad president. The only thing that apparently brought about this change was his "success."

Preston Sturges wrote the screenplay in 1932, during the height of the Depression and the end of the Herbert Hoover administration. Filming began in the days following the inauguration of Franklin D. Roosevelt, and the film was released after the launch of his New Deal programs. *The Power and the Glory* was not immune to the political undercurrent pervading so many Hollywood films of the time. Movies either tackled the Depression head-on in dramas such as *Heroes for Sale*, ignored it completely in escapist fare like *King Kong*, or fell somewhere in between. The Busby Berkeley musical *Gold Diggers of 1933*, for example, began with the toe-tapping tune "We're in the Money" and concluded in part with "Remember My Forgotten Man" as a nod to those who weren't lucky enough to be in the money. *Dinner at Eight* was one of several notable films focusing on high society, but there was an unmistakable reference to the Depression: the "dinner" of the title was increasingly doomed as the movie progressed, demonstrating that even the relatively wealthy were not immune to disaster. *The Power and the Glory*, meanwhile, has a unique perspective on hard financial times. It suggests that the alternative—power and glory—is worse.

Smaller was Better

Pulling one up by one's bootstraps is a well-established American value. But more than one of Tracy's early films sent the message that certain people are meant to accomplish only so much.

In *The Face in the Sky*, Tracy plays a sign-painter who is ambitious within his own field but does not seek to bite off more than he could chew. Instead of wanting to own a railroad, his goal is to marry the daughter of someone who owns a railroad. He doesn't reach that goal, and the film ends happily for him probably *because* that didn't happen. In *The Power and the Glory*, meanwhile, Tracy begins his career as a happy trackwalker, and becomes ambitious only reluctantly. Once he rises to the top, he ends up miserable and as doomed as Charles Foster Kane.

As in *Citizen Kane*, the film begins after the protagonist's death. Henry, Tom Garner's faithful secretary, tells his boss's larger-than-life story. Henry scolds his wife for vilifying Tom. "You didn't judge him by ordinary standards," he says. Henry's narrative shifts back and forth in time, so the audience sees the juxtaposition between old, bitter Tom and young, idealistic Tom. Henry sees a consistent decency in Tom that nobody else (including the film's viewers) sees. The old, wealthy Tom does elicit some compassion, but the Depression-era audience was unlikely to be very sympathetic.

Sturges, like Frank Capra, found the most dignity in the everyman, here exemplified by the old Tom. Trackwalkers, after all, had an important role in America's westward expansion. They would inspect miles of railroads to look for any broken joints and rails, according to a guide published in The *Railroad Gazette* in 1878. At that time, trackwalkers typically lived with a foreman's family. *The Power and the Glory* suggests that married trackwalkers wouldn't stay that way for long.

When Tom meets Sally (Colleen Moore), she is a schoolteacher at the "mountain school," and he is illiterate and ashamed of it. Sally teaches him how to read and write, and they fall in love. Early in their marriage, Sally pushes him into aiming higher.

"Do you want to be a trackwalker all your life?" she asks him. "Won't you try to be somebody?" Maybe then they could have "good clothes and a horse-and-buggy," she says. So Tom goes to business school. They have a son, and Tom tells his wife dreamily, "I'll make so much money for you and that kid we can buy the Southwestern (railroad) and give it to him to play with."

Tom does indeed become the owner of the railroad. Over the intervening thirty years, his personality changes from humble to ruthless. He tramples over his board of directors, bullying it to do whatever he says. He grows bitter and ashamed of his son, who is kicked out of Yale for drunken behavior. "To think I had to sweat for an education," he growls at him. The film's audience sees the contrast between young Tom's enthusiasm for studies and his son's disdain for it.

The story itself seems to question the value of education. Tom is a happy, agreeable person before Sally pushes him into business school. Henry tells us at the beginning of the film that Tom had never gone to school as a child because his father believed that "you didn't need arithmetic to feed hogs or readin' and writin' to milk a cow." Henry's tone and language suggest nostalgia for a time when education was unnecessary. Yet Henry also went to business school, and it's never clear why Henry was content being Tom's right-hand man instead of pursuing his own career path.

As an older man, Tom considers modest work demeaning. He punishes his son—horror of horrors—by getting him a desk job. Sally is disgusted that her son would be a junior bookkeeper. "Especially at *my* age, Mother!" the son complains. "I ought to be taking exercise and having fun. You can't have any fun when you're old." The film has more respect for Tom as a working-class trackwalker than for his son as a wealthy college student who scoffs at the idea of work.

The Belittlement of the Working Man

The portrayal of the labor movement in 1930s Hollywood was mixed. *Black Fury*, for example, implied that the movement was prone to abuse; in that film, the Mob fuels a violent labor strike.

The Power and the Glory under-develops a subplot about a labor dispute, so strikers are characterized as little more than big talkers. A man shouts to the crowd that Tom Garner is a "slave-driver," but clams up when Tom actually shows up. "Sit down, horse-face. You've talked enough," Tom tells him. Tom sees the workers as weak-willed. He addresses the throng: "Listen, boys, you've started something you can't finish." The film presents a labor dispute as a deadly battle of resolve.

Tom had earlier shown his insensitivity to the Depression by complaining about people "whining about the economy." But the script does not fully flesh out why Tom would have been perceived as a slave-driver, so we're left with the impression that he is a target because he is rich and overambitious.

This is the opposite of what he once was. Those who have forgotten their roots are destined to fall with the tree.

This extent of worker anger is largely unrecognizable today, largely because Americans are quieter. The working class is more invisible. The middle class and upper middle class have more political power, and any fury comes primarily from white-collar employees who are victims of colossal corporate fraud. For the working class, the occasional labor dispute, such as the short-lived General Motors strike of September 2007, ends in mutual agreement.

Because the American economy is so dependent on railroads, the strikers in *The Power and the Glory* have little leverage. "There are storekeepers waiting for goods," Tom bellows to the strikers. "Women waiting for food. And there are babies waiting for milk. Well, they're not going to wait any longer. This train moves tonight!" In other words, commerce trumps individual rights. Or, more charitably, Tom was and always would be committed to the railroad.

The Gender Trap

Tom falls in love with another woman, and Sally blames herself for pushing him too hard so many years earlier. "I wanted the power and the money," she says reluctantly. "You wanted to go fishing."

A woman like Sally cannot control the course of a marriage without feeling guilty for it. She takes responsibility for her husband's flaws by finding nonexistent flaws in herself. "I'm a disagreeable old woman, Tom," she concedes when he tells her of the other woman. "Bad-tempered and everything else that goes with it. But I won't be that way anymore."

Tom in turn feels guilty for loving the other woman, the daughter of the president of the Santa Clara Railroad, but narrator Henry explains it this way: the woman was "young and aristocratic-looking. Tom hadn't met this kind very often, so you couldn't blame him much." Perhaps Henry is implying that rich men can be only with their own kind, although Tom never appears to lose an appreciation for Sally's sacrifice.

Sally had been a schoolteacher when she met Tom, but there is no indication that she remains in her job after she is married. It seems that marriage opens the man to career advancement and compels the woman to drop whatever she is doing.

If a married woman works, she does it for her husband's advancement, not her own. Sally offers to become a trackwalker so Tom can go to business school. "Just because a woman never did it doesn't mean a woman couldn't," she tells him. At first he scoffs: "A woman supporting a man!" But she wins him over and lives to regret it.

The Ultimate Regret

Orson Welles studied *The Power and the Glory* as he developed *Citizen Kane*, the chronicle of another fallen titan. Young Tom Garner's frolic in the old swimmin' hole is the warm-weather equivalent of young Charles Foster Kane's play with his beloved sled Rosebud. In both films, rural life seems ideal, while cities are places where men get ruined. Kane's last word is "Rosebud"; Tom's is "Sally," that former schoolteacher in the mountains who had never stopped loving him. Everyone else might have lost money in the Depression, but they would never cry for it in their dying words.

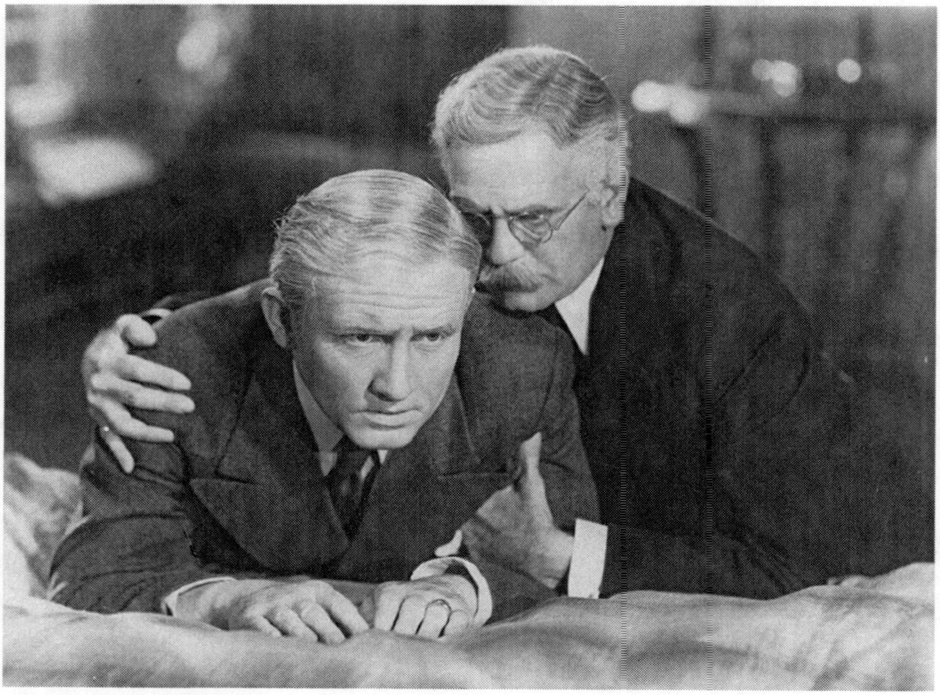

The Power and the Glory, What They Can Do to a Man: Preston Sturges' Dark Vision of Success

Charles Morrow

I. The story behind the story

Over the bleak Christmas holiday season of 1932 and into the first days of the New Year playwright Preston Sturges labored over a curious screenplay of his own devising, a screenplay unlike anything produced in Hollywood up to that time. He created the life history of Tom Garner, a man of humble origins who is encouraged by his wife Sally to educate himself and improve his status in the world. Garner proves an apt pupil and a natural leader, and eventually becomes a powerful railroad magnate, but his rise to great power brings only tragedy to himself and everyone closest to him. Garner becomes corrupt in both his personal and business dealings, inflicts pain on his family and employees alike, and ultimately comes to an untimely and squalid end. *The Power and the Glory*, as it was called, would become an archetype for a number of latter-day films detailing the rise and fall of politicians, businessmen, entertainment figures and other ambitious overachievers who somehow lose their souls on the way to the top. Sturges' tale, written when the Great Depression was at its absolute nadir, is permeated with a deep sense of disillusionment that reflects the national mood in the season of its composition, a sense that the "great men" we had admired and trusted had proven to be all too human, let us down, and even betrayed us. Given the times this theme is not at all surprising, but the structure of the screenplay itself was strikingly unusual for its day: although its key scenes consist of highlights from Tom Garner's life from boyhood to the day of his death, the author chose to eschew a chronological timeline and begin with Garner's funeral, then reveal significant details of his life in a seemingly random order, as a longtime friend of the deceased narrates the story to his own wife. Garner was loosely based on C. W. Post, founder of the company that became General Foods. Sturges had formerly been married to Post's granddaughter, and was fascinated by the stories she told about him: Post had been born in poverty, married young, gained wealth and power as his company prospered, divorced his wife and married a much younger woman, discovered his second wife was unfaithful, then shot himself while still in his 50s and at the peak of his career: these points would all be followed in the story of Tom Garner. Sturges hit upon the novel structure for his screenplay by reasoning that the audience could put together the puzzle pieces of Garner's life the same way he had done as he absorbed the details of Post's biography from his wife: first with the description of Post's suicide, then the earlier details in whatever order seemed pertinent (Spoto 111). As for why he chose to tell this story at this particular historical juncture, Sturges believed the dark times called for a dark tale, especially one exposing the American Dream of success as a fraud (Curtis 79). For generations, the Horatio Alger myth of hard honest labor, steady upward progress, and material reward to the deserving had driven the nation's workforce and inspired innumerable people worldwide to emigrate to the Promised Land, the United States. And now, for unfathomable reasons, the success myth had collapsed, and basic daily survival had become a challenge for millions of formerly comfortable, middle-class citizens. Still, even in the worst period of 1931-33 some 60 to 75 million Americans continued to go to the movies on a weekly basis (Bergman xi), and Sturges felt that these viewers were ready for a bracing splash of reality, the story of a man who was too successful for his own good, a challenging drama that equated excessive material reward with decadence, corruption and failure.

In addition to the unique structure of his story, the author took a course of action highly unorthodox for his time: having conceived the idea for this screenplay himself, Sturges worked on the project at his own pace and without pay (as he was unemployed at the time) with the intention of shopping his script around to any producer who might be interested. One evening at a party Sturges met a man named Hector Turnbull who worked at Fox Films, and this chance meeting brought the screenwriter and his script to the attention of Jesse Lasky, who was at this time producing films independently for release through Fox. Lasky, a Hollywood pioneer whose movie career dated back to *The Squaw Man* of 1914, had recently contributed a piece to the latest edition of *The Film Daily Year Book* in which he noted that the public was weary and anxious, and emphasized the importance of cinematic innovation. "The successful producer of 1932 must be daring," he wrote. "He must discard old formulae. He must go far afield for fresh, startling ideas, for unconventional production brains, for new types of players" (Lasky 39). As it happened, Lasky didn't have to go very far afield to locate an unconventional brain with a fresh, startling idea; when Sturges met with him and described *The Power and the Glory* the producer was immediately interested, and when he read the script he must have believed he'd struck pay dirt. According to subsequent publicity releases and his later autobiography Lasky was "astounded" and considered Sturges' material "the most perfect script I'd ever seen" (Spoto 109), and insisted it should be filmed without any changes. However sincere the producer may have been regarding this promise, however, a comparison of Sturges' original text (published in facsimile by the University of California Press in 1998) with the finished film reveals a number of significant alterations, especially in the concluding sequences. These changes are particularly notable in the scenes concerning the nature of Tom Garner's death and the section describing a strike by railroad employees which leads to violence.

Fox's contract player Spencer Tracy was cast as Tom Garner. Tracy was a Broadway veteran, one of many who had been recruited to come to California during the talkie revolution, and in several respects he was precisely the new type of player Lasky was seeking. Unlike the perfectly groomed 'Arrow collar' leading men of the '20s Tracy was more rugged than handsome, authoritative but with a distinctly blue collar aura. Audiences of the early '30s could imagine riding a bus or working in the same office—or even standing in a breadline—alongside a guy like this. Accordingly, up to this point in his career at Fox Tracy had usually been cast as working class types such as sailors, cops, and the occasional crook, but never a character as nuanced or contradictory as Tom Garner, and never one who wielded such authority. The closest Tracy had come to playing a powerful figure like Garner had been in his notable turn as racketeer Daniel "Bugs" Raymond in the literate and stylish gangster drama *Quick Millions*, released in the spring of 1931. In that film Tracy's character starts out a belligerent truck driver and winds up controlling an entire metropolitan city's trucking business. Raymond isn't as flamboyant as the classic Hollywood crime kingpin, however; he's a cool customer who figures out "the angles" on his own. Once he's on top, Bugs relishes his hard-won ability to force the Establishment businessmen to deal with him on his own terms, surely a satisfying inversion of social roles for viewers at a time when money was scarce and a person's social status could plummet overnight with sudden unemployment. The darkest days of the Depression coincided with the enormous popularity of gangster movies, a genre that took off with the success of *Little Caesar*, released by Warner Brothers in early 1931. In this film and its many follow-ups the American success myth was subverted into a rise-and-fall saga set in the only realm where financial success still seemed possible, the criminal underworld, but even here an individual's success proved to be fleeting and his downfall swift and final. Although the threat of violence is the key to Bugs Raymond's power in *Quick Millions*, Rowland Brown's script suggests that it's Raymond's clever perversion of basic American business practices which gives him the edge over his rivals—for a while, anyway. Tracy managed to imbue the character with an engaging combination of cocky self-assurance and regular-guy modesty: even when he reaches the top of his racket, Bugs jokes about having to get dressed up to go to the opera. But Raymond's doom is assured when he comes to enjoy the trappings of success too much, forgets his roots and shows disdain for his colleagues in crime, who turn against him.

In retrospect this early role can be regarded as Tracy's dress rehearsal for *The Power and the Glory*. Tom Garner, like Bugs Raymond, is another born leader from a modest background who achieves unexpected success but loses his grip on power, though the trajectory of his career and the causes of his downfall are quite different from Raymond's.

II. Sequence by sequence

Fox Films was rumored to be near bankruptcy as *The Power and the Glory* went before the cameras in late March of 1933, at the height of the national banking crisis that coincided with the first days of Franklin D. Roosevelt's presidency (Curtis 85-6). The company would survive, of course, but where this project was concerned certain economy measures were deemed essential; at least some of the changes that would be made in the script, such as the elimination of several minor characters, were undoubtedly made in the interest of saving money. Lasky chose the capable William K. Howard to direct, but Sturges (who would not direct his own work until 1940) was appointed 'dialogue director' and—in yet another break with Hollywood tradition regarding screenwriters—was present for every day of the shooting. Minor dialogue changes were made on the set, but more significant ones were made in post-production, after early preview screenings in June (Jacobs 128). Reportedly, viewers were confused by some of the film's temporal shifts and this led to changes in the narration that would clarify the story, but it seems fair to assume that something other than simple confusion provoked some of these alterations, particularly in the passages concerning the violent strike. This section surely must have hit a nerve with audiences (and caused nervousness in Fox's Front Office) in a country still shaken after repeated violent clashes between the unemployed and law enforcement officials during 1930-32.

The script of *The Power and the Glory* is broken into nine sections labeled A through I. Close comparison of the script with the finished film reveals a number of intriguing developments in the evolution of Tom Garner's personality, his wife Sally's role in his rise and fall, and the ways in which the tragedy of the Garner household reflected the dismal American outlook at the beginning of 1933.

Sequence A begins with the funeral of Tom Garner as the camera pans across the faces of persons we will come to recognize as Garner's son Tommy and widow Eve, both in their 20s and attractive. Sitting further back in the congregation is Henry, Garner's boyhood friend and personal secretary in adulthood. Henry listens impassively as the minister intones platitudes about the deceased, calling him "a truly great man, far-seeing, powerful, and steadfast in his determination." Henry leaves quietly, and then pays a call on the office where he and his friend worked together. He converses briefly with a security guard, but when the man starts to denounce Garner with a harsh remark Henry silences him. Sequence B begins at Henry's home that evening. When his wife expresses her low opinion of the late Mr. Garner, calling him a "good-for nothing," Henry retorts that she didn't understand him, and launches into the series of disjointed reminiscences which comprise the bulk of the film. Henry's wife (unnamed in the script) presumably has heard these stories before and has long since reached her own conclusions, but her role throughout the film is to hold Tom Garner accountable for his misdeeds, while her husband's role is to parry her accusations and defend his friend at every turn. In a 1970 essay critic Andrew Sarris opined that the viewer is expected to accept Henry's account of events in *The Power and the Glory* as objective truth despite his submissive role in Garner's life (Sarris 83), and yet the early introduction of both the security guard and Henry's wife, each of whom is quick to condemn the deceased on the very day of his burial, alerts the viewer that Garner was a controversial figure who excited strong feelings and sharply divided opinions. It is possible and, in fact, likely that Sturges intended the obviously biased Henry to be regarded an unreliable narrator whose version of reality should be questioned; it is also increasingly noticeable as the story unfolds that he is describing events where he could not possibly have been present in person.

Oddly, the first significant fact about the 'Great Man' which Henry chooses to recount to his wife, and thus, reveal to the audience, is that in the course of a protracted strike over *four hundred* men lost their lives in a violent crack-down; Henry's wife bluntly asserts that Garner killed them, to which Henry can only reply "He had to protect the railroad." Next we learn that in later life Garner rejected his aging wife for a younger and prettier one; Henry's response is that "You can't judge him by ordinary standards. They wouldn't fit him. He was too . . . too big." In an effort to establish his late friend's greatness Henry proceeds to relate the story of how they met as boys at the local swimming hole. The exact year is never specified, but based on the age of the characters in 1933 this childhood memory would have taken place around 1890 or so. The sequence, which is the single longest scene in the film, establishes several points: first, that Tom was always the dominant party in his relationship with Henry; second, that he was more daring than the other boys (when he climbs from a tall tree to dive into the pond we're told that "no one had ever dived from there before"); and third, that Tom's boldness leads to grief, as his dive from the tree causes him to lodge his hand between rocks underwater and nearly drown. He emerges, breathless, with only a gash on his hand, earning Henry's lifelong admiration and dog-like devotion in the process. The swimming hole sequence feels sentimental and somehow inauthentic—Sturges, whose unconventional bohemian childhood was spent in Europe, appears to have concocted a typically "American" boyhood from secondary sources—but an additional, important function for this scene is to counter the negative impression we might have started to form of our central character with more positive traits and suggest some complexity in his personality. (For the film's first viewers the sequence would also have provided a nostalgia trip back to a pastoral, Tom Sawyer-like 19th century America that existed primarily in the rose-tinted memories of the elderly.) From what little we've seen thus far, Tom Garner appears to have begun life a decent person. What could have changed him between this childhood idyll and adulthood?

    Sequence C jumps forward to the recent past, i.e. the late 1920s. Tom is now the president of the Chicago & Northwestern Railroad, described in the opening eulogy as the greatest railroad in America, "perhaps in the world." Suddenly, in this non-chronological telling, middle-aged Tom Garner is at the peak of his power and scheming to take control of an additional railroad, the Santa Clara, despite the objections of his board of directors. Now that Spencer Tracy has made his entrance Garner is endowed with the actor's own low-key but unmistakably authoritative presence; we're no longer being told about Garner by third parties, we are permitted into the corporate boardroom and allowed to watch as he demonstrates his command over others and relishes the process. (Tracy celebrated his 33rd birthday shortly after filming began, but plays his opening scene as a gray-haired man in his

50s, looking surprisingly as he would in reality some twenty years later.) With a forceful speech, Garner hectors his reluctant board into agreeing to the purchase of the Santa Clara railroad. One by one the directors are intimidated into acquiescence, and when at last the vote is unanimous Garner informs them with a smile that the deal was actually concluded ten minutes earlier, without their foreknowledge or approval. Immediately after this meeting, Garner arranges to buy stock for himself in the newly-purchased Santa Clara before news of the deal can be made public, and orders his secretary Henry to do likewise. Even in the 1920s such a transaction would have constituted illegal insider trading (in fact, transactions of this nature were outlawed in 1909) and Garner is presumably aware of his transgression; when critic Richard Corliss called Garner a "financial gangster" he must have had this scene in mind. There are similar scenes set at testimonial dinners, backroom meetings, etc., in the gangster movies predating *The Power and the Glory* in which Rico Bandello, Tony Camonte, Tom Powers, and Bugs Raymond of *Quick Millions* demonstrate their command over their men and make 'em like it. When Garner grins and informs his board that they've already purchased the Santa Clara, and then coolly ignores the law to enrich himself further, we're reminded of the moment when Bugs Raymond grinned in a similar fashion and announced that "racketeering's just getting what the other's guy's got, in a nice way." Latter-day viewers might also be reminded of *Wall Street*'s Gordon Gekko, Oliver Stone's amoral go-getter who would assert, in the very different financial climate of the mid-1980s, that greed is good (a line borrowed from real-world financial gangster Ivan Boesky), a baldly stated credo which would have been unthinkable coming from Tom Garner. At some point after completing work on the first draft of *The Power and the Glory* Sturges conceived a joke for Tracy to deliver in this scene and penciled it into his copy of the script, a bit where Garner would quip to his board that he doesn't care whether he dies with fifty million dollars to his name—or only thirty million. The line wasn't used in the finished film, and it's difficult to imagine it would have provoked even hollow laughter when the movie premiered. More to the point, the quip is out of character for the Tom Garner presented in the finished text, the man Tracy came to embody. As it stands, Garner never expresses any particular fondness for wealth or luxury items for their own sake, nor does he gloat about the power he wields over others, though it's clear from Tracy's performance that this power, once it's achieved, is something he's comfortable with and quietly enjoys. But what motivates Garner is one of the central mysteries we're meant to consider as the story unfolds.

In Sequence D we jump back to the turn of the century: Henry and Tom are now about 20 years old. Henry is away at a business college, while Tom is working for the railroad as a track walker, an unskilled worker who inspects mile after mile of track on foot. In this sequence we learn that Tom, whose father felt he didn't need to go to school to feed hogs or milk cows, is still illiterate. Having received a letter from Henry, Tom visits the local school teacher, Sally, to cajole her into reading it to him. Recognizing the problem, Sally offers to tutor Tom in reading and mathematics. Their private classes quickly lead to romance. In the film's best known scene, Tom decides to propose marriage to Sally and awkwardly attempts to do so during a hike up a mountain on a hot summer afternoon, but is unable to bring himself to propose until they have hiked almost to the top. The scene is a comic high point in this otherwise somber film, and the nostalgia for bygone days feels more sincere in than the swimming hole sequence. It would appear too that this scene, beyond its primary function as an important story element and its secondary one as comic relief, also served as a tribute of sorts to the recently departed silent cinema. The scene was shot silent and is accompanied only by music and Henry's voice-over; our narrator even supplies brief bits of dialog synchronized to match Tom's and Sally's mouthed words. This scene could also be regarded as the only opportunity Spencer Tracy (who made his screen debut in 1930 and appeared only in talkies) ever had to perform silent comedy. Tom and Sally's period clothing, plus the fact that Sally is portrayed by one-time silent star Colleen Moore, underscores the elegiac effect. It is striking too that the man we know will metamorphose into the powerful, commanding Tom Garner is retroactively reduced to an awkward comic figure by the prospect of proposing marriage to this physically unprepossessing young woman, his teacher no less. Not coincidentally, by the end of this sequence Tom Garner has earned his first measure of audience sympathy.

In Sequence E we are brought back from the turn-of-the-century hilltop to the recent past, just after Garner has concluded his take-over of the Santa Clara railroad, and now we are permitted another look at the mature Garner at the peak of his success, and at the very moment the seeds of his downfall are planted. Mr. Borden, current president of the newly-acquired Santa Clara, pays a nervous call on Garner, who relishes the opportunity to humiliate his adversary. ("He kept me out of a club once," Tom tells a visibly uncomfortable Henry, "I guess he thought I was too common," a remark worthy of racketeer Bugs Raymond.) But Borden is accompanied by his beautiful, recently-divorced daughter Eve, brought along in a calculated effort to interest Garner and influence his next moves, a stratagem which succeeds easily. After one lunch sitting across from Eve, Garner is smitten. Narrator Henry naturally absolves his hero of blame, but in post-production Sturges strengthened his description of Garner's motivation with a heightened element of class envy. In the script, Henry says only "[Eve] sure was a beautiful woman. You couldn't blame Tom much," but in the finished film he says: "[Eve] sure was a beautiful woman: young, and sort of aristocratic looking. Tom hadn't met that kind very often, so you couldn't blame him much." This change reminds us of both Tom's and Sally's modest backgrounds, and while it doesn't absolve Garner in any respect Henry's words say something about the attitudes of the period. The nod to Eve's pedigree spoke to deep-seated audience desires in the depths of the Depression: this young woman is not merely beautiful, and not merely rich (so is Garner, by this point), she represents old money: she's got *class*, and therefore is protected by that imagined social safety net that presumably keeps such people from hitting bottom. After the Bordens depart Garner's adult son Tommy arrives in the office and reveals that he's been expelled from college because of a drunken indiscretion. Garner chides his son and orders him to take a low-paying bookkeeper's job with the railroad. In contrast with the poised, aristocratic Eve, Tommy Garner is immediately established as a spoiled and callow young man, an impression reinforced in the family home that evening when he pleads with his mother to take his part in the matter. Our first view of the mature Mrs. Garner is startling: suddenly she is a prematurely aged, bitter old lady. Sally angrily confronts her husband, condemns his well-intentioned intervention in their son's affairs, and needles Tom with the reminder that he wouldn't have achieved anything without her. We know this to be true, but Sally's nasty tone combined with her coddling of their son puts her in an entirely unsympathetic light, and introduces a second mystery to the narrative: what happened to the pleasant young woman we saw in the schoolhouse, and hiking up that hill? Is Sturges suggesting that the accumulation of wealth, in and of itself, is ruinous to good character, or are we to infer that a violation of some unwritten rule of social class is the key factor here, and that Tom and Sally have broken the rules by hoisting themselves out of the class where they naturally belonged? There is reason to believe Sturges suspected this was a factor in the downfall of C. W. Post (Curtis 79). Where Sequence E is concerned, meanwhile, it is worth pointing out that this is one of several scenes Henry narrates from what could only have been second-hand knowledge. He is not present, and therefore must be repeating the version of events Tom Garner later recounted to him; and because he's tailoring his narrative to form a defense of the man, delivered to his own Garner-hating wife, the narrative itself must be viewed as doubly filtered: this is Henry's version of Garner's version of events, delivered to a skeptical listener.

  In Sequence F we are taken back to the early years of Tom and Sally's marriage, before the birth of their son. Tom is still a track walker and apparently content with his lot, but Sally urges him to make something of himself so that they can improve their standard of life. She suggests that he go to college while she assumes his track-walking duties herself. When Tom objects that a woman supporting a man is unthinkable, and that his boss Mr. Robinson would never permit the arrangement, Sally reveals that she's already approached Robinson and secured his approval. We now see where Garner learned the maneuver he used on his board of directors in Sequence C, and this realization underscores Sally's point in the previous sequence: she not only taught her husband to read, write and do math, but taught him interpersonal techniques he would put to use later. Sally's crucial importance to her husband's future career is plain, but Tom's lackadaisical character as presented in this scene feels jarring. We can accept that a young man who is still illiterate at age 20 could learn to read, educate himself, and *possibly* become the president of a railroad by the age of 50, but the man we see here who is perfectly content to live in a cabin and work as a track walker resembles neither the daring boy of the swimming hole nor the forceful businessman who acquires the Santa Clara railroad over his directors' objections. Tracy's smug boardroom gangster is suddenly a rural simpleton, and although his performance is equally credible in both scenes it is difficult to reconcile the two Tom Garners. It would appear that Sally's gentle-but-firm prodding is all that's required to reawaken Tom's dormant leadership qualities. Oddly, William Troy's favorable review of this film in *The Nation* would summarize it as a parable of "the self-made American businessman being pressed on by a hard-driving, power-mad American female to misery and self-destruction," but this scene represents the only evidence of Sally Garner's alleged hard-driving, power-mad qualities. In any event, Tom goes off to college and works hard, while Sally walks track in the snow. Sturges wrote Garner a comic scene in a saloon to conclude this sequence and perhaps lighten the film's tone, but it was cut; audiences saw only an earnest young man who (at his wife's urging) applies himself at school, rises in his profession, and earns the seemingly accursed wealth that brings misery and destruction in its wake.

Sequence G brings us back to the recent past. In a swanky restaurant Tom tells Eve with evident sincerity that he's in love with her, "more than any man ever loved a woman." When Eve asks what he's going to do about it Tom replies that he could never divorce Sally. (In the script Eve replies "You're not asking me to become your mistress, I hope," a line not used in the film or in any case not present in surviving prints.) Eve indicates that their relationship is at an impasse until he can choose between them, and departs. Tom is back at his office when Sally arrives and proposes that the two of them travel to Europe together in an attempt to repair their relationship. She delivers a speech taking the blame for their difficulties and acknowledging that she's become a "disagreeable, bad-tempered" old woman, though she does not speculate as to why this is. In response, Tom gravely informs her that he's in love with someone else. Dazed and angry, Sally again blames herself, this time for pushing Tom beyond his own desires ("I wanted the power and the money . . . you wanted to go fishing.") She leaves her husband's office, pauses to give her purse to a puzzled old lady peddling flowers in front of the building, and deliberately steps in front of a streetcar, killing herself. In the script Henry narrates Sally's every move, but his voice-over is much simplified in the finished film, with one notably ironic observation added in post-production: "She looked up at the big building, where Tom had become so great." An additional irony is not underscored, i.e. that Tom's "greatness" came about through his management of a railroad, and that Sally chooses to die by throwing herself in front of an oncoming locomotive. Sally's suicide is followed by a scene not found in Sturges' script of January 1933, therefore most likely written and shot after the movie's first previews that summer. In this new scene Henry and his wife disagree about the happiness of Tom and Sally's marriage. Henry's wife calls Garner "rotten" and asserts that Sally was never happy from the day they married; Henry insists that Tom treated his wife with kindness and devotion for thirty years, and that his affair with Eve Borden represented a singular lapse after decades of fidelity. In Henry's view, Tom couldn't help falling in love with Eve because "he was too honest." It would appear that the viewer is free to agree with either of these opinions and is not expected to accept either as the unfiltered, objective truth, and that the filmmakers did not necessarily side with either speaker.

Sequence H, originally the most complicated and cinematically sophisticated section of Sturges' screenplay, was considerably altered and simplified for filming, this time, unfortunately, to the detriment of Sally Garner as a forceful character in her own right. The sequence is set in the early years of Tom and Sally's marriage, and concerns the day Sally informs her husband that she is pregnant. By this time Tom's rise in status is underway: he has graduated from college and become a construction engineer, and is supervising the building of a bridge. As originally written, Sturges placed Sally at the construction site where Tom is working. When she learns that Tom is at the top of the bridge, she insists on being taken up to him on a girder, and compels the reluctant foreman to comply with her request. Interestingly, Sturges chose to cut back and forth between this joyful sequence and a somber conversation shortly after Mrs. Garner's suicide, twenty-some years later, between the middle-aged Tom Garner and his callow son. One moment, the smiling young Sally is being hoisted to the top of the bridge to tell her husband the good news, and the next we observe as Tom awkwardly informs his son that he intends to marry Eve Borden. Tommy is unhappy at the news, but pleased when his father relents on his plan to force him to work as a low-paid bookkeeper. Instead, Garner invites Tommy to come live with him and his young bride, and enjoy life. The two men reconcile, at which point we were to be taken back twenty years to the top of the bridge, as Sally arrives and informs her startled husband that they're going to have a baby. The next scene in the script occurs months later, as Tom anxiously awaits the birth of his son in their modest home. When the baby is born Tom is deeply moved: "My son, I've got a son. Oh Sally, they'll never stop me now. Thank you." In Sturges' script Sequence H ends here. The finished film substitutes a far more conventional sequence set in the Garners' home. It is here, not atop a bridge, where Sally announces the news to her husband, though the author added a mildly comic touch as Tom and Sally initially speak at cross-purposes: he is excited about his promotion to foreman and she is dazed at the thought of having a baby, but they are only half-listening to one another and each at first misunderstands the other's meaning. Once they're on the same page, so to speak, Tom is stunned and then ecstatic to learn that he is going to be a father. The elimination of Sally's scene riding a girder to the top of the bridge is unfortunate, but was most likely made for budgetary rather than aesthetic reasons: the process work involved would have added greatly to the cost of a project which perhaps only Jesse Lasky believed would be a sure-fire box office champ. Aesthetically speaking, meanwhile, the simplification of this sequence means that Tom Garner is the only "climber" in this story: he climbs the tall tree by the swimming hole and practically drags Sally up a mountain to propose, but Sally is not granted comparable ability and can only urge her man onward verbally. The childbirth scene which follows Sally's announcement hews to the script fairly closely, but concludes Sequence H with a speech Sturges had originally intended to save for the film's finale: Tom Garner's fervent prayer of thanks to God for the birth of his son, a prayer which incorporates a passage from the Lord's Prayer that gave the film its title: "for Thine is the power and the glory, Amen." The words of Tom's prayer are immediately and ironically echoed by our narrator Henry, who intones a line apparently conceived in post-production, much-quoted in subsequent reviews, which serves as the film's thesis statement: "The power and the glory, what they can do to a man." Tracy plays the birth scene with intensity and is especially moving, for here we see Tom Garner at what was undoubtedly the peak of his life, but the sequence is disturbing in whichever version it's experienced, whether one reads the screenplay or watches the finished film, and for the same reason: we know how Tom and Sally's son is going to turn out, and that Tom's hopes will be dashed. By this point in the story the young adult Tommy is already well established as unworthy of both his parents, a lazy wastrel ruined by inherited wealth—and by ineffectual parenting—and this knowledge makes his father's joyful prayer painful to witness. Garner happily predicts that their son will be "someone we can be proud of when we're old," but thanks to the non-sequential structure we've already heard the middle-aged Garner tell his recently expelled, no-good son that he's ashamed of him. Richard Corliss would call this time-defying quality "an oppressive sense of predetermined pastness" and compare it to the noir classics of the 1940s, those crime sagas narrated by characters already in desperate or doomed situations. In such scenarios even scenes of cheer or optimism recalled from earlier days are clouded by a fatalistic irony, by our knowledge of what the future holds for these characters. Our sympathy for Tom Garner peaks at this moment but we have no time to dwell on it, for Garner's prayer is followed by the scene, twenty years later and shortly after Sally's suicide, when Garner informs his son that he is soon to marry Eve. The style in which this conversation was staged and performed must have been calculated to destroy all sympathetic feelings generated by the previous scene: Garner and his son wear tuxedoes and sit puffing cigars on a veranda overlooking a moonlit lake or river; the men resemble the decadent, fat-cat 'Capitalists' who appeared in newspaper editorial cartoons of the '30s (and beyond). And when Tom Senior backs off from his earlier insistence that his son take a low-paying job, all Tommy can say is "Gee father, that's swell!" Even in 1933, audiences must have hooted with laughter.

At this juncture, as our protagonist has morphed from an earnest railroad worker into a pompous railroad baron, the strike mentioned in the opening sequence erupts. In Sturges' script our narrator is quite voluble about the situation. "The Aurora yard men were on strike, but the freight had to move so we sent down some strike-breakers." Next, over night-time shots of a burning warehouse: "The boys didn't like that, so they burned the warehouse. There just happened to be a few strike-breakers inside." Here the script indicates that the strike-breakers run out of the flaming warehouse, accompanied by police, as Henry says: "and when they came out, *somebody* started firing." The script indicates that a strike-breaker "clutches his belly, spins, and falls." When a policeman fires in response, a fusillade of shots follow. Henry mildly remarks that "there weren't so many killed, but it started the big strike . . . It was a swell chance for somebody so the I.W.W.'s [i.e. Industrial Workers of the World] jumped in and then the REAL trouble started." All of this voice-over material was deleted from the finished film, but the shots of the flaming warehouse and the action involving the victimized strike-breakers and police was retained, and so was Tom Garner's subsequent confrontation with the striking railroad men. We've seen Garner take on a room full of executives and intimidate them into submission, but this is something else entirely: a warehouse full of strikers, hundreds of men who are hostile to him and who could easily overwhelm him. This is a genuinely dangerous environment. Garner ignores a security guard who warns him not to enter the warehouse and strides into the crowd. The men are listening to an angry orator, described in the script only as "a wild-looking man." In the film he's also given a distinctly Eastern European-sounding accent, a not-so-subtle indication that he is an outside agitator—and, implicitly, a Radical of some sort, possibly Jewish. His speech is indistinct at first because of the echo-y acoustics of the hall, but we're able to distinguish his line "You work and slave and give [Garner] the best years of your life and what does he give you in return? STARVATION WAGES—just enough to keep you alive." Greater emphasis is placed on the orator's denunciation of the boss: "He's a dirty bum and a crook and a slave-driver. If I could lay my hands on him, I'd—I'd—" The orator's words die in his throat as Garner himself calls out from the crowd: "You'd what?" Garner takes the stage as the orator weakly backs away. It's Garner's turn to address the men but he says nothing about their wages, living conditions, complaints or demands. He addresses the men sternly as if they were naughty schoolchildren and flatly informs them that "storekeepers are waiting for goods, men and women are waiting for food, and there are babies waiting for milk. They won't have to wait any longer. THIS RAILROAD RUNS TONIGHT." Garner adds that five thousand men are en route—he doesn't call them strike-breakers, but his implication is obvious—along with a thousand state militia men to "keep order." He concludes by saying he hopes there won't be trouble, but that anyone who is looking for it will find it. There are no catcalls, no replies whatsoever as Garner leaves the warehouse. Our narrator, Garner's faithful defender Henry, brings the episode to a close by informing us that four hundred and six men were killed in the ensuing violence.

It's difficult to imagine how the filmmakers intended this scene to be received or to learn how it was greeted when *The Power and the Glory* was first previewed in the summer of 1933. Garner's confrontation with the strikers is mentioned only in passing, if at all, in contemporaneous reviews of the film. Is this the "steadfastness" cited by the minister in his eulogy in the opening scene? When Henry's wife angrily denounces Garner for his actions and mentions the strikers' widows and children, are we expected to agree with her or to admire Garner's toughness? Even Henry seems to falter in his advocacy for Garner in this matter, offering only a limp "Maybe it was his fault, I don't know"—hardly a ringing defense. Whatever his admiration for Sturges' screenplay producer Jesse Lasky may well have been uneasy about this passage: almost all of Henry's lines describing these events were deleted from the final cut, including a reference placing the strike in Illinois (no geographical location is mentioned), his citation of the specific unions involved, and all references to the I.W.W. or "wobblies" as they were nicknamed and originally called in the script. Lasky had reason to be concerned; the first three years of the Depression saw some of the worst civic violence in the United States since the race riots that followed the First World War, and tensions ran high as economic conditions worsened. Only four months after the stock market crash of October 1929 large-scale violence related to unemployment had broken out in several cities across the country. Newly formed councils of unemployed workers, some organized by a subsidiary branch of the Communist Party of America called the Trade Union Unity League, chose March 6, 1930, as a day of organized protest in several major cities across the country (Watkins 118). In Chicago and in New York's Union Square the clashes between protesters and police turned violent, and scores of marchers were beaten. Over the next two years unemployment and hunger marches were common, though no single incident was as bloody as that day in 1930. Then on March 7, 1932, the Unemployed Council of Detroit, Michigan, organized a march on the Ford Motor Company's River Rouge plant in Dearborn. Henry Ford—who, like Sturges' Tom Garner, had climbed his way up from modest circumstances to a position of great personal power—had cut his factory workers' wages to an annual average of just over a thousand dollars a year, less than half the minimal subsistence level a family required at the time. Production lines were speeded up, in order to get maximum efficiency from exhausted workers and keep expenses down. Ford's employees were also subject to spying by his ubiquitous security forces, and union agitation was suppressed (Watkins 126). The protest of March 7 was intended to publicize worker unhappiness with these conditions and demand changes, including the right to organize. Shortly after the protest began tear gas was fired, then water hoses were turned on the marchers. The rally seemed to be over when shots were fired into the crowd. Four workers were killed, one of whom was a teenager. Worse was yet to come. That summer, President Herbert Hoover called out the Army to rout several thousand peaceful protesters from their encampment in Washington, D.C., driving them across the nation's capital with tanks, tear gas, bayonets, and swords. They were the "Bonus Army," unemployed American war veterans who were seeking their pensions from the government, and the violence directed at them by Federal troops produced more casualties and lasting bitterness (Watkins 139-40). Whether or not Sturges had these specific events in mind while he was composing his screenplay several months later is, strictly speaking, irrelevant; these disturbing, shameful episodes haunted the nation and were part of the era's Zeitgeist. The appalling body count Sturges devised, which goes far beyond the worst death toll of any civic violence in U.S. history, surely reflected the rampant pessimism and paranoia then abroad in the land. America's worst financial and social catastrophe had not, to date, provoked civil strife on this scale, but as the crisis worsened over the winter, with no certain foreknowledge that newly-elected President Franklin D. Roosevelt would have the ability to reverse the downward spiral, who could say matters would not get worse? In 1932 calls for an American dictatorship could be found even in middle-brow publications such as *Vanity Fair* and *Liberty*; that was also the year that a Senator from Pennsylvania named David Reed remarked: "If ever this country needed a Mussolini, it needs one now." (Bergman 268). If Preston Sturges intended to express any particular political point in *The Power and the Glory* it is unclear what it might have been; Tom Garner is no union man but he's also a deeply flawed character who is not the author's spokesman. [For the record, in private life Sturges was essentially apolitical; remarkably, in his correspondence and other writings from the 1930s he never expressed any opinion in writing of Franklin D. Roosevelt or the New Deal, either pro or con (Jacobs 125)]. But even if we admire Garner's brass when he enters that warehouse and calmly addresses the strikers, his tough-talking speech is undercut for the viewer almost immediately, for at this point we learn something that Garner himself does not yet know: while he was away dealing with the strike his new young wife and young adult son, who are approximately the same age, have begun an affair.

Sequence I, the film's finale, covers the day of Tom Garner's death. He and Eve have now been married exactly two years, although the ever-faithful Henry must remind Tom that today is his anniversary. Tom decides to buy Eve an expensive gift—along with a toy for their baby son—and then stop off at home early to surprise her. It's Garner who gets the surprise, however, for upon entering their home he overhears his wife having an intimate conversation with some unknown party on the phone. She turns to the subject of her baby boy, and Garner is horrified to hear her say: "He looks just like you." When she realizes she's been overheard Eve attempts to talk her way out of the situation. Tom, stunned, returns to his office but is unable to work, so Henry accompanies him back to his house. Tom confronts Eve, demands to know the identity of the baby's father, and (in an action quite explicit in the script but de-emphasized in the film) threatens to harm their infant son to force a confession from her. Tommy arrives at this juncture. In Sturges' script, their confrontation is prolonged and melodramatic, and reveals a heretofore unexplored, sadistic side of our protagonist. As originally written, Garner points a pistol at his son's chest but then, in a moment of cruel inspiration, turns the gun towards his own heart, grabs Tommy's hand and forces it around the gun's barrel, and compels him to pull the trigger. When Henry bursts into the room, however, Garner whispers the word "Suicide" to him with his dying breath. Readers of the script may interpret this act as Garner's revenge on his son, who must live with the knowledge that his finger was on the trigger when the shot was fired. The scripted finale 'twists the knife' for the reader even more, in a manner of speaking, by following this scene with young Tom Garner's fervent prayer of thanksgiving to God upon the birth of his son. In the finished film, however, once Garner has learned the identity of the baby's father he simply goes into a bedroom, closes the door, and is alone (and off-camera) when he shoots himself. Tommy arrives in time to hear the shot, but never speaks to his father beforehand. Garner's final word before dying, uttered to Henry and Tommy after they've entered the room, is "Sally." In the film this scene is followed by a brief, wordless coda featuring Henry and his wife in their home. Henry has finished reminiscing and sits sadly before the fireplace; his wife pats his shoulder, dims the light and proceeds upstairs to bed. Henry's hero Tom Garner, a man able to take on a warehouse full of angry strikers without flinching, has been driven to self-destruction by a betrayal of trust in his own family.

III. The Residual

Preston Sturges once wrote that the success or failure of any piece of writing rested in the *residual*, i.e. that which lingers with the reader or viewer after reading a book or seeing a play or film (Horton 9). What exactly is the "residual" we are left with after experiencing *The Power and the Glory*? In essence, it's Horatio Alger gone terribly sour: the story of a boy from a humble background who works hard, betters himself, wins the girl, and gains power and wealth, but never achieves any meaningful personal fulfillment through his efforts, and ultimately inflicts only pain on his family, his colleagues, and himself. This is a twisted take on the archetypal Alger success story, composed at a time when the disillusioned generation raised on Alger's stories was struggling for basic survival. And yet, although *The Power and the Glory* in both written and cinematic form is very much a product of its era, it contains no explicit reference to the Depression; during the boardroom confrontation in Sequence C one of the directors exclaims "Business is bad anyway!" but the line is lost in the general din. Most of the flashbacks are set long before the 1930s, and even during the contemporary scenes it appears that the Garner household is untouched by hard times: on the day of his death, Tom Garner impulsively buys his wife Eve a string of pearls said to cost thirty-five thousand dollars in the script (although the price is not specified in the film). Sturges' story expresses the malaise and bitterness of its historical moment but no specific allusions are necessary. Besides, it wasn't the Depression that destroyed the House of Garner; the problem, it would appear, is that Tom Garner's rise in the world is not accompanied by concomitant growth of character. For a man who climbs as high as he does, Tom Garner remains stubbornly unsophisticated and morally undeveloped.

When he wants to acquire another railroad, he bullies his directors into going along through sheer intimidation, then ignores the law to enrich himself from the transaction. Faced with a strike, he ignores its causes and threatens the strikers with violence, then delivers it on a horrific scale. And just in case we wonder whether this catastrophe causes the Great Man any self-recrimination, guilt, or even a moment of reflection, his faithful apologist Henry is quick to assure us that Garner was "happy as a lark" in the period following the massacre because "his conscience was clear." After all, he had to protect the railroad. Based on the evidence at hand the sole element of Garner's life that he believed made it worth living was the existence of his eldest son. But for all his apparent sincerity in praising God when the baby is born—and Tracy's performance in this scene is achingly real without descending into mawkishness—we have to question what being a father really means to Garner. When Sally tells him the news, Tom exclaims: "They'll never stop me now, honey! I'll make so much money for you and the kid, we'll buy the Great Western and give it to him to play with." This marks the sole occasion we hear Tom express a desire to become rich, or any attitude toward money as such (aside from the joke Sturges deleted). It's the birth of the boy, more than Sally's gentle urgings, that motivates Garner's drive to succeed, but if Tom is egotistical enough to regard Tom Jr. as a merely an extension of himself then the story's resolution should come as no surprise to anyone but its unhappy protagonist. Garner's belated realization that his son is an unworthy heir is the revelation that destroys him. Not merely unworthy, Tommy actually cuckolds his father—in his own home, under his own roof—and in the process fathers a child whom the horrified Garner perceives as some kind of monstrous, semi-incestuous mockery. Ultimately, it isn't the betrayal by his second wife that destroys Tom Garner, it's the betrayal by his son.

IV. Release, obscurity, influence

The Fox Film Corporation was in desperate condition as 1933 began, but from the moment he read Preston Sturges' script producer Jesse Lasky believed *The Power and the Glory* would be one of the studio's major releases of the year and a great success at the box office, and its release was trumpeted as an epochal event. Publicity material touted Spencer Tracy as a rising star and saluted the "comeback" of Colleen Moore, a major star of the silent era who hadn't appeared in a film since 1929. The accomplishments of director William K. Howard were dutifully acknowledged as well, but, extraordinarily, the real star build-up was reserved for the screenwriter and his work. The reverence Lasky accorded Sturges was evident at an early preview of the film, when it was noticed that the opening credits featured Sturges' name in larger type than Howard's, but the "mistake," if that's what it was, was rectified in subsequent prints (Jacobs 128). Meanwhile, someone in the Fox publicity department coined the term "narratage" to describe the story's structure, a term Lasky and Sturges promptly embraced. "Narratage" was subsequently ballyhooed as the greatest cinematic innovation since the development of the soundtrack. After the previews and subsequent cuts and alterations had been made, *The Power and the Glory* premiered in New York at the Gaiety Theatre—an ironically named venue for such a grim attraction—in August of 1933. Colleen Moore made a personal appearance at the theater and posed for photos alongside a bronze plaque touting the accomplishment of Lasky and Sturges in bringing the first "narratage" production to the screen. A copy of the film's shooting script could be viewed by patrons in a glass case.

In general the critics greeted *The Power and the Glory* as an interesting and unusual accomplishment, although the "narratage" campaign provoked a fair amount of skepticism and sarcasm. Reactions ranged from Regina Crewe's breathless rave in the New York *Sun* ("The production is so distinctive as to establish a new criterion in pictorial story telling, and it is illuminated by unwavering histrionic brilliance") to Charles Hammond's exasperated pan in the New York *Evening Post* ("The picture could have been much better had the story not been so saccharine and so utterly sentimental"). Most critics regarded Sturges' unconventional storytelling technique as little more than a novelty of limited utility, but all were united on one point: Spencer Tracy had given a first-rate performance. "His is the exquisite artistry that makes acting seem natural," lauded the *Sun*'s Crewe, while the *New York Times*' comparatively low-key Mordaunt Hall asserted that "no more convincing performance has been given on the screen than Spencer Tracy's impersonation of Tom Garner." Other reviews, even those that were less than enthusiastic about the film itself, sang the praises of the leading man. Tracy had every reason to believe that this performance would mark a turning point in his relationship with his employers and set a new course for his career; and every reason to be unhappy when the Powers That Be at Fox subsequently resumed casting him in unchallenging roles in routine pictures such as *The Mad Game* and *Now I'll Tell*. In 1935 he would leave Fox for greener pastures (i.e. more challenging roles, and genuine stardom) at MGM, his home studio for the next twenty years.

Meanwhile, after a successful two-week run in New York, *The Power and the Glory* went into general release throughout the country, where it did not fare so well. Perhaps some found the unconventional structure of the narrative confusing, but more to the point the story itself was undoubtedly too bleak and depressing for most audiences. At a time when one-quarter of the American workforce was unemployed, and even those lucky enough to have jobs were struggling to put food on the table, who needed to hear that—Mr. Alger notwithstanding—riches earned through hard work and honest toil could only lead to corruption, misery and death? Among other things, this a story in which two major characters respond to personal trauma by committing suicide, and it arrived in theaters not long after the suicide rate in the United States had reached an all-time high (Watkins 54). Moreover, no matter how humble his origins, Tom Garner's eventual status as a highly successful captain of industry could hardly encourage much audience sympathy at a time when big businessmen were widely held in low esteem. Garner's brutal response to the railroad strike would only alienate viewers further, reminding them of the real-life response of Henry Ford's armed security forces to the River Rouge marchers the previous year. And by the time *The Power and the Glory* went into general release in the autumn of '33 a politically engineered shift in the nation's mood was underway. The fledgling creations of President Roosevelt's first hundred days in office, New Deal programs such as the Civilian Conservation Corps and the National Recovery Administration, had been launched with considerable ballyhoo of their own. The Depression was by no means over, but the public was being encouraged to rediscover optimism and consign pessimism to the Hoover Era past. Whether the reasons were aesthetic, cultural or political, box office receipts for *The Power and the Glory* did not live up to Lasky's expectations. As it turned out, Fox Films' biggest hits of the year were *Cavalcade*, Noel Coward's stiff-upper-lip tribute to Mother England, and *State Fair*, a folksy comedy-drama featuring the studio's two biggest stars, Will Rogers and Janet Gaynor. *The Power and the Glory* managed to turn a modest profit before all prints were returned to the Fox vaults. The film was gradually forgotten by all but a few ardent admirers such as Billy Wilder, who saw the movie several times during its first run in Paris. In the late 1930s the film's camera negative and master lavender were destroyed in a vault fire (Curtis 88); prints that survive today derive from a dupe master painstakingly pieced together from various sources.

In April of 1941, a few weeks before Hollywood's new Wunderkind Orson Welles released his already-controversial first movie, journalist Sidney Skolsky ran a column in which he relayed his assistant Philip Hevema's impressions of *Citizen Kane*. Hevema, who had seen the film at a preview screening on the RKO lot, found *Kane* impressive but noted its similarities to *The Power and the Glory*, and reported that Welles had screened the latter several times while preparing his debut feature. In later years Welles spoke highly of Sturges but insisted that he had never seen *The Power and the Glory* and that any similarities between the two movies were coincidental (Welles 51). Certainly their similarities are striking: each begins with the death of its central character whose biography is then related in flashback, ignoring linear chronology in order to jump back and forth in time; both protagonists marry early and use their wives to get ahead in the world, but ruin their marriages when they're caught in affairs with younger women; both men are widowed and both remarry. Each film presents an essentially downbeat tale of a man who rises to great wealth and prominence but fails in his personal relationships and ends his life in misery. The two films also differ in a number of significant respects: although C. W. Post was Sturges' primary inspiration in creating Tom Garner he used only the basic outlines of Post's life and avoided identifying him explicitly; Welles based his Charles Foster Kane directly on William Randolph Hearst and deliberately used a number of recognizable parallels to identify him in viewers' minds. Welles' film is considerably longer than *The Power and the Glory* and is populated with a number of colorful supporting players, several of whom narrate Kane's story from contrasting and sometimes overlapping perspectives; Garner's story is shorter and simpler, and strikingly under-populated (in part because several small roles were cut, probably for budgetary reasons). We hear Garner's story only from the perspective of poor, dull old Henry, a lifelong subordinate who appears to be Garner's only "friend." While *Citizen Kane*, despite its downbeat theme, is exuberant and frequently funny, *The Power and the Glory* maintains the solemnity of its opening funeral throughout—which is surprising, considering Preston Sturges' overall body of work, and those manic farces of the '40s for which he is best remembered. Perhaps he felt that the seriousness of his theme and the bleakness of the times called for a more somber tone. In any event, decades after the films were made the renaissance of Preston Sturges' reputation as well as the ongoing popularity of *Citizen Kane* have kept interest in *The Power and the Glory* alive. Perhaps too, we are more accustomed by now to the cinematic subgenre it initiated: the exposé of a supposedly great figure who, we discover, was not as great as commonly believed. Variations on this theme have included *The Keeper of the Flame* (1942) which also featured Spencer Tracy, *All the King's Men* (1949), Welles' *Mr. Arkadin* (1955), *The Great Man* (1956), Elia Kazan's *A Face in the Crowd* (1957), and revisionist biographical treatments debunking everyone from Buffalo Bill to Howard Hughes. In an age when TV, print media and the Internet supply all the information anyone could possibly want (and then some) about public figures, it's difficult if not impossible to be shocked by any additional revelations about these individuals, post mortem or otherwise; but then, our expectations of great men (and women) are no longer so unreasonably high. There are no larger-than-life Tom Garners or Charles Foster Kanes in our popular culture today, certainly not in the realms of business or politics. In recent times, revelations concerning massive fiscal improprieties at Enron produced genuine, widespread shock and indignation, although this was primarily in response to the very scale of the fraud itself. Nonetheless, Kenneth Lay and Jeffrey Skilling, the key figures in the scandal, would appear to be the closest current equivalents we have to Tom Garner, which makes the documentary film *Enron: The Smartest Guys in the Room* (2005) our closest cinematic equivalent to *The Power and the Glory*. While parallels between the careers of these men and that of Tom Garner may be somewhat tenuous—Lay came from a poor family; Skilling suffered a nervous breakdown under stress and reportedly considered suicide—the melodramatic and highly public saga of their downfall suggests that the basic storyline conceived by Preston Sturges seventy-five years ago can still be applied to certain once-powerful individuals in our world. Sturges' perversely twisted version of the Horatio Alger "success" story continues to play itself out, in reality, in 21st century America.

Sources

All quotes from Preston Sturges' *The Power and the Glory* screenplay come from *Three More Screenplays by Preston Sturges*, edited with introductions by Andrew Horton. Berkeley: University of California Press, 1998.

Books

Bergman, Andrew. *We're in the Money: Depression America and Its Films*. New York: New York University Press, 1971.
Curtis, James. *Between Flops: A Biography of Preston Sturges*. New York: Harcourt Brace Jovanovich, 1982.
Deschner, Donald. *The Films of Spencer Tracy*. New York: Citadel Press, 1968.
Jacobs, Diane. *Christmas in July: The Life and Art of Preston Sturges*. Berkeley: University of California Press, 1992.
Seldes, Gilbert. *The Years of the Locust (America 1929-1932)*. Boston: Little, Brown and Company, 1933.
Spoto, Donald. *Madcap: The Life of Preston Sturges*. Boston: Little, Brown and Company, 1990.
Swindell, Larry. *Spencer Tracy: A Biography*. New York: World Publishing Company, 1969.
Watkins, T. H. *The Hungry Years: A Narrative History of the Great Depression*. New York: Henry Holt and Company, 1999.
Welles, Orson and Peter Bogdanovich. *This is Orson Welles*. New York: Da Capo Press, 1998.

Articles, essays, etc.

Corliss, Richard. "Preston Sturges." *Cinema* (spring 1972).
Horton, Andrew. "The Power and the Glory: 'You can't judge him by ordinary standards.'" From *Three More Screenplays by Preston Sturges*. Berkeley: University of California Press, 1998.
Lasky, Jesse. Untitled essay in *The 1932 Film Daily Year Book of Motion Pictures*. Jack Alicoate, editor. 14th annual edition. New York, 1932.
Sarris, Andrew. "Preston Sturges in the Thirties." *Film Comment* (winter 1970-71).

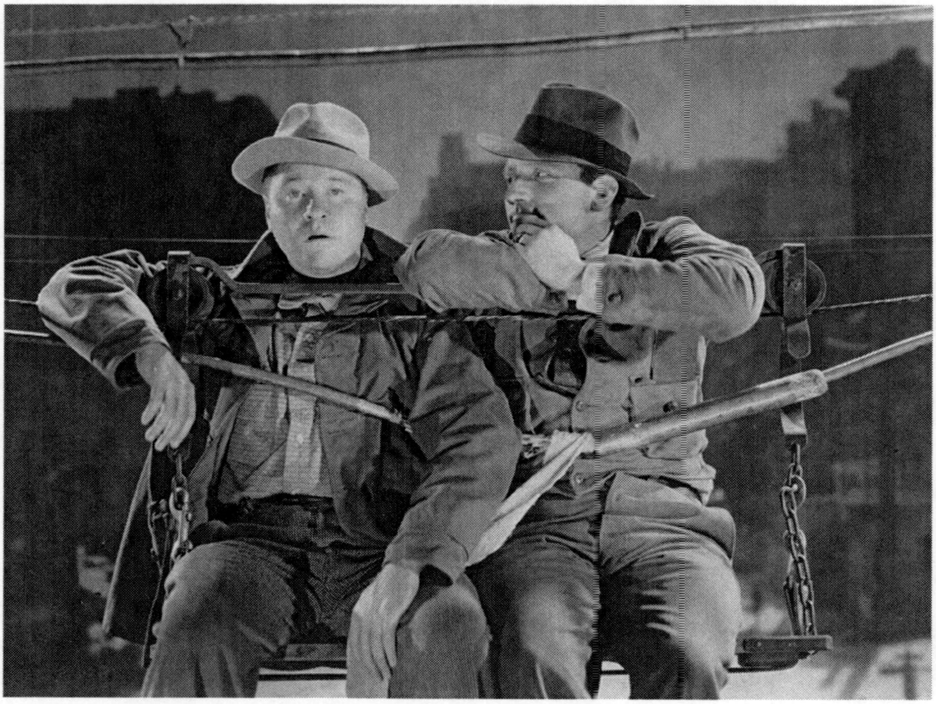

LOOKING FOR TROUBLE

William Wellman, Director
Darryl F. Zanuck, Producer
Story by J.R. Bren
Leonard Praskins and Elmer Harris, Screenplay
James Van Trees, Cinematographer
Produced by 20th Century Pictures
Released March 29, 1934
80 minutes

Cast
Spencer Tracy . . . Joe Graham
Jack Oakie . . . Casey
Constance Cummings . . . Ethel Greenwood
Morgan Conway . . . Dan Sutter
Arline Judge . . . Maizie Bryan
Paul Harvey . . . James Regan
Judith Wood . . . Pearl La Tour
Joseph Sauers . . . Henchman Max
Robert Elliott . . . Captain Flynn
Franklyn Ardell . . . George Martin, Troubleshooter
Paul Porcasi . . . Cabaret Manager
Charles Levinson . . . Switchboard Operator

And other cast

Looking for Trouble and Finding Contentment: The Exciting Life of a Telephone Trouble Shooter

Jeremy Bond

Spencer Tracy's earliest films have a discernible pattern. When Tracy plays a character who overachieves—such as in *Now I'll Tell* and *Dante's Inferno*—the character gets his comeuppance. When Tracy plays someone who is content in a livelihood beneath his potential—such as in *The Face in the Sky* or *Looking for Trouble*—he lives happily ever after. The distinction is the most evident in *The Power and the Glory*, in which Tracy begins as a perfectly happy trackwalker and ends up a perfectly miserable magnate. In *Looking for Trouble*, Tracy plays a telephone lineman named Joe Graham who, despite (coincidentally?) sharing a common name with the inventor of the telephone, doesn't aspire to much. Working for work's sake, the film implies, is an admirable American trait.

Tracy was occasionally loaned out to other studios during his five-year tenure at Fox Film Corp. *Looking for Trouble* was produced by 20th Century Pictures before the company merged with Fox. It was directed by William Wellman, who had already achieved popularity with films such as *Wings* (1927) and *The Public Enemy* (1931). Wellman was not associated with one particular studio, but *Looking for Trouble* reflects the same modest American values as Tracy's Fox films: honesty, humility, and loyalty. Tracy had become the antithesis of the swaggering leading man exemplified by Douglas Fairbanks Jr. The Depression-era audience might come to the movies to escape, but Tracy reminds them that their life is okay as it is.

The Good Americans

From the start, the film venerates Joe Graham's profession. An opening title reads: "The producers wish to express their appreciation to that vast array of telephone repairmen and trouble shooters who made this picture possible." We meet Joe's boss, Mr. Regan (Paul Harvey), an avuncular man with an omnipresent cigar—the kindly employer of yore who rewards loyalty and integrity. He offers Joe a promotion and is surprised when he turns it down. "Have you lost your mind?" Mr. Regan asks him. "You'll have fourteen men under you. Better hours. Easier work."

"Yeah, yeah, and get calluses on my can from sitting in a stuffy office all day," Joe replies respectfully. "And double my laundry bill sending out those white collars."

Joe then has a short monologue that demonstrates that he values both hard work and independence:

> Some people live for riches and luxury. Others like a fireside, a shady tree, a comfortable bed. But I'm a guy that lives for the thrill and excitement I get out of life. I broke my old man's heart when I wouldn't go to work in his paint shop. That was ten years ago. Ever since then, I've been doing the things I wanted to do most. No matter what and where they are. And right now, I think being a trouble shooter is swell. The constant hurry, the everlasting change, the unexpected adventures got under my skin.

In a sense, Joe is contradicting himself. He broke free from his father, and yet he is drawn to working under a father figure. He wants excitement, and yet he is content fixing people's phones. Mr. Regan doesn't push the promotion issue any further. "Heh heh heh," he chuckles. "I wish we had more like you, Joe."

Joe's fiancée, Ethel (Constance Cummings), is an operator with the phone company and doesn't dismiss Joe's intransigence so easily. "I just heard you turned down an offer of promotion," she complains to him. "Oh, Joe, why did you?"

He replies, "Now listen, baby, if you want me, and I don't see how you can help it, you've got to take me as I am, and I ain't the sort of a guy who could sit in an office all day. You know that. And I can't wear white collars. They don't fit the size or the color of my neck. I've got to work with my hands."

Today, his self-identification as a redneck wouldn't be seen as a compliment.

The Women Have Their Place

Joe sounds humble to his boss when he rejects the promotion. When he makes the same argument to his girl, however, he seems to take on a superiority complex. He establishes gender roles in the most traditional way.

Joe and Ethel enter the company cafeteria, and Joe doesn't let her choose her own lunch. She orders a salad, but he tells the cafeteria worker to give her roast beef instead. She doesn't like spinach, but Joe orders it for her anyway. "Are you going to bully me all your life?" she asks, not at all angry.

"Yup. If taking care of you is bullying you, that's what I'm going to do."

But Ethel soon stands up to him. Joe becomes angry with her for associating with Dan, Joe's devious co-worker, but Ethel dismisses Joe's protectiveness.

"You've been everywhere. All around the world. Seen everything," she protests. Now Joe has no interest in going out with her because everything is old news to him. But "I get a kick out of stepping out and enjoying myself like any normal girl would.

"After we're married, if we ever are, I'll be perfectly willing to sit at home and darn your socks and listen to your stories about Asia and Africa and South America or what-have-you," she adds. "But right now I want a little fun and a few laughs." Here, she makes a curious distinction: that a woman without a man is self-sufficient, but a woman who has given herself to a man lives only to please him.

Ethel and her friend, Maizie (Arline Judge), straddle the line between independent womanhood and tying the knot. Joe and Ethel's extended engagement probably speaks to their uncertainty about the concept of marriage. Maizie acts indifferent toward men and makes fun of Joe's goofy assistant Casey (Jack Oakie), but she plays along when Casey jokingly pretends to be a Southern colonel. Casey kisses her passionately without warning, and she apparently doesn't see herself in a position to protest. Maizie ends up marrying him—as if marriage was inevitable for her anyway. Societal expectations are well-established.

Notably, the woman in the movie with the most self-assuredness—Pearl (Judith Wood), Dan's partner-in-crime—doesn't survive. She is the opposite of passive. She is a seductress, but Joe uses her only as a means to an end.

No Ordinary Joe

Joe's tendency to take control extends beyond women. He seems to be the leader among his humble fellow trouble shooters. When he (temporarily) resigns, the men, in tattered clothes and hats, line up as if Joe were royalty. Joe suggests to Casey that his departure would open Casey to a higher position, but Casey says dejectedly, "Who wants your job? You're the only guy I've ever met [whom] I'd work under." Suddenly, a request comes in for a wiretapping investigation, and Joe abruptly "un-resigns" to take the assignment—with no objection from his fellow workers. While Joe respects the modesty of his occupation, he clearly relishes being a big fish in a small tank.

No one is an authority over Joe. When Casey is injured in a fire, Joe tells a fireman what to do: "Go on, get a doctor, would you? He's burned bad." Later, after an earthquake, Joe bravely climbs a telephone pole with crackling wires. No wonder the film has such high regard for telephone repairmen: they act like superheroes.

The telephone business itself seems to live by its own authority. Joe and Dan fight right in front of a police officer, but Mr. Regan keeps the cop from intervening. Joe obtains a list of phone numbers dialed from a certain line, without anyone bringing up the appropriateness or legality of releasing such information to an ordinary citizen. Ma Bell is a monopoly, and as such, it is all-powerful.

A Little Bit of Everything

Looking for Trouble was filmed just before the enforcement of the Production Code, and the leniency shows. Judith Wood does a Mae West routine (her phone isn't broken—but why don't you come up to her place to fix it anyway?). Casey accidentally calls a whorehouse and writes an asterisk next to the phone number. Joe starts to call Dan a "son of a—" before stopping himself.

It also presents 1930s America as we more or less know it. A newspaper seller walks through the streets shouting, "Extra! Extra!" Operators at the phone company are women with nasally voices. People pick up the phone and say, "Hello, operator?"—something that people probably did only in movies, to fill the audience in.

The film also presents a slice of time and place and an unusual confluence of talent. The earthquake scene is actual footage of the quake in Long Beach, California, in March 1933, in which more than 5,000 people were injured or killed. At MGM, Tracy would end up in another prominent California earthquake scene, in *San Francisco* (1936). Others associated with the film would prosper as well. Oakie's most famous screen role would be that of Benzini Napaloni, the dictator of "Bacteria," in Charlie Chaplin's *The Great Dictator* (1940). William Wellman, who used Oakie in a small handful of other films, would move on to direct two of the most popular films of 1937, *A Star Is Born* and *Nothing Sacred*. And Ma Bell would survive another fifty years.

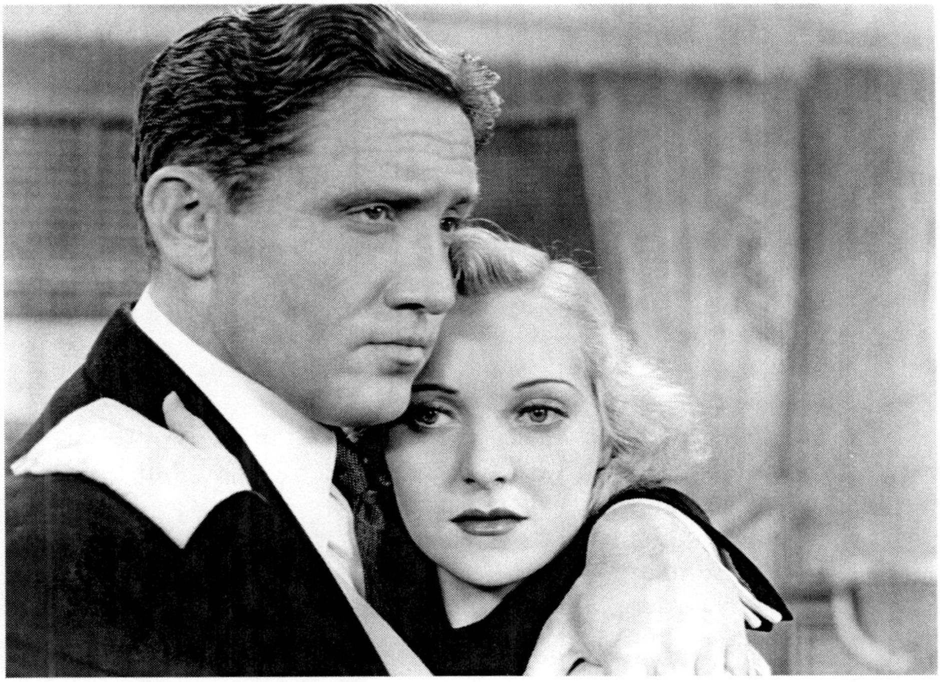

BOTTOMS UP

David Butler, Director
Buddy G. DeSylva, Producer
David Butler, Story & Screenplay
Buddy G. DeSylva, Story & Screenplay
Sid Silvers, Story & Screenplay
Arthur C. Miller, Cinematographer
Produced & Distributed by Fox Film Corporation
Released April 13, 1934
85 minutes

Cast
Spencer Tracy . . . 'Smoothie' King
Pat Paterson . . . Wanda Gale
John Boles . . . Hal Reed
Sid Silvers . . . Spud Mosco aka Reginald Morris
Herbert Mundin . . . Limey Brook aka Lord Brocklehurst
Harry Green . . . Louis Baer aka Wolf
Thelma Todd . . . Judith Marlowe
Robert Emmett O'Connor . . . Detective Rooney
Dell Henderson . . . Lane Worthing
Suzanne Kaaren . . . Wolf's Secretary
Douglas Wood . . . Baldwin

And other cast

Bottoms Up: Spencer Tracy Comes Out on Top as a Hollywood Hero

Cinzi Lavin

Introduction

When one considers Spencer Tracy's film legacy, his enduring on-screen persona invariably involves his timeless appeal as a forceful, nurturing masculine figure. He protects the weak, fights for the truth, and is honest enough to face his own doubts squarely and without flinching. He is the Perfect Man, able to blend strength and sensitivity, to earn the affection of women and the respect of men. Tracy brought multitudinous, unchartered facets of leading-man talent to the Hollywood scene, markedly different from those of his peers. With his easygoing manner, passionate courage, self-abnegating attitude (plus a healthy splash of spunk and vigor), Tracy was a surprising composite of the range of cinematic potential. He understood that screen acting was about more than merely filming a *de facto* stage performance, and played to the hearts and minds of his viewers in a way far more intimate than his contemporaries. Tracy showed moviegoers that there were dimensions of on-screen depth and vulnerability of which they had never dreamed . . . and literally took their breath away with his stark sincerity. Tracy, a consummate actor, draws us into his inner world—not only makes us believe, but makes us *want* to believe that he is his character—*and we do*—and therein lies his genius.

The Story

In the musical *Bottoms Up* (1934), Spencer Tracy is wondrously suited to the part of dreamer/schemer Smoothie King, a hardscrabble huckster with a heart of gold. He knows which side his bread is buttered on, but he's always willing to share more than a morsel with his friends. He blows into Tinsel Town with pal Limey Brook (Herbert Mundin) who spent time in jail for not being very good at signing names. Together, they miraculously meet up with Smoothie's old friend, Spud Mosco (Sid Silvers), who stands outside an opening-night film-debut, hawking sheet music for the show's hits. ("'I Surrender, Dear' for only ten cents!" constitutes one of the most memorable laugh-lines in the film.)

Inside the theatre, the opening song, "Turn On the Moon," is the perfect *entree* for a movie experience that is all about Hollywood. Cinema sheik Hal Reed (John Boles), with his impeccably clipped moustache and film-star good looks, sings in *bel canto* style reminiscent of pop-tenor John McCormack, with a mouthful of preponderant lyrics and rolling r's, surrounded by an overproduced set, gorgeous costumes notwithstanding (kudos to designer Russell Patterson).

In short, everything has been laid on thick. How refreshing, then, for the viewer, when Reed exits the theatre and confronts producer Louis Wolf (Harry Green), saying politely that he believes the film is "the most stupendous piece of junk" he's ever seen. He greets the throng of fans around him with a macabre sense of duty, knowing he knows something which they do not: that he is nothing more than a pitiful alcoholic bit-player who has been wrongly exalted, by popular demand and the machinations of Hollywood, to the ranks of fame.

He is then approached by Wanda Gale, a waifish fan (Pat Paterson) who cadges his autograph, remarking that she thinks he's wonderful. He replies that he wishes he did and sends her off with a bitter, self-mocking smile.

Moments later, Smoothie, Limey, and Spud find themselves enjoying a jolly, if sparse, meal at the local drug-store (the fast-food equivalent of the day). Smoothie sees Wanda enter and notices her sitting alone at the other end of the counter, furtively scarfing a half-sandwich concealed in her handbag. (One assumes she has only ordered a glass of water.) Concerned for her welfare, Smoothie chats her up and treats her (on Spud's largesse) to a slice of pie. He discovers that she is a beauty contest winner, come from Canada to become a Hollywood movie star, and that the contract she had been offered by one of the studios only cast her as an extra. Worse yet, the brief contract has expired, leaving her out of work and at embarrassing loose ends. She doesn't want to return home to face her friends and family and their high hopes for her stardom until she has become a success. As the four exit the diner, Smoothie susses out that Wanda intends to wander the town for the evening, as she hasn't paid her rent and her landlady won't let her back into her apartment. He offers her to spend the night with him and his comrades at Spud's accommodations, smoothing over their reservations with the same irresistible charm a child does when bringing home a stray pet.

Arriving at Spud's digs (the open-air underbelly of a large outbuilding on a miniature-golf course), Smoothie gallantly creates a private sleeping-area for Wanda, turns on the radio for her amusement, and then joins the boys to collect some firewood. As they return, they are captivated by a mesmerizingly lovely voice performing a song on the radio. However, approaching the hovel, they see that the voice belongs to Wanda, who is touchingly shown in all her delicate beauty, singing "I'm Throwing My Love Away" to a radio instrumental. (It is worth noting that Gus Kahn, one of the film's songwriters, is famous for creating the hits "It Had To Be You," and "Makin' Whoopee.")

Smoothie, ever the opportunist, is instantly convinced that Wanda has talent worth promoting. He enthusiastically cooks up a scheme in which Wanda takes Hollywood by storm, arriving from England (in ostensible secrecy) with her father, Lord Brocklehurst (to be played by Limey) as an up-and-coming screen hopeful. Smoothie's confidence that the plan will work rests in his conviction that Hollywood cannot tell the difference between a silk purse and a sow's ear, and that any hint of the arrival of foreign gentry will send the town's gossip-mill into overdrive to fuel Wanda's publicity and (ultimately) acceptance.

Setting the plan into action, Limey and Wanda (clad in expensive-looking garb they have rented from a costumer's) alight from an incoming Los Angeles train and are interviewed by a crowd of reporters, who have been tipped off about their arrival. Meanwhile, the pair of pretenders feign modesty at having been recognized. The gang then settles into a posh hotel suite, arranged by Smoothie (who has taken on the role of Wanda's promoter), and it is all they can do not to ravage the complementary fruit-basket, a sad testament to their actual status, which is, in reality, being held together by no more than a lick and a promise.

Smoothie knows it will only be a matter of time before they get a break, but he is taken aback when actress Judith Marlowe (Thelma Todd) forces her way up to their rooms, claiming to know Lord Brocklehurst. He is horrified that she actually may, and wonders how they are going to pass Limey off to her until it becomes apparent that Marlowe is nothing more than a social bounder, even phonier than they are. The smarmy Marlowe invites the lot to a *soiree* welcoming Wanda and her father. After Marlowe's exit, as Wanda expresses her gratitude to Smoothie for helping her, he makes it a point of telling her he "ain't the marrying kind."

At Marlowe's party (in which a young Lucille Ball—two years into her film career—appears in the uncredited role of "Blonde Party Girl"), Gale again meets up with depressed screen-idol Hal Reed, who gets himself drunk enough that she offers to drive him home. Reed accepts. When they arrive, she gives him buttermilk to drink and listens to his sad-sack story about having become a caricature of himself. In contrast to his discouragement and disappointment about his career, she is hopeful and supportive . . . and also clearly falling very much in love with him.

The remainder of the plot, for brevity's sake, consists of Wanda being offered a starring screen role and Smoothie's scheme appearing successful until it is revealed to producer Lou Wolf that *Burke's Peerage* does not list a Lord Brocklehurst, and that he and his "daughter" are *poseurs*.

Smoothie confronts Wolf, passionately arguing that Wanda's talent is genuine despite her fabricated provenance, and that she deserves to be in pictures. Wanda's director petitions for keeping her in the film, which is still in production. Meanwhile, Reed has emerged from his addictive stupor and is feeling more optimistic about his acting potential thanks to Wanda's efforts. Unfortunately, the lovers have been driven apart by the hoopla surrounding Wanda's being outed as an imposter.

In the midst of this drama, Smoothie (who has been conveniently blind to Wanda's adoration of Reed) has decided to ask her to marry him. At the moment of his intended proposal, Wanda (who considers him nothing more than a dear friend), unburdens herself to him about her heartbreak at losing Reed's love.

In a bold move, Smoothie then pays a visit to Reed in order to ascertain his worthiness for Wanda. He finds Reed every bit as crushed as Wanda by the turn of events, and judges him to be a fit partner for the woman he himself loves. He advises Reed to contact Wanda, thereby securing her happiness at the cost of his own.

The film closes with Wanda and Reed, newly affianced, appearing before the Hollywood press, Wanda making a radio-broadcast statement thanking Smoothie. Meanwhile, back at the miniature-golf-course hovel with Limey and Spud, Smoothie, hearing her message, wistfully remarks that she and Reed make a good couple, adding (with obvious regret over losing her) "maybe it's just as well that I wasn't the marrying kind."

Analysis

As easy as it would be to label *Bottoms Up* old-time, throw-away, B&W entertainment, the film sheds some pretty merciless light on a Hollywood that has remained largely unchanged since the movie was made.

From an historical perspective, the openly expressed assumption of the film is that true talent holds less *cache* in Hollywood than connections. American entertainment in general has long had the infamous international distinction of allowing the business of politics to dominate sheer artistic ability. Within this once and future climate, Louis Wolf's character is particularly easy with which to sympathize—he is the consummate Hollywood middleman, yearning to create art, yet always at the mercy of the studio heads. It is no wonder that he is beset by so many nervous ailments, the physical manifestation of trying to serve two masters: art and commerce.

From a social standpoint, little has changed the plight of the stage or screen artist since *Bottoms Up* was made. The starveling actor is still very much with us, and judging by the fact that this mainstay of the entertainment business has been around since before Shakespeare's era, not likely to vanish from the scene any time soon. Art, the most luminous and attractive of all human endeavors, exacts a terrible cost from those who would pursue it, and in the process, many poor moths get their wings singed. Back in the days of New York City's famed Automat cafeteria, crackers and "tomato soup" (*read*: ketchup and hot water), all of which could be had for free, were the mainstay of the artist's diet, keeping hope alive and body and soul together.

The dark side of shattered artistic dreams—and the depths to which one can fall in following them—was brought shockingly to the fore in cinematic history by *Midnight Cowboy*, the story of a would-be actor who prostitutes himself to men and women. This evergreen reality is fleetingly (and discreetly) alluded to in *Bottoms Up* when Limey tells Marlowe, who lashes out at Wanda after her cover has been blown, that while he acknowledges the little charade he and Wanda have pulled on the film industry to achieve fame, "I'd hate to know what you had to do to get into pictures."

The political and economic relevance of this film to today's society and our current movie industry is clearly apparent. Hollywood, in the spirit of good-natured amusement—now as then—is ever willing to poke fun at itself. Films such as *What Price Hollywood* (1932), *A Star is Born* (1937), *Sunset Boulevard* (1950), and *The Player* (1992), prove that Hollywood is willing to take a pie in the face from time to time—a small price to pay when one considers the magnitude of artistic loss caused by the everyday workings of bottom-line thinking and under-the-table deals that dominate business behind the scenes. In short, Hollywood can afford to expose itself or it would not do so. That alone is evidence of how deeply entrenched—how very *secure*—its system is.

Turning to Tracy's performance, it is well worth noting how exceptional his ability to be a "real" character was, given his time and place in history. Moreover, his ease at weaving "feminine" characteristics into his leading-male roles is nothing short of groundbreaking. Considering he was working in front of the camera prior to the advent of "metrosexuals," he nevertheless made it seem natural and unthreatening to his masculinity to be extraordinarily nurturing. To offer but a few examples from later films, in *Boys Town*, he was both father and mother to the children in his care. In the *Father of the Bride* series, he exposed unmistakable tenderness towards his daughter in stark contrast to the gruff, bottom-line "how much is this wedding/grandchild going to cost me?" stance that would've been the obvious approach to the role of most actors of his time. *Bottoms Up* shows him not only as an ardorous suitor to Wanda, but a man who is equally concerned with and unquestionably capable of keeping her warm, well-fed, comfortable and contented.

Conclusion

Spencer Tracy had the rare gift of understanding his potential within the industry and utilizing it to magnificent ends, as few actors before or since have done. Even in his early works, such as *Bottoms Up*, we see him—not fumbling to create his persona as a performer—but eloquently giving voice to a vision that was already within him, which we are invited to relish in each gesture and each spoken line, as he does in delivering them. Tracy arrived on the scene ready-made for a public that hungered, suddenly, for artistic authenticity and diversity within a gender-role. And that he made it all look so easy demonstrates the immense artistry he brought to his craft. Tracy looked within the heart of his characters and lent them the compassion that resonated within himself as he considered his powerful connection to them. Before we even knew it ourselves, Tracy knew we all needed a Smoothie King in our midst, a forgivably presumptuous, starry-eyed, larger-than-life friend with a pocket full of dreams to cheer us through our rough times and champion us on to glory. If Tracy has bequeathed anything to film history, surely his contribution involves his innate ability to embody characters that bring light to our lives, to breathe into existence archetypal heroes whom we are only dimly aware that we want—and need—standing beside us. He always does, and therein lies his profound and lasting gift to the art of movie-making.

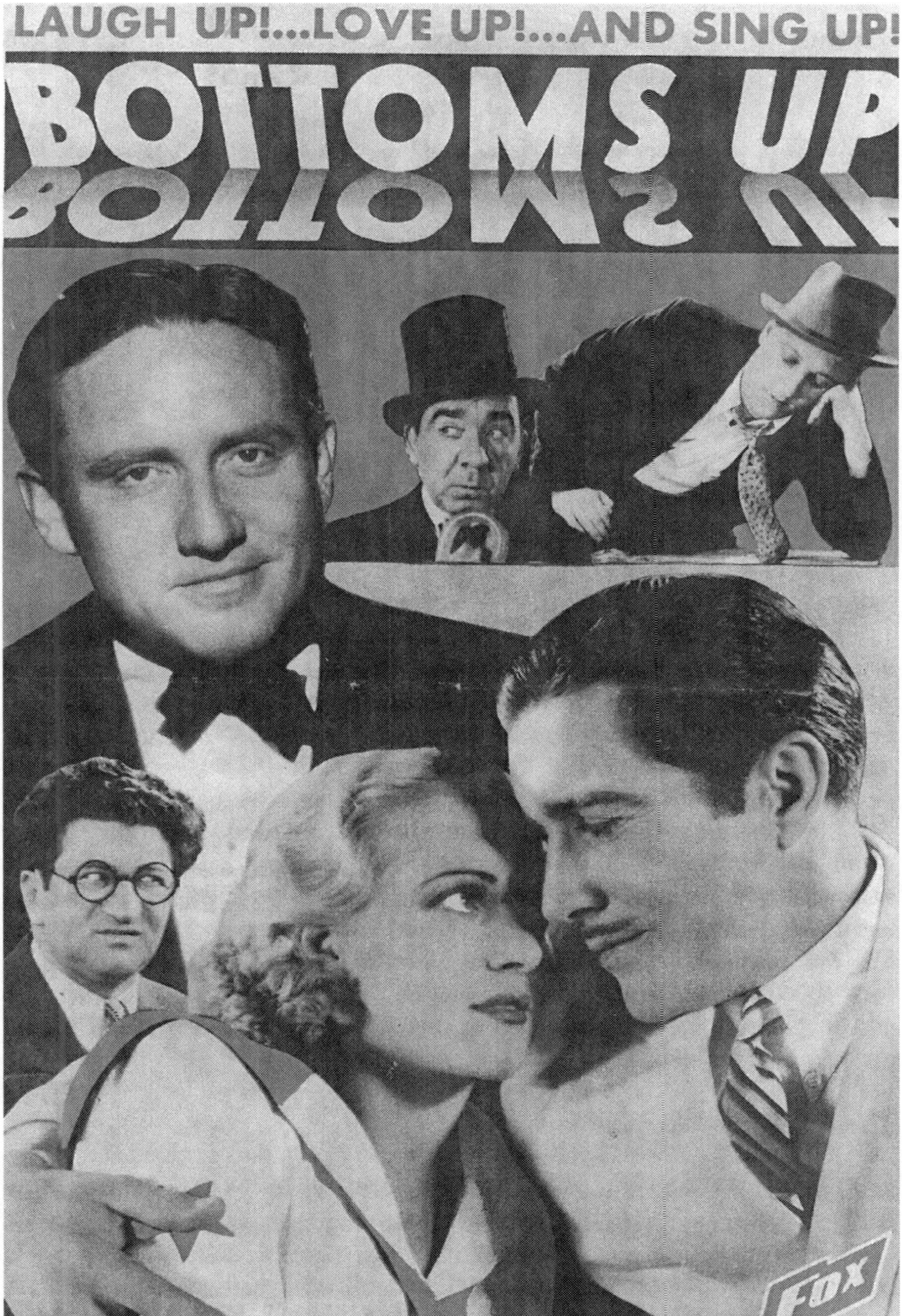
LAUGH UP!...LOVE UP!...AND SING UP!
BOTTOMS UP
FOX

Bottoms Up to Hollywood: Anyone Can Beat This Racket

Jeremy Bond

In the Hollywood of *Bottoms Up*, it's easy to get into the movie business if you have a plan. Talent has little to do with it. A good "little girl" hoping for her big break cannot succeed without help from a man, while a bad girl probably made it by sleeping with someone. For a film with such a critique, *Bottoms Up* is decidedly good-natured. It was made in Hollywood, after all, so it believes in the system. Its cynicism gives way to romanticism.

The Spencer Tracy role, "Smoothie" King, represents an average American man with the rather unlikely ability to manipulate the Hollywood system in whichever way he chooses. "I figure a guy like me could make a lot of dough in this motion picture racket," he says confidently, as if "a guy like me" means anything more than an ordinary guy. He had already tried the "Bible racket," the "glass-eye racket," and a few rackets "I made up myself," so how hard could it be? In this fantasy-world look at Hollywood, not very hard at all.

The Limits of Womanhood

The good girl in the film is Wanda Gale, played by Pat Paterson, the British-born future wife of Charles Boyer. Wanda ends up hitched with a (fictitious) handsome movie actor named Hal Reed, but if Paterson's real life is any indication, marriage to a star will mean little advancement in Wanda's own livelihood. Paterson retired from the screen before hitting 30, soon after her marriage to Boyer. Boyer's career continued to flourish, and presumably Hal Reed's would too—being the male half of an acting couple.

Wanda's passion for success seems muted. She came to Hollywood because she had won a "personality contest" in her hometown of Toronto. "I got a free trip out here and six weeks contract with Supreme Pictures," she tells Smoothie. "I thought I was made. But I only worked [as an] extra in two pictures. They didn't seem to know I was alive." She acknowledges being homesick, but she had had such a big sendoff in Toronto that "I wanted to go back [only] after I'd made good."

It is no wonder that Wanda has not made it very far. She has singing talent, but she lacks ambition. The only passion she displays is when she gets to be alone with the dashing Hal Reed for the first time. "You don't know what you've meant to me," she gushes to him. "Just seeing you on the screen. It wasn't the parts you played. They didn't matter. I saw something in you that—oh, I just had to admire."

So it turns out she is just another starry-eyed girl. But she also sees Hal Reed as a model for how to handle fame. "Instead of being conceited and content, you want to do something better," she tells him. That "proves you're all right inside."

Hal Reed needs proof of his worth because on the outside, he is a drunk. His behavior agitates the studio head. The implication is that fame can ruin people, but not to such an extent that falling in love with a dreamy girl can't turn a guy around. That is why this film is not cynical after all. Perhaps it should be at least a little more skeptical, given the odds of the typical Hollywood marriage between two successful stars. But in Hollywood's first decades, characters who fell in love generally wed. The Production Code would not allow the representation of alternative relationships outside the confines of marriage, despite the realities of the world outside; for decades, Tracy and Katharine Hepburn were content with an alternative arrangement.

Wanda's success ultimately relies on Smoothie, who refers to her as a "little girl" whom he has to "take care of." When Wanda thinks Hal Reed has rejected her, she runs to Smoothie begging him to "take me away from here." Wanda had been enough of a big girl to arrive at Hollywood herself, yet once a man arrives, she depends on him completely. As soon as Smoothie secretly patches it up between Wanda and Hal Reed (which Smoothie does dejectedly, as he had planned to propose to Wanda himself), Smoothie announces to Wanda that he is leaving. "But Smoothie, what am I going to do here without you?" Wanda says.

"You don't think I'd go away and leave you if I didn't know everything was going to be all right with you, do you?" Smoothie replies sweetly. Wanda will be all right without him because there is another man to take his place.

Keeping Up Appearances

The bad girl in the film is a movie actress named Judith Marlowe (Thelma Todd), who sees phoniness and schmoozing as a way to get ahead. "What a delight it is to meet people of my own kind. People of refinement," she says, thinking she is meeting royalty. She is actually speaking to Smoothie's buddy, a British thief called Limey, and Wanda, whom Smoothie has passed off as a visiting lord and the lord's daughter as a scheme to get Wanda into the movies.

When Judith is told of the ruse and confronts Limey about it, he replies, "It's true we practiced a little deception in order to get some honest work. [But] I'd hate to know what you had to do to get into pictures." The Production Code would soon crack down on such a suggestion that a woman would sleep her way to the top. The theme had certainly been tackled before. The previous year, Warner Bros. had made a whole movie about that subject: *Baby Face* with Barbara Stanwyck.

Smoothie, after Wanda's lament that studio executives "didn't seem to know I was alive," makes some pointed criticism at the way Hollywood chooses its darlings. "I can't get over these Hollywood producers," Smoothie says. "Here they have marvelous talent right under their nose, and what do they do? They import some hag from the New York stage, give her the parts with all the gravy, then they lose a million dollars." He might easily have been alluding to an actual real-life actress. Once Smoothie comes up with the royalty hoax, he makes clear references to particular people.

"The only way to get into pictures is to put up a front," he says. He refers to a "girl from Iowa" who pretended to be an Englishwoman and "got herself a big part in *Cavalcade*," a blockbuster that would win the Best Picture Oscar the same month *Bottoms Up* was released. The phony Englishwoman "made a hit, and then she told the studio the truth," Smoothie says. "They were tickled to death." Smoothie is talking about Margaret Lindsay, who was born in Dubuque in 1910—the same year Paterson, the actress playing Wanda, was lucky enough to be born in England. Lindsay had been unable to find work in New York and found much better success in England. She used this to her advantage when she returned to New York and did not dispute the false assumption that she hailed from Britain. Smoothie might be right that the studio was "tickled to death" over Lindsay, because *Cavalcade* was produced and distributed by Fox Film Corp., the same studio that produced *Bottoms Up!* Far from being embarrassed by Margaret Lindsay, the studio seemed to welcome the opportunity to allow *Bottoms Up* to plug *Cavalcade*, not to mention the studio itself.

Smoothie assures Wanda that deception is part and parcel of Hollywood life, citing a more famous con artist. "Why, they go for anything out here. Look at what this prince/count Romananoff and that phony countess got away with." This is a reference to "Prince" Mike Romanoff, whom a 1971 *Time* magazine obituary referred to as "Hollywood's reigning restaurateur-raconteur for more than two decades." Romanoff might have been born Harry F. Gerguson, the son of Russian immigrants, but he misrepresented himself as everything from Rasputin's assassin to a cousin of Czar Nicholas II to the son of Victorian Prime Minister William Gladstone. "In Hollywood, Romanoff was accepted as an off-camera actor in an actor's town," according to *Time*. Given the reference to Romanoff in *Bottoms Up*, Hollywood was not disputing its hospitality to tricksters. Romanoff would open his first restaurant in Hollywood a few years after this film's release.

Smoothie and his buddies, Limey and Spud, have no qualms hanging out with the Hollywood elite because they show the same penchant for con artistry. But Limey has the upper hand because of his British accent. Never mind that he's a thief (his specialty is writing bad checks); he is British, and thus he is cultured and refined. Spud constantly misunderstands Limey's urbane words and phrases such as "fortnight" and "arriving *in cognito*" ("I think it's much better coming from Pasadena," Spud remarks.)

Driving home the contrast between boorish Americans and sophisticated Britons, Wanda performs an "impression of an English girl trying to sing an American song." She opens her mouth wide and repeats a refrain in a squeaky voice evocative of Betty Boop: "Oh gee, oh gosh, gee whiz . . ." Wanda sounds British herself, as if Canadians always speak that way. It is a curious choice for the screenwriters to have Wanda hail from Toronto instead of Middle America (Dubuque, for example). She is as innocent and wide-eyed as farm girl, even though Toronto and Los Angeles had comparable populations around 1920. (Both cities grew rapidly in the first two decades of the twentieth century, although Los Angeles grew at a much faster rate after that, having twice the population of Toronto by 1930.) Technically, Wanda might have been a city girl, but she was a Canadian; the film provides no other explanation for her simplicity and naïveté.

Wanda and Limey, posing as royals, arrive in Hollywood by train (not exactly the transportation of choice for royalty today). Reporters ask the phony lord the purpose of his visit, and Limey replies, "To look over your cinema factories. I'm thinking of starting one myself. Purely as a hobby, of course." This could be dismissed as a humorous aside of how anybody with a certain amount of wealth or status could easily break into the movie business, but Smoothie had been fully serious when he said, "With my noodle, I oughtta control one of these [movie] companies in about six months." The film industry in *Bottoms Up* is apparently ripe for exploitation, not the exclusive domain of studio bosses.

The studio head in *Bottoms Up*, Louis Wolf, is a weak man who can be manipulated and easily flustered. He is Jewish, and the writers remind us of that constantly through blatant Jewish stereotypes. His voice is raspy and grating. When he clutches his chest of a stress-induced ulcer, he whimpers, "Get me a cheap doctor." Wolf is played by Harry Green, who was born Henry Blitzer and was regularly typecast in stereotypical Jewish roles (in 1930, he played a cigar store owner in "The Kibitzer"). Wolf probably is not meant to represent any one of the many prominent Jewish men who dominated the early film industry—Louis B. Mayer, Samuel Goldwyn, Irving Thalberg—but his characterization suggests an unfounded impression that a Jewish person in authority is more Jewish than authoritative.

The demeaning portrayals of African Americans in Hollywood's first decades might have reflected the dearth of African Americans in the major film studios, but it also reflected the culture; White, Anglo-Saxton, Protestant audiences preferred to see characters that reflected their impressions of certain groups. Those who felt threatened by the prominence of Jews in the film industry could take comfort in a character like Louis Wolf, because throughout *Bottoms Up*, he was never really the one calling the shots. That lack of authority was certainly a fantasy, although apparently the Jewish studio heads—including William Fox, the founder of Fox Film Corp.—did not have the power or interest to prevent distasteful portrayals of Jewish studio heads from popping up in movies like this one.

From the Bottom to the Top

Some of the studio founders were children of immigrants who had grown up in poverty. The phrase "bottoms up" is used in the film in its traditional sense (as part of a toast), though the title clearly refers to Hollywood allowing people of modest means to work their way up.

Classic Hollywood enjoyed making fun of itself and the victims of fame, from Jean Harlow's *Bombshell* in 1933 to Gloria Swanson's doomed Norma Desmond of *Sunset Boulevard* in 1950. *Bottoms Up* takes a few digs at the system, but it lacks the bite of those films. It ultimately celebrates Hollywood and ties the story up in a Capra-esque happy ending. Hollywood is still the stuff of dreams.

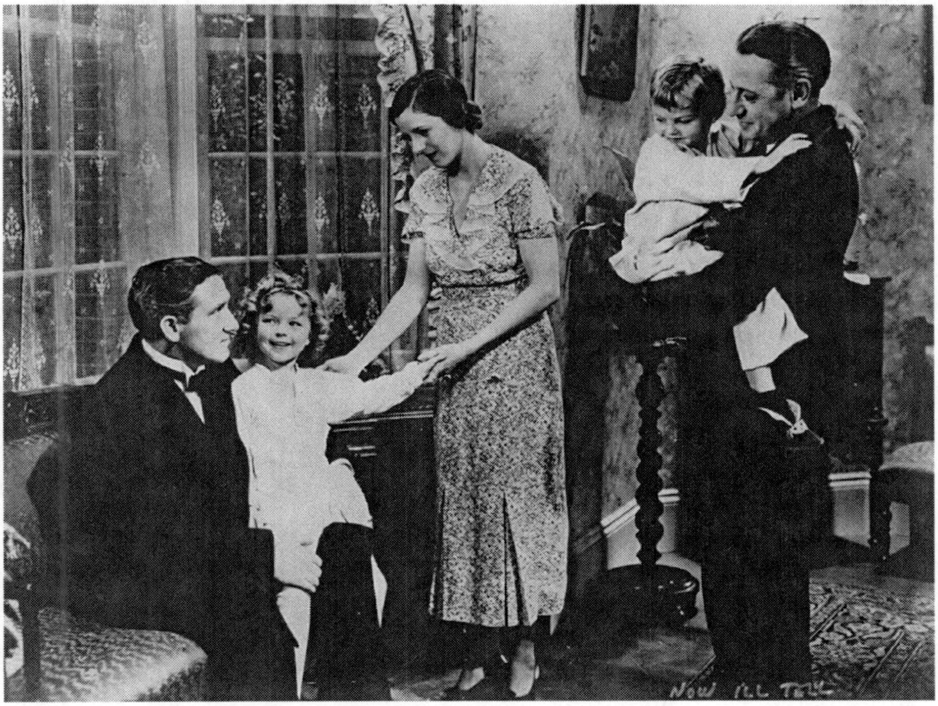
NOW I'LL TELL

NOW I'LL TELL

Edwin J. Burke, Director
Winfield R. Sheehan, Producer
Screenplay by Edwin J. Burke based on the book by Mrs. Arnold Rothstein
Ernest Palmer, Cinematographer
Produced and Distributed by Fox Film Corporation
Released June 8, 1934
72 minutes

Cast
Spencer Tracy . . . Murray Golden
Helen Twelvetrees . . . Virginia Golden
Alice Faye . . . Peggy Warren
Robert Gleckler . . . Al Mossiter
Henry O'Neill . . . Tommy Doran
Hobart Cavanaugh . . . Freddie
G.P. Huntley . . . Hart
Shirley Temple . . . Mary Doran
Ronnie Cosby . . . Tommy Doran Jr.
Ray Cooke . . . Eddie Traylor
Frank Marlowe . . . George Curtis
Clarence Wilson . . . Attorney Davis
Barbara Weeks . . . Wynne
Theodore Newton . . . Joe
Vince Barnett . . . Peppo
James Donlan . . . Honey Smith
Leon Waycoff . . . Max

And other cast

Now I'll Tell: Crime Pays, At Least for the Story Rights

Jeremy Bond

The opening title establishes the plot: "This is the story of a girl who married a gambler—and the career of Murray Golden, the man to whom nothing was wrong except failure." Actually, *Now I'll Tell* is a fictionalized account of Arnold Rothstein, the real-life gambling Goliath who was blamed for fixing the 1919 World Series, among other things. The awkward title of the film used to be even more awkward—*Now I'll Tell* by Mrs. Arnold Rothstein"—because this was the story as told by his widow. (Carolyn Rothstein's book, titled *Now I'll Tell*, was published in conjunction with the film.) Arnold Rothstein had been murdered under mysterious circumstances, which certainly set the stage for a juicy story. Mrs. Rothstein used the opportunity to portray things as positively as possible. In the film, the wife is presented as innocent and loving, and her husband as flawed but ultimately selfless: the film ends with the gambler arranging his own death for his wife's financial advantage. By this point, the real story has clearly taken a back seat to Hollywood fantasy.

The script is co-written by director Edwin J. Burke, and the film is ultimately more of a macho crime drama than a love story. It belongs in the era's pantheon of gangster films and reflects the appetite for tawdry real-life stories in twentieth-century America. The Charles Lindbergh baby had just been kidnapped and murdered, a crime accompanied by the same type of media frenzy as the Lizzie Borden case was in the 1890s and the O.J. Simpson case would be in the 1990s. But despite the title, *Now I'll Tell* doesn't tell us much. Carolyn Rothstein, after all, was a bit player, and her husband's murder remains as unsolved as Jimmy Hoffa's. Audiences at the time, and even the studio, were largely indifferent.

Good Ol' American Gambling

Outside the realms of the rich and prominent, the America of *Now I'll Tell* reflects the Depression. Murray's sidekick Freddie asks a telegram messenger, half-seriously, what he is paid and if there are any openings in his business. Murray is troubled to see that a former acquaintance has become a beggar. A diverse group of children dances in the street for spare change.

For Murray, the only reliable moneymaker is a racket. Like Jim Carter, Tracy's character in *Dante's Inferno*, Murray is unconcerned with sin. "You can do anything you can get away with," Murray says. "You're only wrong when you fail." Also like Jim Carter, he appears to learn from his misdeeds and tries to do right by his former wife, Virginia. Murray purposely gets himself shot so that life insurance money could be used to buy back Virginia's jewelry, which he had pawned. This paves the way for a dramatic finale by Golden's hospital bedside.

Gambling is depicted as not only highly profitable but also as a favorite American pastime. The film opens in the Saratoga Springs of 1909, complete with a carnival atmosphere and ladies doffed in their very best. In contrast to the British depiction of horseracing in *My Fair Lady*, this American form is more criminal. And it's not just horseracing that is linked to dishonest gambling methods. Murray successfully bribes a boxer to throw a match (before his opponent can do the same), and boat-racing, hockey, and the quintessential American pastime of baseball are shown in montage to suggest that they all fell victim to Rothstein's dirty dealings. (The montage is the only possible reference to Rothstein's alleged hand in the Black Sox scandal, in which Chicago White Sox players were bribed to throw the World Series to the Cincinnati Reds. Rothstein's role, if any, is uncertain.) Given the subsequent decades of sporting scandals, Murray's schemes fail to shock today.

Virginia (Helen Twelvetrees) is portrayed in the beginning of the film as completely ignorant of her future husband's criminal behavior. This may be a fiction Mrs. Rothstein perpetuated to protect herself, but she does so at the expense of making herself (and by extension women in general) appear flighty and naïve. Virginia does eventually leave Murray when she discovers another woman in his life. This move makes Virginia seem more empowered, but also indifferent; she doesn't even become angry when she discovers that Murray had pawned her jewels.

Virginia dreams of climbing in social status, an ambition widely shared in the middle of the Depression. (So can you blame her for loving a crook?) She wants "money enough to travel, leisure enough to read nice books," and she hopes to "live among nice people." Murray fakes a telegram from a prominent citizen, and promises that "one of these days I'll be getting *real* telegrams from the Vanderbilts and the Whitneys." Like other Americans, the Goldens are always aiming higher, but this commonality with average folk is superficial. The kind of money Murray and his compatriots throw around—gambling thousands upon thousands of dollars on a whim—would unlikely endear them to movie audiences of the time.

The "other woman," Peggy, is certainly not a paragon of virtue. She is a blonde cabaret singer who tells Murray she was born in the Virgin Islands. "You must have left there when you were quite young," Murray replies—a suggestive remark that wouldn't have passed muster after the enforcement of the Production Code. [Peggy is Alice Faye's first role in a full-length feature film; in a few years Faye would play beside Tyrone Power and Don Ameche in two well-received chronicles of Americana, *In Old Chicago* (1937) and *Alexander's Ragtime Band* (1938).]

The ideal American seems to be Tommy Doran (Henry O'Neill), Murray Golden's childhood friend who is now a police detective. Doran is the consummate family man, with two children (one of whom is played by Shirley Temple) and a house in the suburbs. "Must be nice," Murray remarks in all honesty. But Doran knows that his moral standing is more valuable than his possessions. When he refuses to get involved in a bribe, he tells Murray, "I've got so much, and you've got so little." The implication is that when you remain moral, you can achieve the American dream.

The Jewish Gangster

Now I'll Tell is a rare example of a mainstream 1930s Hollywood film in which the lead character is Jewish, but the fact is never mentioned or implied and is treated as irrelevant. Rothstein was Jewish, and a Jewish name—Murray Golden—is chosen for the fictitious character representing him. There is no obvious reference to his religious background in the film, unlike in the Tracy-Fox film *Bottoms Up*, which featured a stereotypical Jewish film-studio head in a prominent role.

Rothstein was no stereotype. He was wily with money, but he also was a gangster—a role not typically associated with a Jewish American. Spencer Tracy, an Irish Catholic, could play the role as convincingly as anyone. (Four years later, in *Boys Town*, Tracy would win an Oscar for playing an archetypal Roman Catholic, Father Flanagan. Another actor, Henry Hall, would play the Jewish pawnbroker who provides the money to help Flanagan build the home for troubled boys.) Hollywood had at least one other film in 1934 focusing on Jewish crime, *Straight Is the Way*, in which Franchot Tone plays an ex-con named Benny Horowitz.

Hollywood would tell Rothstein's story, both directly and implicitly, in several other films, including *Street of Chance* (1930), *The Rise and Fall of Legs Diamond* (1960) and *King of the Roaring Twenties—The Story of Arnold Rothstein* (1961). In *The Godfather, Part II* (1974), Vito Corleone nicknames a hoodlum "Hyman Roth" after Rothstein. Both Meyer Wolfsheim of *The Great Gatsby* and Nathan Detroit of *Guys and Dolls* were reportedly inspired by him.

After Its Time

Today, eighty years removed from Arnold Rothstein's murder, the story of *Now I'll Tell* has become just another 1930s Hollywood message film about why crime doesn't pay. Watching Spencer Tracy play a gangster doesn't leave the same indelible image as James Cagney did in *The Public Enemy* or Edward G. Robinson did in *Little Caesar*, even though Rothstein's story was just as timely.

By 1934, the first brief Golden Age of the gangster picture had already passed. With the New Deal and the repeal of Prohibition, the scourge of organized crime so vilified in Tracy's second film, *Quick Millions*, was no longer a paramount concern. *Now I'll Tell* remains simply an instructive piece of historical fiction.

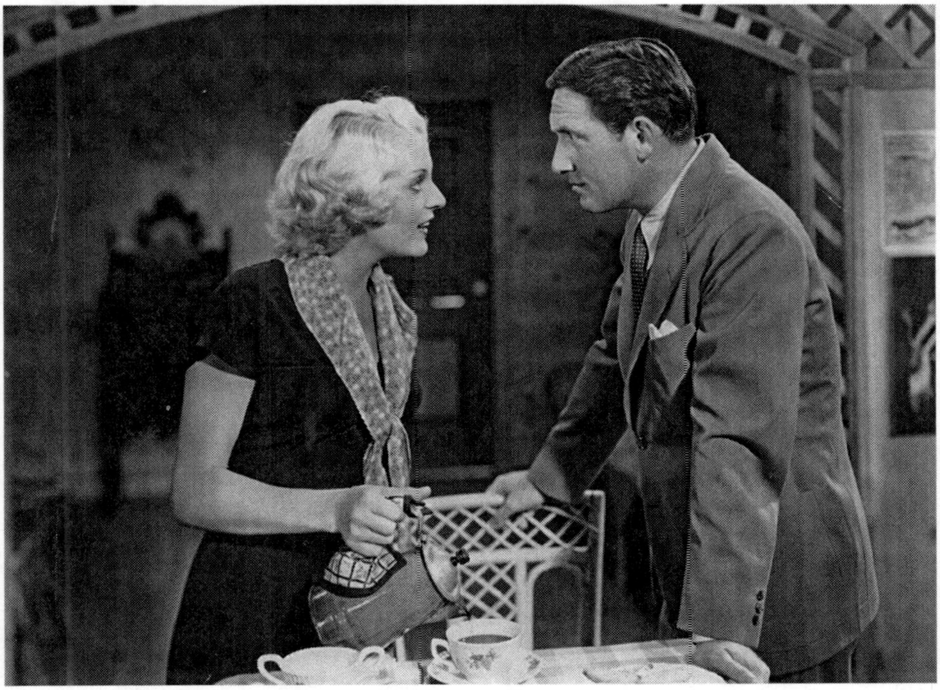

MARIE GALANTE

Henry King, Director
Winfield R. Sheehan, Producer
Story by Jacques Deval
Screenplay by Reginald Berkeley
John F. Seitz, Cinematographer
Produced and Distributed by Fox Film Corporation
Released October 26, 1934
88 minutes

Cast
Spencer Tracy ... Dr. Crawbett
Ketti Gallian ... Marie Galante
Ned Sparks ... Plosser
Helen Morgan ... Miss Tapia
Sigfried Rumann ... Brogard
Leslie Fenton ... General Saki Tenoki
Arthur Byron ... General Gerald Phillips
Robert Loraine ... Ratcliff
Frank Darien ... Ellsworth

And other cast

Cultural & Racial Stereotyping in Marie Galante

Sean Connell

The film *Marie Galante* is considered a classic for many reasons but innovative character development is not one of them. Most of the roles in the movie come across more as caricatures than as characters. Remarkable cinematic techniques are displayed, coupled with some fine acting within the constraints of the roles provided, but the film fleshes out most of the major roles and one minor role through racial and cultural stereotypes, the notable, yet still limited, exception being Spencer Tracy's character, Corbett. For the majority of the roles, commonly held notions of certain racial and cultural groups act as a replacement for actual character development, while presumably providing contemporary audiences with easy-to-fill expectations. Marie is the innocent girl, naive and unworldly. The British are proper and—for a tropical country like Panama—typically overdressed. There's even the obligatory lounge singer, and song numbers, that come with the bar.

Two stereotypes (one more pronounced than the other but both blatant to modern eyes) stand out in the film: Tenoki, played by Leslie Fenton, and Stepin Fetchit's unnamed waiter. The former character was written into the film, whereas the other was the creation of the actor and part of his image. While Leslie Fenton would play Asian men again, he also found success in other roles (in addition to his work on the other side of the camera). Fetchit, by contrast, made his fortune playing a single character, the "coon" persona, and that character is on obvious display in *Marie Galante*.

Fetchit's routine of the bumbling, mumbling black man caused a great deal of controversy in its time, and even the modern eye feels an undeniable discomfort. While the actor himself was a pioneer in the Hollywood's Black community, Fetchit's character was perceived as feeding into the more hurtful racial prejudices of the white community and ultimately made his legacy a difficult one. What saves the performance in *Marie Galante* is the knowledge of two things, one found in the film itself and one found in film history.

The latter stems from why Fetchit created a character that so blatantly and bluntly played into the negative expectations of whites. Though largely unrecognized at the time, and therefore unappreciated by contemporary audiences of both colors, Fetchit's caricature was intended to mock those expectations. The shuffling black man only shuffled on the outside, hiding his true nature from those who didn't respect him. This hiding in plain sight is arguably a little too effective.

Fetchit's waiter betrays himself in one crucial line of dialogue that is almost overlooked even as it is mumbled. When asked what brought him to Panama, Fetchit replies, in the midst of giving a shave, that he had once shaved someone "too close." Little else is said about this back-story, and it is played mostly for comedic effect in the film itself. However, keeping company with spies and international agents, it is the waiter shuffling along in the background who is also very dangerous. It was too much to hope for that his role would prove to be a pivotal one—it turns out he is no piano-playing Sam to Spencer's Corbett—but there are depths to Fetchit's character that go beyond what's on the surface and they are, unfortunately, left unexplored.

The other racial role is played by a white guy in Asian blackface. If *Marie Galante* were in color, it is likely that Fenton's portrayal would have been all the more obvious, but even in black and white to a modern eye it is obvious that Fenton is not Japanese. This was an era in Hollywood when Asian actors where few and far between—if around at all. In some ways this makes Fenton's portrayal all the more stereotyped. Whereas Fetchit is a black man playing on white expectations of Negroes, Fenton is a white man playing out white expectations of the Japanese.

In real life, beyond the movie, the Japanese are ostensibly still allies. Though the Japanese Empire has begun by this point to expand its aims in Asia, the Western World still views them as friends. Empires were not something to be distrusted, after all, the French and English still had one even if it they called it something else. The character of Tenoki represents some of the misconceptions about the Japanese, misconceptions that blind the West to Japan's ambitions. These are played out in the two sides of his character.

On the one hand, British-born Fenton plays what he is, the proper Englishman in natty suits. He looks—except for the slick, black hair—as though he could be one of the British agents. He wears his suit better than Spencer Tracy does, with that proper British crispness. Then he composes haikus and wears a kimono, which marks him as "other" in a way that even the affected hairstyle cannot. Now he is obviously Japanese, and it is really that facet of the character, more than anything else, that sets him up as the diversion, the red herring.

And what of the hero, Spencer Tracy's character, the American Corbett? A stereotype again, and one that has yet to die out in cinema. He's the one who knows what's really going on, and who maintains his belief in his convictions despite the admonishing of his superiors. In the film he is the one who believes Marie even when no one else does, and who ultimately uncovers the plot. It is to Tracy's credit that, despite being another caricature, the character is fleshed out as much as possible. Tracy gives Corbett a bit more presence, a bit more passion as befits the central protagonist. Corbett's doubts about Marie's innocence are as scripted as the rest, and typical of this kind of story, but they do give Tracy the opportunity to do something with his character that the others are not given.

The one place characterization stands out as progressive is in the movie's portrayal of the villain, Brogard. Ironically, it is far more likely that the pre-World War II Japanese would have hatched a plot about the Panama Canal than some faceless terrorist, despite the prevalence of the arch-villain in early twentieth century movies. No matter how preposterous, the idea of some madman fostering a nefarious terrorist scheme to blow up the Panama Canal and the American Fleet is all too real for modern audiences. And while modern movies have stereotypes of their own (i.e. madmen hatching nefarious schemes!), at least modern films seem to have overcome the blatant racial and cultural stereotyping deliberately on display in *Marie Galante*.

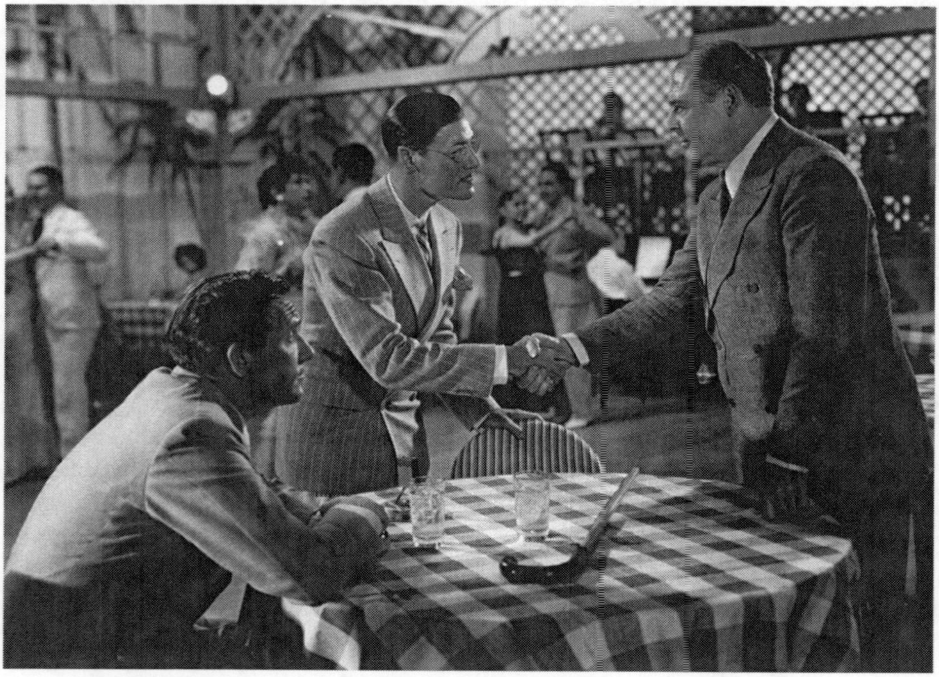

The International Perspective of Marie Galante: As Long as You Speak Our Language

Jeremy Bond

In *Marie Galante*, people of different nationalities and races are treated with respect even as they are stereotyped. Characters who are nonwhite or non-American are no more or less likely to be villains; in fact, a presumed villain, a Japanese man, turns out to be one of the good guys. But he still represents a type rather than an individual. His mannerisms and way of speaking mirror the typical depiction of 1930s or 1940s movie characters of Oriental descent, of any nationality.

The title character is French, other characters are British, and Spencer Tracy, as usual, plays an American, and everyone's presence in the Panama Canal Zone lends an international flavor to the whole film. But the film does not challenge the perceptions (and misperceptions) that clearly existed about certain groups of people.

The Language Barrier

The film begins with an extended sequence in Paris, where the characters speak French without subtitles. An English-speaking monolingual audience understands the gist of the action: that Marie is a messenger sent to deliver a telegram. But the language barrier between the characters and the audience is jarring until Marie reaches the recipient of the telegram, an American sea captain. It is the first time we hear English. The American speaks to the French woman as if she were a child. "Thatta baby!" the captain tells her. "You're not only cute, but you're smart." He invites her onto his ship, and we realize he is inebriated. He inadvertently lets the boat leave the port with Marie aboard, and after traveling across the ocean he dumps her in Mexico. She winds up in the Panama Canal Zone, where she laments (in English) that nobody speaks French, and we are left wondering how she suddenly acquired a good command of English. The early scene had given the audience the sense of being a stranger in a strange land, but for us to feel for Marie, she has to speak our language.

In later films with language barriers, such as *The Search* of 1948, the non-English speaker learns English over the course of the film. *The Search* focuses exclusively on the relationship between the American soldier (Montgomery Clift) and the young concentration camp survivor, and the audience experiences the communication through English-speaking Clift. In the setting of *The Search*, postwar Berlin, English is not necessarily the default language. In *Marie Galante*, by contrast, Spencer Tracy's role as the facilitator of communication is much more muted because Marie spends just as much time with the owner of a Parisian bazaar (who speaks English with a German accent) and the (supposed) owner of an adjacent curiosity shop (who speaks English with a Japanese accent). And in this film, because of the choice of setting (the Canal Zone is U.S.-run but is populated by people from all over the world), everyone speaks English, and the film is from an American perspective. So, for the benefit of the audience, we are no longer forced to wade through somebody else's language.

Tracy plays the film's key American, Dr. Crawbett, who represents himself as a researcher from Wisconsin but is actually a government agent. He insinuates himself into Marie's business just as British intelligence officer Ratcliff (Robert Loraine) is investigating a plot to blow up the power house to the canal. Marie unwittingly becomes entangled in the investigation because she sees the Parisian store owner Brogard—ultimately the mastermind of the plot—as a possible source of a ticket home. Unfortunately for her, but conveniently for us, he is not French. Afterward, Crawbett asks Marie about her meeting with Brogard and remarks, "That's funny. Two French people talking English." Marie corrects Crawbett's misperception of Brogard's nationality, but Crawbett's remark draws attention to the fact that the film avoids having two characters of the same non-English speaking country.

Simplistic Portrayals

The Japanese character Tenoki is played by a Briton, Leslie Fenton. The studio, once it became known as 20th Century Fox, would later use non-Asian actors to portray characters in popular serials who were of Oriental descent. Charlie Chan, the fictional detective on the Honolulu police force, was long played by Warner Oland, a native of Sweden. Mr. Moto was played by Peter Lorre. Similarly, the small studio Monogram Pictures used Boris Karloff in the *Mr. Wong* series. Fenton is convincing as an Asian, but he speaks with the slow, philosophical tone that has since become a clichéd manner of portraying Asian characters. Like Charlie Chan, Tenoki comes up with wise sayings to fit any particular circumstance—which is more disarming in a comedic context and more difficult to take seriously in a drama such as this film. Still, Tenoki as a character is an actor; after he is nearly framed in the canal plot, he finally reveals himself as a Japanese naval officer sent to find the actual mastermind. So this is a character who *should* speak with great deliberation. His clerk, meanwhile, speaks in short, declarative sentences less eloquently (and less grammatically) than he does—and, solely for the benefit of the audience, in English.

Ketti Gallian seems authentic playing Marie because she is a French native in real life. As far as French typecasting goes, she is dreamy and romantic. She is captivated by anything French, from the doodads in Brogard's shop to Tenoki's explanation of the history of France's role in the Panama Canal. It is hard to imagine an American woman lost in another country acting as childlike as Marie does.

Finally, the African American character (Stepin Fetchit) is stereotyped as he would be in most other Hollywood films of the era, regardless of the film's setting. He is apparently a servant—the most fitting word—of Plosser, played by Ned Sparks (who himself was typecast as a cranky sarcastic-type). Fetchit as an actor was controversial in the African American community at the time for his characteristic servile, slow-on-the-uptake demeanor, mumbling his words through protruded lips. (Stepin Fetchit, a stage name, would be used as a code name for other portrayals of this type.)

Fetchit's character is immediately judged by his looks. Crawbett and Ratcliff, ostensibly well-studied in biology, show off their knowledge by treating the servant as an anthropological subject. "Incredible!" Ratcliff exclaims upon looking at him.

"Cranial capacity, ninety-four," Crawbett says.

"I should say, ninety-five," Ratcliff replies. "Facial angle, minus seven."

"Ah, student of criminology, eh?"

"I have a bowing acquaintance with some of the criminal type."

This "acquaintance" is a reference to Ratcliff's role in British intelligence, but his association of the "facial angle" of an African American man with a certain degree of criminality is unsettling today.

The servant, meanwhile, is not impervious to conducting his own quick anthropological analysis of other races. When Tenoki's clerk comes by, the servant describes him to Plosser this way: "He's a yellow man. He ain't Chinese. He ain't Philippine. He ain't Japanese. Just yellow." Plosser identifies the visitor from this description alone.

Because of their exaggerated accents, these supporting characters could use subtitles even when they are speaking English. But like most movie characters speaking lines from scripts, Crawbett and Plosser understand them without once asking, "What?"

The Changing Enemy

Marie Galante was made with the assumption that espionage focused on attempts by individuals, rather than governments, to rock geopolitical balances. This was a simpler time. Once Tenoki reveals he is an undercover officer, he describes the plot mastermind as someone "whose business it is to create wars, and [who] is being highly paid by certain individuals who desire war, because war brings to them immense profit." Apparently this was once considered a scandal and not the basic functioning of a military-industrial complex like the one that exists today.

At the end of the film, ships move freely through the canal to the sound of victorious, patriotic-sounding music. Commerce continues unabated because the bad guy—whose portrayal by a German actor might not have been arbitrary—is dead, and the Americans and Britons are triumphant. The geopolitical picture was already starting to get more complicated than that in the real world. Tenoki, for one, would have ended up on the other side.

The film is not particularly interested in an accurate representation of the relationship between nations, however. Its characters are standard depictions of particular races or nationalities. And as a Hollywood film, it places the American—Tracy—in the position of the hero.

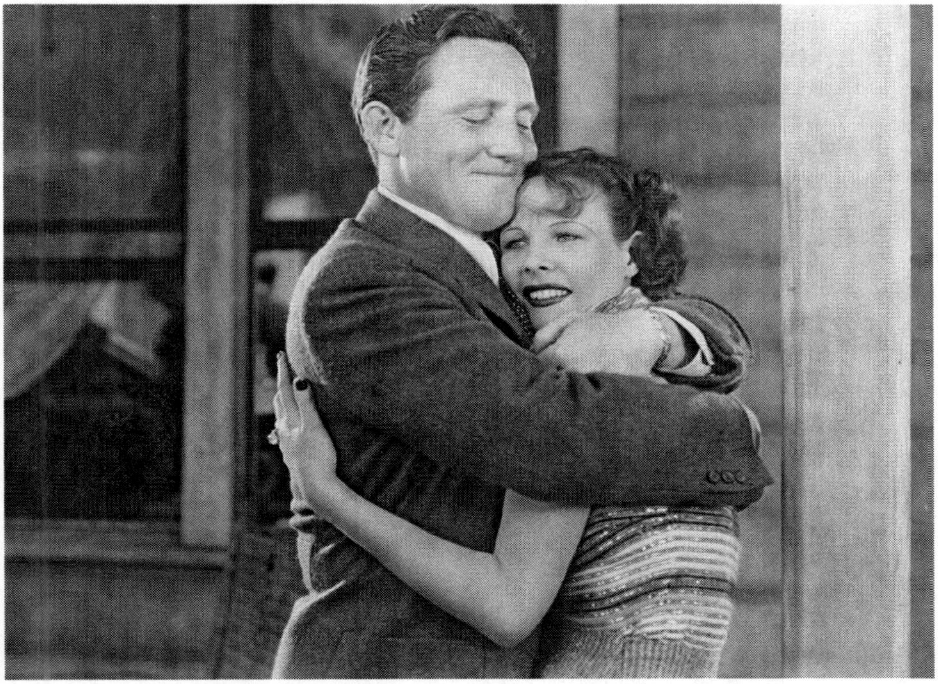

IT'S A SMALL WORLD

Irving Cummings, Director
Edward Butcher, Producer
Albert Treynor Novel "Highway Robbery"
Screenplay by Sam Hellman and Gladys Lehman
Based on Albet Treynor's short story "Highway Robbery"
Arthur C. Miller, Cinematographer
Released April 12, 1935
70 minutes

Cast
Spencer Tracy . . . Bill Shevlin
Wendy Barrie . . . Jane Dale
Raymond Walburn . . . Julius Clummerhorn
Virginia Sale . . . Lizzie
Astrid Allwyn . . . Nancy Naylor
Irving Bacon . . . Cal
Charles Sellon . . . Cyclone
Dick Foran . . . Cop
Belle Daube . . . Mrs. Dale
Frank McGlynn Sr . . . . Snake Brown Jr.
Frank McGlynn Jr . . . . Snake Brown, Junior-Junior
William Gillis . . . Snake Brown, Sr.
Ed Brady . . . Buck Bogardus
Harold Minjir . . . Freddie Thompson
Charles R. Moore . . . Doorman

And other cast

It's a Small World After All: City Folk Run Smack-Dab Into Americana

Jeremy Bond

Spencer Tracy's last film for Fox Film Corp. has a soft spot for small-town Southern life. In Hope Center, Louisiana, a rich girl from the city discovers love. In the city, she is cynical and supercilious; in the Louisiana backwater, she becomes humbled and gracious. As in previous films Tracy made for Fox, *The Power and the Glory* and *The Face in the Sky*, life always seems to go better in the country.

It's a Small World is adapted from an Albert Treynor story called *Highway Robbery*, and it clearly aims to model the spectacular success of another recent film adaptation: Columbia's Oscar-sweeping *It Happened One Night*. In both films, the woman is wealthy but bored with her privilege. She is a willing fish out of water but takes a while to feel comfortable in her new modest surroundings. And she finds happiness with a man she initially dislikes. But *It's a Small World* is less of a road picture; the protagonists' journey is almost entirely in Hope Center. It's the place where dreams are made of—though ultimately it's not the place for outsiders. In the final scene, the lovers drive out of town.

The Two Worlds Collide

The contrast between wealthy urbanites and rural simple folk is established early. Jane Dale (Wendy Barrie), a young woman of privilege, plays tennis and drives fast cars. (Issuing her yet another speeding ticket, a cop tells her sardonically that it is a ticket for a "matinee" in traffic court. She is unfazed, undoubtedly because any fine is negligible to her family.) Jane bickers with her famous cousin Nancy Naylor, whose multiple marriages and divorces are dutifully reported in the gossip columns. Jane then takes off in Nancy's car with her little white terrier (reminiscent of Asta of the *Thin Man* series).

Meanwhile, Bill Shevlin, a lawyer who has worked enough divorce cases to despise women like Nancy Naylor, had escaped into the woods to go duck-hunting. The highway on which they travel is classic backwoods America, labeled as U.S. Route 61 but resembling a dirt path. Cattle lounge in the middle of the road. The cars collide, and the accident leads them to Hope Center.

Neither complains outright about being stuck there, although Bill parodies the town's motto, "You can exist anywhere, but you live in Hope . . . Center." (Bill says, "But you die in Hope . . . Center.") Near the end, when Jane's mother comes to town, she scoffs, "Can you imagine anybody choosing a place like *this* for an accident?"

Hope Center is the kind of place where one man, Julius B. Clummerhorn (Raymond Walburn), serves as judge of the local courthouse, owner of the local hotel, owner of the auto repair garage (next door), a taxi driver, a barber, and the deputy game warden (among other things, we assume). His "taxi" is virtually a Model T with a bicycle horn, and it brings Bill and Jane to town after their accident. The two stay at Clummerhorn's hotel, where a hammock hangs on the porch and a woman named Lizzie rings a bell outside to signify a meal. The jail cell (in which Jane sits temporarily) looks out to the town, so the occupant can hear what goes on outside. The local men hang around chewing (something) and watching strangers in fascination, calling them "stranger." It is vintage Americana.

Clummerhorn is the quintessential "Big Daddy" Southern gentleman. He is paunchy, wears a white suit (even in the woods) and chews a cigar. He boasts about owning the "best little garage in the district. And I built it up from two little bolts and a nut." He is about to describe his hotel in a similar fashion, but Bill finishes his sentence for him: "Yeah, built it up with a couple of towels and a soup spoon, huh?" Walburn also would play to type for a prototypical chronicler of Americana, Frank Capra, in *Mr. Deeds Goes to Town* (1936), *Broadway Bill* (1934), and, once again portraying a judge in a film starring Spencer Tracy, *State of the Union* (1948). He was a favorite of Preston Sturges, too, who cast him as a mayor in *Hail the Conquering Hero* (1944).

Clummerhorn's jurisprudence does not instill confidence when Bill is hauled into court over the accident. The jury includes "Snake Brown," "Snake Brown Jr.," and "Snake Brown Jr. Jr." (the latter two played by real-life father and son Frank McGlynn Sr. and Jr.). Bill Shevlin, representing himself, requests that Snake Brown Sr. be removed from the jury. "I challenge this gentleman," Bill says.

"To what?" the judge replies, temporarily thinking in terms of a good-ol' Southern duel. "I mean, on what grounds?"

Bill appears to know more about the law than the judge does, reminding him of his constitutional right to a preemptory challenge. But the Browns try to stand their ground. "What you got again' my pappy?" Brown Jr. says. "Nobody can talk again' my grandpappy," Brown Jr. Jr. chimes in. These lines are enough to present an image of small-town simpletons who stick together and all talk the same way.

Another name befitting small-town life is Calhoun Calhoun (Irving Bacon), the garage repairman who takes Jane's side. The judge refers to him as "our witness," as if the judge were not a neutral party—then quickly corrects himself and refers to Cal as a witness of "the state" (and then inexplicably refers to Cal as *Bill's* witness). Bill calls for Cal's statements being stricken from the record, and the judge replies, "We ain't got no record."

The next witness is an old man who does not hear the judge dismissing him from the witness chair. The judge kicks him and says, "Git off that, you psycho! Dismissed!" Bill announces he is ready to make his summation, and the judge says, "Go ahead, make a—what you said." So much for wise, respectable judges.

Rural judges were not always pigeonholed as ignoramuses. Irving S. Cobb's Judge Priest character, played by Will Rogers in a 1934 adaptation directed by John Ford, was a turn-of-the-century Southern judge with grace and dignity. His mind might have wandered in the middle of a trial, but he knew the law and treated everyone with respect. (Ford liked the character so much he remade the film in 1953 as *The Sun Shines Bright*, with Charles Winninger as Judge Priest.)

In the *It's a Small World* trial, the jury does not come off particularly well either. The members shout "Guilty!" in unison immediately after Bill's summation, without any deliberation. Jane knows how to ingratiate herself with the jury, however, pretending her name is "Jasmine E. Lee" and speaking with a phony Southern accent. She lies her way through her testimony without consequence, even when the judge later learns her real name. As soon as she is finished speaking, the jury shouts, "Not guilty!"

"Jasmine E. Lee!" Bill later complains. "What chance would a Yank have against a name like that?"

A Woman's Place

Bill is lucky enough to be in Louisiana, which uses the Napoleonic code. Jane owes him money for the car repair, and under the code, "the body of the debtor may be served" to the person who is owed. Jane scoffs, "I'd just like to see [Bill] try and seize my body." It sounds risqué, perhaps unintentionally so.

Louisiana's Napoleonic law, which originates from the state's history as a French colony, differs from the other 49 states' systems, which are derived from English common law. (Other states modeled their laws after Napoleonic code as well, but the code's strongest roots are in Louisiana—though even Louisiana has gradually changed its codes to be more in line with common law.) As long as Napoleonic codes are on the books, lawyers like Bill Shevlin could take advantage of them. Most of the traditional Napoleonic codes addressed the right of property, and many placed women in an inferior position. One passage read: "The husband owes protection to his wife, and the wife owes obedience to her husband." It was easier for a man to get a divorce on grounds of adultery than for a woman to do so.

As the brutish Stanley Kowalski in *A Streetcar Named Desire*, Marlon Brando cites Louisiana's use of the code as a means to control Stella (Kim Hunter):

> "Did you ever hear of the Napoleonic code, Stella? . . . Now according to that, what belongs to the wife belongs to the husband also, and vice versa . . . . It looks to me like you've been swindled, baby. And when you get swindled under Napoleonic code, I get swindled too, and I don't like to get swindled."

The code is used more playfully in *It's a Small World*, especially since Bill and Jane fall in love and his legal control over her becomes irrelevant. But Jane's character immediately becomes suspect when she is mistaken for her divorce-happy cousin Nancy, who was married at 17 and again at 19 (at ages exceedingly unlikely today for a woman from a well-to-do family). When Bill thinks that Jane is Nancy, he grumbles to her, "Your kisses are a dime a dozen."

Apparently marrying multiple times would be a worse crime than any crime Jane had committed (like stealing Nancy's car). Later, when Bill discovers that Jane is *not* Nancy, and the real Nancy arrives to retrieve her car, Bill helps Jane escape.

"You mean you'd help me even if I stole a car?" Jane asks him.

"If you committed eleven murders I'd help you just so—as long as you're not that Naylor woman."

Jane as a character is more free-spirited and independent than many women portrayed on the screen. The appeal of the film version of "It Happened One Night" was that the millionaire heiress of the original story became a woman struggling to break free from her roots. Jane is much the same way, to her mother's chagrin.

"If you'd only get married and settle down," the mother tells Jane, referring to one particularly "lovely" boy named Freddie.

"'Lovely' is the word," Jane scoffs. "Freddie, that boneless cactus. You know, he's the kind of man who'd wait for a full moon to come out and then get down on his knees to propose."

"What's wrong with that? Your father got down on his knees to propose."

"Yeah," Jane replies. "And he never got up."

Jane apparently has an inherent disdain for traditional gender roles, perhaps because she cannot be categorized. She is out of place trying to wash dishes. In that scene, Bill appears to be the domestic. But she isn't rugged either; when Bill later takes Jane hunting with him, she is completely unfamiliar with the concept. Unlike Jane's British counterparts—the wealthy denizens of Robert Altman's *Gosford Park*, for example—hunting is represented as something outside the repertoire of the American elite. Bill briefly leaves Jane alone in the brush, and she panics.

The Other Side of the Mountain

When Tracy takes to the road at the end of *It's a Small World*, singing "The Bear Went Over the Mountain" for the umpteenth time, he was about to leave Fox for good. He had begun to develop the persona of the nice guy who was there to help somebody out. Instead of the glitzy heroes of British swashbucklers, or the wealthy citizens of all-star Hollywood films, he almost always played a character from the working class—like most of the members of the audience. The characters were the direct precursor of the rugged Manuel of *Captains Courageous* and the saintly Father Flanagan of *Boys Town*, the roles for which he would win back-to-back Oscars. Bill Shevlin might not have been much of a hero, but he knew where he was heading.

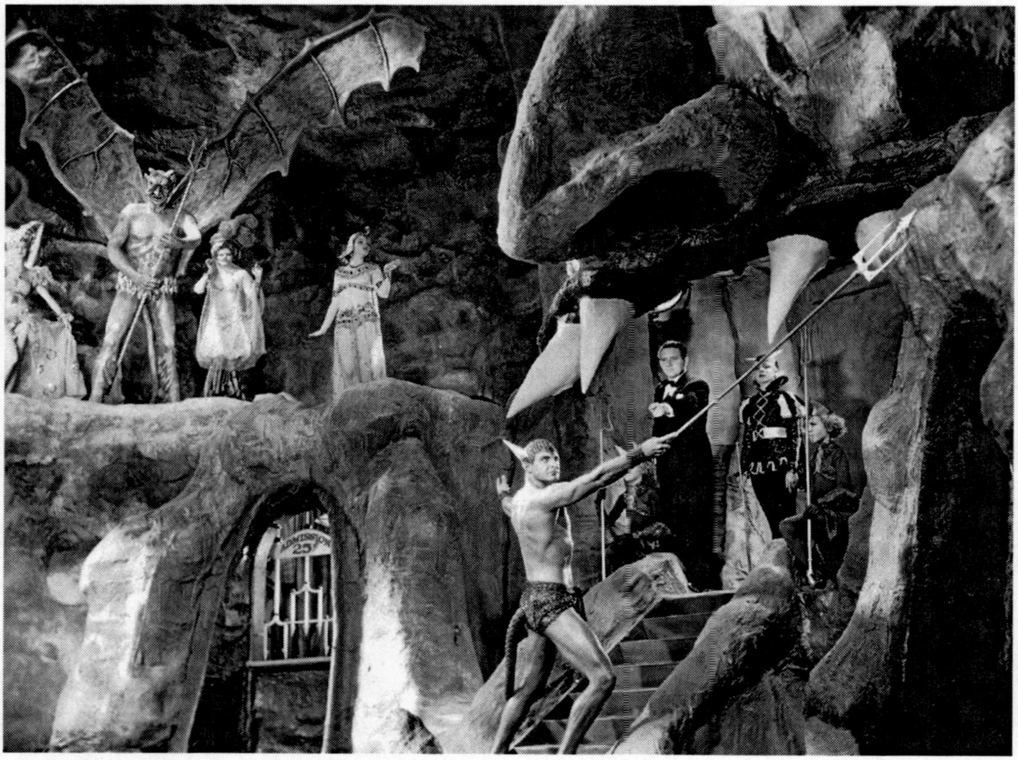

DANTE'S INFERNO

Harry Lachman, Director
Sol M. Wurtzel, Producer
Screenplay by Philip Klein & Robert M. Yost
Rudolph Maté, Cinematographer
Distributed by Twentieth Century-Fox Film Corporation
Released July 23, 1935
89 minutes

Cast
Spencer Tracy . . . Jim Carter
Claire Trevor . . . Betty McWade
Henry B. Walthall . . . Pop McWade
Alan Dinehart . . . Jonesy
Scott Beckett . . . Alexander Carter
Robert Gleckler . . . Dean
Rita Cansino (Rita Hayworth) . . . Dancer
Gary Leon . . . Dancer
Willard Robertson . . . Building Inspector Harris
Morgan Wallace . . . Captain Morgan

And other cast

Dante's Inferno: Pre-Code Decadence Falls to the Flames

Jeremy Bond

Dante's Inferno marked a transition in the Fox Film Corp.: the Production Code was newly enforced, Fox merged with Twentieth Century Pictures, and Spencer Tracy, who played the lead role, had just left for MGM. The new 20th Century Fox distributed *Inferno* in summer 1935, the last time audiences would see Tracy in a newly released Fox film. (*It's a Small World* was the last movie Tracy filmed at the studio, but it was distributed earlier.) The protagonist of *Inferno*, Jim Carter, was not a radical departure from Tracy's previous roles. Carter exhibited the ruthlessness of Tom Garner in *The Power and the Glory*, the tenderness of Joe Buck in *Face in the Sky*, and the wiliness of Smoothie King in *Bottoms Up*. So at the end of his Fox tenure, Tracy was no longer given the opportunity to expand his repertoire. That would change at MGM, which handed Tracy Oscar-winning roles two years in a row.

As the title suggests, *Dante's Inferno* is a story of morality. The film takes sin very seriously, a notable difference from Tracy's lighter fare in the pre-Code era such as *Goldie* and *Me and My Gal*. Here, the protagonist learns his lesson as if he were being led by Virgil through the seven terraces of Purgatory. Yet the transgressions here are trifling compared to the behavior of Tracy's previous characters. As in *The Power and the Glory*, the offense is self-made success gone too far. This doesn't seem like pure sin, but it is treated that way.

The Sin of Success

The film begins with the image of a fire, which has the same significance in the film as it does in the original *Dante's Inferno*. The opening shot peers inside the furnace of a ship, foreshadowing a disastrous ship fire at the film's conclusion.

Fire is a constant in Carter's life. After losing his job as a stoker, Carter is hired by a carnival proprietor nicknamed Pop (Henry B. Walthall), who runs a sideshow called "Dante's Inferno" in which visitors are led through the seven terraces of Purgatory. The implication is that Carter would go through Hell himself after committing at least some of the seven deadly sins: Lust, gluttony, greed, sloth (which Dante defined as a failure to love God), wrath (vengeance), envy, and pride (the original and most serious sin, which Dante defined as "love of oneself perverted to hatred and contempt of one's neighbor"). If Carter follows Dante's path, he would have to purge himself of each sin in order to escape Hell.

The sins in the film, however, do not seem serious enough to warrant this drama. Carter's worst offense is his callousness when he induces the other concessionaires to invest in a massive expansion of the inferno exhibit. One man, Dean, refuses to give up his property right away, and Carter forces him out. Later, in an unnerving scene, Dean startles Carter inside the Hell exhibit and jumps to his death. We had just been reminded that suicide is a sin: a grotto in the inferno is reserved for "those who laid violent hands upon themselves, destroying life, which God alone controls," Pop says. By driving Dean to suicide, the sin was apparently Carter's.

The film's righteousness seems aimed toward villanizing real-life entrepreneurs whose quest for profit overrode their moral compasses. Carter's transgressions mirror theirs.

A safety inspector warns Carter that the inferno exhibit is unsafe. Carter complains that the renovations would be expensive and bribes the inspector under the table. (He reminds the inspector that he got him his job; certainly the practice of business leaders handpicking their regulators is familiar today.) It isn't long before the ceiling of the exhibit collapses onto the screaming crowd inside, and Carter has to fight a civil suit against him. Carter's wife Betty (Claire Trevor), who is Pop's daughter, is forced to perjure herself to keep Carter out of prison.

The disaster is reminiscent of the fire that destroyed Dreamland, a sprawling attraction at Coney Island, in 1911. Dreamland had a religious theme and included a "Hell Gate" attraction in which visitors rode small boats through dark caverns to represent a trip through Hell. The attraction had been created by William H. Reynolds, a prominent businessman with links to crooked politics and New York's corrupt Tammany organization. According to some sources, Dreamland was built over many fire hydrants, assuring free water for the park but not a lot of extra water in the event of a fire.

Just before the season opening of Dreamland in May 1911, workers were using tar to seal a leak in Hell Gate when light bulbs began exploding, a bucket of hot tar spilled, and Hell Gate burst into flames. Without the hydrants, water pressure was low. Area merchants apparently tapped into whatever water supply was available to save their own properties, so the Fire Department had to use fireboats from the ocean. The burning Dreamland Tower collapsed dramatically just as Dante's Inferno would collapse in the film. In the end, Dreamland was not rebuilt and more than 2,500 people lost their jobs.

The film's second disaster is a fire on Carter's other business enterprise, a massive gambling ship ironically named *Paradise* (as in, Dante's destination after the inferno). Pop tells Carter that he is troubled by a venture that would promote vice, but Carter insists that there is "no moral law on the high seas." Here, the coming disaster is not Carter's fault—a drunk spills his alcoholic beverage on flaming burners of food—and yet the film treats the disaster as just as blameworthy as the one caused by Carter's selfish negligence. Sin is sin: the revelry on the ship had been downright bacchanalian, which should be considered sinful, and the fire had begun quite literally as a result of sin (overindulgence of alcohol).

This catastrophe also shares similarities with a real-life tragedy, which happened just before the film was produced. Like the fictitious *Paradise* in the film, the *Morro Castle* had plenty of drinking and carousing, particularly when the ship sailed beyond U.S. waters in the Prohibition years. The *Morro Castle* was used during the Great Depression, and the fare was cheap, so to remain profitable the ship sailed constantly. There was significant turnover in the crew, so much of the crew did not know safety procedures and was not particularly loyal to the welfare of the ship. The fire hydrants on the *Morro Castle* were apparently capped, and no fire drill had been conducted on the voyage in early September 1934 when a fire broke out on the ship off the coast of New Jersey.

In *Dante's Inferno*, the ship workers go on strike, but Carter insists that the ship sail without them. "There are hundreds of men around the dock who would jump at the chance," he says, probably suggesting that menial laborers were not hard to find during the Depression. But these workers end up being slackers, and during the fire, they are about as reliable as those on the *Morro Castle*. More than 130 people died in that real-life fire, and the wounds were still fresh in 1935, so Carter's blunders probably seemed more egregious at the time of the film.

Until the climax, Carter is unapologetic for his aggressive brand of capitalism and considers morality irrelevant to success. "Since the beginning of time, there's only been one sin, and that's failure," he tells Pop. "People don't care how you win, so long as you win." When his wife is devastated from having to commit perjury, he defends himself by saying that he "didn't do anything that any other businessman wouldn't have done." There might be an element of truth to that; this Depression-era film clearly is targeting certain real-life businessmen as well.

Carter seems genuinely committed to making sure their young son has a better life than he had, an anxiety certainly shared during the Depression. "You don't think I wanted Sonny to go through all the things that I had been through, do you?" he tells Betty. "I wanted him to start at the top, to have the best of everything that money could buy." But money didn't help us in the end, Betty snaps back.

With money, Carter has to worry about status. He is chagrined when Sonny isn't accepted to a private school. "We haven't got any, whaddaya call, any social background," he observes. He teams up with "society dames from the Social Welfare League" in order to gain that status, not to do good.

The fixation on societal standing, at the ultimate expense of a moral compass, is reminiscent of Theodore Dreiser's 1925 work *An American Tragedy*; Josef von Sternberg had made the first film version of that novel four years before *Dante's Inferno*. Dreiser's theme would become more pertinent at the onset of the Depression, when an audience struggling financially might have to be reminded that an obsession with wealth was not healthy.

At the beginning of the film, Carter feels humiliated by virtue of his low status. He is a stoker on a ship with wealthy guests, who watch the stokers as a source of entertainment. When a supervisor disciplines Carter, an onlooker says, "Isn't this priceless? I wouldn't miss this for the world." Carter, ashamed, grumbles to her that some day he would be "right up there where you are, and then maybe I'll be laughing, too." It is notable that he does not bother to stand up for the dignity of stokers. Seven years later, when he owns a ship himself, he reveals that he was once a stoker but fibs that he had done it only once after he "got in a little jam in Australia." Carter might atone for his sins at the end of the film, but it's not clear whether he ever regains respect for the working class. This is far from a fanfare of the common man typical of Frank Capra films.

Problematic Characterizations

In the beginning, Carter is a stoker who places bets on the skills of another stoker to avoid working himself. (This other stoker is played by

Warren Hymer, who apparently was destined to play dim bulbs outsmarted by Spencer Tracy characters. One of his other films with Tracy was *Goldie*, which also had extended scenes at a carnival.) Carter is not portrayed as particularly ambitious, yet as a newcomer to the carnival sideshow racket he winds up controlling the destinies of all of the other concessionaires. His only obvious advantage seems to be his position as a young, white, American-born man.

As if to underscore this, Carter wears a racist disguise during an extended scene at the beginning of the film. After being kicked off the ship, he tries his hand as a chump in a carnival who throws insults at the patrons while wearing blackface. (The version of the game portrayed in the film involves throwing a baseball in the person's face, rather than the less violent version today of throwing water balloons or hitting a target that drops the chump into a tub of water.) The chump's blackface and a wig of short, tightly coiled hair is uncomfortable to see today, but it puts his character in the context of being degraded.

The American carnival is depicted as a miniature melting pot, perhaps because the work is not desirable to native citizens. Many of the carnival workers are immigrants, such as a man of Arab descent with a name that sounds like "Abdullah." After a baseball socks him in the eye, Carter abruptly quits the "chump" concession and wanders off to a food stand run by a quick-tempered Italian immigrant named Tony. Carter asks for raw meat for his swollen eye but has no money to pay for it.

"What you mean, you no pay?" Tony says in a stereotypical Italian dialect. "Three time-a-today people told me, 'Charge it.' Now I-a get mad. If you don't pay right-a now I call the cops!" Soon enough, Tony is another sucker who gives up his own business to buy stock in Carter's venture. When it fails to deliver, he confronts Carter: "But you say stock is just like-a money." Carter is able to stave him off. Tony represents the immigrant as a naïve pushover.

Pop is a white American, but he is old, and thus is no match for the youthful Carter. But he is the film's moral conscience. The actor portraying Pop, Henry B. Walthall, has frequently represented the quiet American hero, from his role along Tracy in *Me and My Gal* (1932) as a paralyzed military veteran who ends up saving the day, to a reverend in John Ford's *Judge Priest* (1934) who stirringly defends the patriotism of an accused assailant. But he also depicted a character with infamously mixed-up morality, Roger Chillingworth, in Robert Vignola's 1934 film version of Nathaniel Hawthorne's *The Scarlet Letter*. Chillingworth, who as husband of Hester Prynne is a victim of his wife's adultery with Arthur Dimmsdale, becomes so obsessed with torturing Dimmsdale that Hawthorne compares Chillingworth to the Devil: "Had a man seen old Roger Chillingworth, at that moment of his ecstasy, he would have had no need to ask how Satan comports himself when a precious human soul is lost to heaven and won into his kingdom." Soon afterward, in *Dante's Inferno*, Walthall plays someone who is fascinated by the Devil and quips that his sideshow creation is "a little glimpse of Hell, [with] a few suggestions of how to keep out of it." Walthall's roles of the period seem to reflect the awkward balance between America's Puritanism and debauchery.

A Moral Turning Point for Tracy Onscreen

Dante's Inferno is no satire about piousness. It believes in it. Its opening score is dark, and it includes an extended dream sequence of the actual Inferno, with (distant) naked bodies falling off cliffs and writhing in agony. (The footage is said to be taken from a 1924 silent film also called *Dante's Inferno*, which likewise told the story of a scrupulous businessman.) The film's earnestness is dead serious, even if today it is difficult to take seriously.

Spencer Tracy, then, was no longer playing the likeable rogue of his earliest films. The Production Code, firmly enforced by 1935, might have rejected Tracy's earliest films, such as the lighthearted prison picture *Up the River*, if the implication was anything other than that crime doesn't pay. Tracy, though a real-life rebel, seemed to fit naturally into the image of the reluctant American hero—Father Flanagan of *Boys Town*, Henry Drummond of *Inherit the Wind*—without abandoning the everyman image in his pairings with Katharine Hepburn. Unlike Jim Carter, most of Tracy's subsequent characters led by example. They didn't need to scare wrongdoers with the images of *Dante's Inferno*.

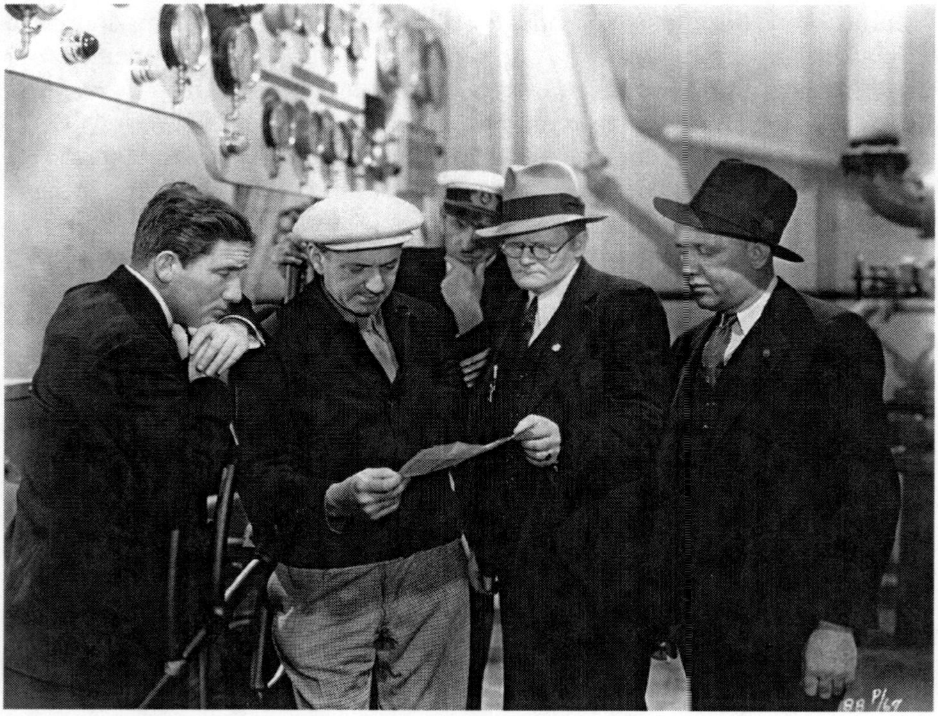

Dante's Inferno: Tracy's Trial By Fire

William Russo

After making his final Twentieth Century Fox film, Spencer Tracy ascended from the ashes of hell.

What nadir could better describe his misuse at Fox—and the belief of Louis B. Mayer that the great studio of MGM could turn around the fortunes of the benighted actor. Yet, the success at Metro could only derive from the abysmal depths to which he fell in the earlier stage of his film-acting career.

Amateur psychoanalysis dispensed frequently in the tabloids of cinema seems to be one of the fates suffered by Spencer Tracy; no one really knew him, and he maintained his privacy for a lifetime and more. One fact is certain, during the last days at Fox, he was not a happy man. For five years at the studio, he brokered his on-screen appeal with fans to his dissatisfaction as a professional actor—and man. He seemed to hate his roles, his colleagues, and showed it in a series of notorious drunken benders.

Fox awarded Tracy with an interesting role—an instructive moral lesson, assigned to him (whether inadvertent or not) to teach him with hard insights. To play Jim Carter, a man with a gift for winning the trust of the public, no matter how little he deserved it, Spencer Tracy would have to face the hideous punishment of men who shirk ethics, playing someone whose personal behavior was reprehensible despite having redeeming love for his family and friends.

Dante's Inferno owed its title and central imagery to the great Italian epic poem about eternal justice, taken from *The Divine Comedy* (whose title is often misunderstood). After all, the tale is a dark satire of human folly, a kind of *opera bouffe*. Done with the usual updates to modern America, the movie version seemed to befit the Great Depression era mentality that believed entrepreneurs made money with corrupt motives and attitudes. At the heart of the motion picture's tale, cruel and ruthless men needed to be given their comeuppance. Detractors of the film cite the fact that it makes a shallow mockery of the original Dante Alighieri Renaissance poem, or that the depictions of hell seem like graphic novel pleasures of certain sado-masochistic elements. Yet, the conceit of the film is a modern dress commentary on American ambition, and one man's sardonic demeanor.

The plot of *Dante's Inferno* detailed a man who rose from nothing—working in the bowels of a ship as a stoker in the fiery hell of the engine room—who saw a chance to better himself. Meeting a professorial man named Dante who runs a cheesy beachside carnival sideshow about the lessons of history, Carter (with Tracy's appealing tough guy with a gift of gab) takes the operation and turns it into a demonic entertainment. Tracy would play a charming man who had sociopathic emptiness inside him. Loving and devoted to his wife and family, he could as easily manipulate, bribe, and toss aside any life that blocked his climb up from the bottom. He could turn the switch on and off instantly—which in many ways resembled Tracy and his own daily regimen.

After putting up with Spencer Tracy's hair-trigger, alcoholic and physical bouts, the studio gave him a cautionary tale about good and bad behavior. If there was a wink in the executives' attitude, it had to arise from forcing Tracy to look at a potential end that befitted him. If they wanted to scare the living fury out of Tracy, they found their screenplay. The script was an early mishmash of Federico Fellini-style grotesqueries, using the circus and carnival atmosphere as a metaphor for all life. The studio, no saintly institution above profit, took the old tale of fire and brimstone and dropped it on a fallen Catholic with a heavy sense of guilt: Spencer Tracy.

Director Harry Lachman (who later went on to direct Charlie Chan mysteries and one of the Laurel & Hardy comedies) was a post-impressionist painter—and used his eye to help design the two infernos that would comprise this picture. The first was the carnival barker vision of Carter—a papier-mâché sideshow of freaks, complete with "she-devils of history" to lure in the customers. Tracy's peppy talk draws the paying public because, as he notes, hell is "popular." The grottos of the movie's cheap carnival are horrific in their own inexpensive and intentionally unreal way—with a

Satanic Majesty in a silver loincloth to cover his modest well-oiled and buff body. The second inferno was a brilliant use of an imagined descent into the grottos of hell, in which Tracy never appeared.

The stairs to the various levels that Tracy has built on his Coney Island business may look like a cardboard cutout version of Carlsbad Cavern, with boiling vats and silly demonic faces leering. Tracy delivers his lines with cavalier bravado: "Failure is the only sin," and "Human Nature doesn't change." Likening his project to that of the great theme parks at Coney Island at the turn of the 20th century, Carter plans to build an amusement entertainment to rival all. As Tracy notes in the film, he will create the "biggest hell on earth."

Approximately fifty minutes into the movie comes one of the greatly remembered sequences in film history—the Descent into the Inferno. This happens as a plot device after the second suicide caused by Carter's ambitions; here, the elderly Professor Dante, also Carter's father-in-law, recalls the original poem to Tracy who sits at his hospital bedside, opening up the eight minute clip. So different from the rest of the movie is this scene that it's clear to most viewers that it has been dropped here from another motion picture: indeed, it has.

Most experts know the images of figures of men in cowls marching in a prehistoric mist and the lamenting chorus of pained victims is from the silent 1924 *Dante's Inferno*, which had a similar message—modern life's punishment coming the old-fashioned way. Though some state the sequence is five minutes, or nine minutes, it is almost exactly eight minutes in length.

With walls of flame, featuring a population of tiny naked people struggling against their fate, the picture shows boulders being pushed up hill by a throng of oiled and exquisitely defined bodies. Suicides are shown becoming part of trees and vines, their arms and chiseled torsos melding into the woodwork. Naked bodies fall from cliffs, and the art design resembles that of Hieronymous Bosch, not Gustav Dore as others contend. The scene was clearly filmed in the era before the Hays Code and may have worried the editors and producers at Fox. It may have also worried Spencer Tracy.

The star actor had to perform the role of a man who suffers as one of the "tormented souls who live ruthlessly." Tracy admits in the scene, "We make our own heaven and hell on earth." It was clear he had taken the wrong road, but he continues to expand his ambitions—a company called Amusement Enterprises with a gambling ship casino next on his agenda. After all, the road to hell is paved with good intentions. He will bribe society matrons with "charity," and he will pursue the notion to make "history in the annals of vice." With an oil portrait of Alexander the Great over his shoulder in many scenes, Tracy plays a soul chained to his own foibles.

In the midst of filming this picture Tracy grew increasingly agitated. Though he normally worked well once a production started, he snapped suddenly and disappeared for two weeks. The character kept his professional life and personal life separated by a gulf of personal love and frightening power. Highly protective of his family, Carter can buy the lease out from under a business opponent and cause him to descend into suicidal depression. Tracy's own "lost weekends" were perplexing, inexplicable, and dangerous.

Those who loved Carter, like those who loved Tracy, protected him and swallowed their own integrity to keep him safe and secure. In one of the most disturbing scenes for Tracy, Carter goes on trial for the culpability of driving one of the city inspectors to suicide over ignoring under-code building violations at the carnival site. Tracy gives the hard edge to a man who simply denies his own wrong-doing—but when his wife, played by Claire Trevor, goes to the witness stand, knowing her husband's unethical behavior, she lies completely to save him. Tracy squirms and shows utter shame as Carter. How much like Tracy's own life the scene resonated; the punishment fit.

What effect this performance had on Tracy's psyche can only be imagined. Before long an out-of-control Tracy was chasing director Harry Lachman around the set. In his drunken, violent condition, Spencer hated everything about the film. In the midst of production, he went off for a few weeks to seek oblivion in drink. Upon return, Tracy threatened the director with bodily harm. Still intoxicated and out of control, he terrified all on the set with his rampages.

One of the producers at Fox then evacuated the entire stage area. Tracy finally fell asleep on the set of Carter's apartment in New York. When he awakened, he was locked in the sound stage—utterly alone. This strategy backfired, frightening both Tracy and everyone at Fox Studios. Witnesses outside could hear him smashing props, cameras, scenery, even hearing the explosions from studio lights as he demolished them. His tantrum continued for an hour. The studio fined him, as there was somewhere around $100,000 worth of damage. Yet, they wanted him to finish the movie. After a short rest in which he regained self-control, he returned in March morose and facing a wary edge among the entire crew.

When the film resumed production, Lachman picked up where wife Betty leaves Carter, accusing him of the "loss of everything decent." Carter's rebuttal is to argue that he is like "any other businessman." But Trevor's sweet but disappointed wife counters, "Nothing can stop you, but you are going alone." Indeed, Tracy's character embarks on his biggest money-making project—the ship casino, based on the true story of scandal in the news, the disaster of the *Morro Castle*, a pleasure ship off New Jersey that caught fire and killed over 130 people.

In the film Carter proceeds with his plan, despite a strike of workers. He endangers all by hiring scabs to fill in—and takes the cruise ship out to sea. Unknown to Carter, his son has been kidnapped by his right-hand man and brought to the ship. When it catches fire, he must save his son, descend into the bowels of the engine room and try to make amends for his wayward life.

In a mock of the *Morro Castle* catastrophe, or echoing the *Titanic*, and even the *Poseidon*, the ship burning sequence was a major climax after the vision of hell. It allowed Tracy's character to find redemption. He admits, "I've been through a hell of my own making . . ." Whether he dies at the closing credits may be more of a personal interpretation, but he seems reconciled with wife and his soul. Yet, the experience of making this picture at Fox may have tried Spencer Tracy and found him guilty. After this at MGM, he seemed to play strictly decent men, not amoral monsters.

His costar, Claire Trevor, later said of the experience: "Usually you can connect with Spencer's eyes. That intense contact with his fellow actors is one of the major keys to his brilliance as a performer. It was missing this time." Indeed, in late March, the studio "released" him, a code for firing the actor. It also meant the $750,000 picture was relegated to the backburner. It barely broke even—despite the fact *Dante's Inferno* was an A-list picture. By the time of its release in August of 1935, Spencer Tracy was ready to begin again with MGM.

Louis B. Mayer saw the moral edge in Tracy's personality—and built carefully a future series of roles that emphasized the optimism and gentleness of the actor. Here, away from antiheroes and dubious shady figures, Spencer could use the same dimensions that went into Jim Carter to create a Manuel in *Captains Courageous*, or even an enterprising Father Flanagan in two films. He could play a priest with venal worries and maintain his basic decency in *San Francisco* and *Boys Town*. Though Tracy would have other incidents throughout his life, he was better able to harness his energies into film roles after *Dante's Inferno*. For a lapsed Roman Catholic with demonic urges, his foray into hell on screen and on the set may have altered the future for him. Fortunately, Spencer Tracy was able to acquit himself on screen.

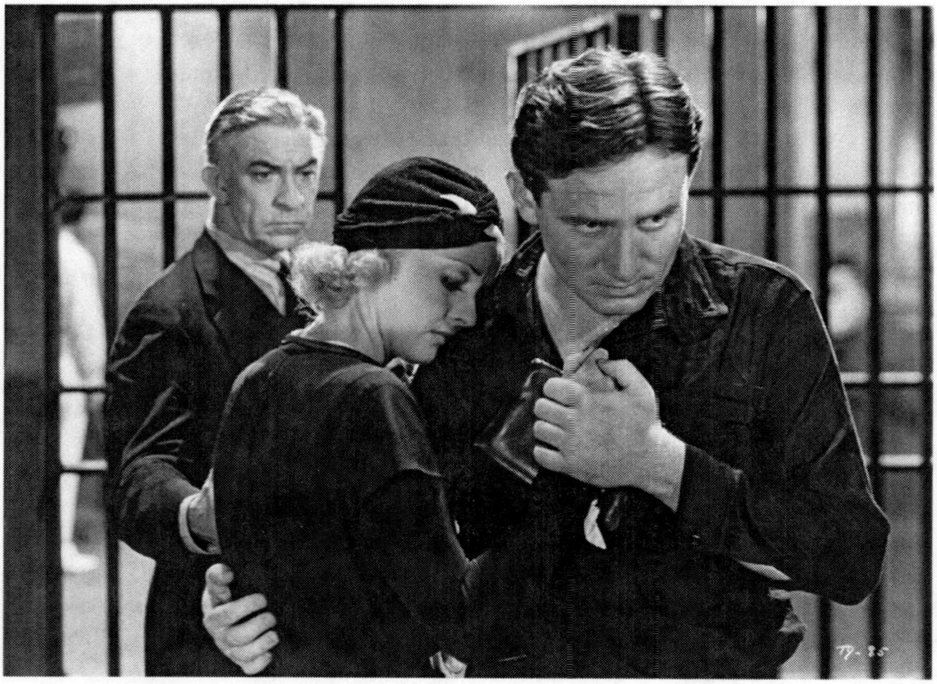

Spencer Tracy: King of the Underworld

James Fisher

"What difference does it make... Whether laws are made by a bunch of lawyers for other lawyers to break, or whether they're made by hoodlums for other hoodlums. They're all man-made laws."

Daniel J. "Bugs" Raymond in *Quick Millions*

"Come on and I'll show ya how tough I am!"

Tommy Connors in *20,000 Years in Sing Sing*

James Cagney, Edward G. Robinson, Humphrey Bogart, Paul Muni, George Raft—one can almost hear machine gun fire at the mere mention of their names. For cinephiles, they were the definitive 1930s screen gangsters (mobsters, hoodlums, or New York street toughs, if you prefer). During the Golden Age of the Silver Screen, each of these actors made numerous "gangster pictures" and typically made them at Warner Bros., a major Hollywood studio specializing in everything from musicals to dramas, all featuring a gritty realism and streetwise characters—even Warner Bros. animated characters like Bugs Bunny and Daffy Duck sported comically exaggerated Brooklyn accents and street "cred." As the acknowledged home of the cinematic tough guy—and a few tough "dames" too—Warner Bros. carefully developed the careers of these actors around a range of topical, rapidly (and often cheaply) made films about contemporary crime and punishment "ripped from the front pages," as their advertisements often claimed, despite the fact that at least four of these actors—Cagney, Robinson, Muni, and Bogart—ultimately proved to be far more versatile when afforded opportunities to put away their gats and prison stripes for more varied roles. Cagney, the hoodlum sprite, even appeared in Shakespeare (the 1935 Max Reinhardt-William Dieterle classic *A Midsummer Night's Dream*) and tap-danced his way through the George M. Cohan biopic *Yankee Doodle Dandy* (1942).

Spencer Tracy is rarely if ever mentioned among this elite group of cinematic thugs, yet during his first five years as a movie actor (1930-1935) under contract to the Fox Studio, Tracy occasionally played gangsters with the distinction that would mark all of his screen work—from his first two feature films, *Up the River* (1930) and *Quick Millions* (1931), to *20,000 Years in Sing Sing* (1932) and *Now I'll Tell* (1934). And, like most of his screen performances, Tracy put a unique stamp on these underworld figures and, it might be argued, his achievement added dimensions to a type of screen character that would appear in various guises over the subsequent seventy-five years as gangster films became a staple of American cinema.

It is worth noting that although Tracy made approximately twenty-five films during his five year stint at Fox, most movie fans only know his work from the great films of his Metro-Goldwyn-Mayer era (1935-1955) and his last dozen years as an independent player and the acknowledged "Dean of American film actors" (1955-1967). On one hand, it is perhaps not surprising that these later two phases of Tracy's career merit most attention; the films he made during these thirty-two years were typically done with a quality rarely evident in the cut rate production values of an early 1930s Fox film. In his post-1935 performances, Tracy demonstrates a versatility matched by few screen actors (Cagney is perhaps the only actor of Tracy's generation to rival him). Tracy's best-remembered screen appearances after he went to work at M-G-M are those in which he becomes, in various guises, a romanticized icon of the "typical" American male, as seen most vividly in his "buddy films" playing sidekick to Clark Gable (particularly in *Test Pilot* and *Boom Town*), in lavish adventure epics (*Captains Courageous* and *Northwest Passage*), in a nine film screen partnership with Katharine Hepburn (at their best—and most iconic—in *Woman of the Year, Adam's Rib*, and *Pat and Mike*), and, in his final years in such socially-conscious "prestige" films as *Judgment at Nuremberg, Inherit the Wind,* and *Guess Who's Coming to Dinner* in which the ordinary "mugs" he often played had grown in wisdom to become embodiments of integrity, decency, and progressive vision.

Those who seek out Tracy's Fox films (not an easy feat, since few have found their way on to VHS or DVD and rarely appear in art houses) discover that those first twenty-five films prove decisively that the unmatched versatility and skill found in his later movie performances are evident from the beginning and, in fact, it can be argued that there is an even greater diversity in genre and range of characters in these vital, albeit more cheaply produced, films. That diversity includes the Tracy gangster roles—a character type he never again returned to in his post-1935 career, a fact that may explain why his name is not found among the pantheon of cinema hoods including Cagney, Robinson, Muni, Bogart, and Raft; with the exception of Muni, they returned to the gangster genre literally through the end of their long careers (Cagney, particularly, developed every nuance in the type, from the unthinking street punk of *The Public Enemy* [1931] to the sympathetic "big shot" of *The Roaring Twenties* [1939] and the psychopathic monster of *White Heat* [1949]). Tracy took different paths and his few gangster films faded into cinematic obscurity as these early pre-production code films languished in oblivion, rarely to be found in revival cinemas or on vintage film channels on TV.

The Fox films, which might reasonably be thought of as lost, or at least woefully ignored, prove to be informative in understanding the entire Tracy oeuvre, especially so in the case of his gangster roles, which reveal the roots of his darker screen characterizations (in such later diverse films as *Fury, Sea of Grass, Edward, My Son, Malaya, Plymouth Adventure, Broken Lance,* and *The Devil at Four O'Clock,* not to mention *Dr. Jekyll and Mr. Hyde*). These roles also reveal the reasons versatility, not to mention intelligence, a rough sensitivity, and a vital humanism, emerge as dominant defining characteristics of his style as a screen actor.

A minor prototype of the Tracy gangster made a first screen appearance in the Warner Bros./Vitaphone short subject *Taxi Talks* (1930). In this crudely made little film from the dawn of the sound era, a cab driver, played by Vernon Wallace, is interrogated by police after witnessing a murder. Tracy is the murder victim, a tough hood stabbed to death by his girlfriend (played by Katherine Alexander, who also appeared with Tracy in another Warner Bros./Vitaphone short, *The Hard Guy*, also in 1930), and actress Mayo Methot, later the wife of Humphrey Bogart, appears in a small role, as do Roger Pryor and Evalyn Knapp. *Variety* called it "one of the most entertaining and diversified of short subjects" (Waly.), but this film is virtually unknown. Tracy made it under the direction of Arthur Hurley from a screenplay by Frederic and Fanny Hatton while appearing on Broadway in a fortuitous stage appearance that led to his next gangster role, this time in a broadly comic vein, in his first feature-length film, John Ford's *Up the River* (coincidentally featuring Humphrey Bogart's first screen appearance—in an innocuous role as a genial young man]). Ford had seen and greatly admired Tracy's stage performance as hardened death row prisoner "Killer" Mears in John Wexley's socially-conscious prison drama *The Last Mile*. Critics of this hit play rhapsodized about Tracy's "tour de force" (Barton 18) performance, remarking on the "relentless fury and drive" (Hutchens 278) of the portrayal. The reviews led almost every film studio to test Tracy, but no offers were forthcoming until Ford saw the play and convinced Fox to hire him.

Ford planned *Up the River* as a realistic prison melodrama in the vein of *The Last Mile*, but M-G-M had the same idea and beat Ford to the screen with *The Big House* (1930), starring Wallace Beery. Undaunted, Ford refashioned *Up the River* as a comedy (in fact, a spoof of prison films) and to his surprise and relief, Tracy, the intense dramatic actor he had seen in *The Last Mile*, proved to be an adept comic actor. Tracy is cast as "Saint Louis," a hood from the streets who aspires to the high life, imprisoned with his bumbling compatriot, Dannemora Dan (Warren Hymer, playing the sort of role Victor McLaglen regularly portrayed in Ford's later films). Although they mostly like jail, Saint Louis and Dan escape at the behest of a winsome female prisoner, Judy (Claire Luce), who enlists them to rescue the reputation of her guileless lover, Steve (Bogart), who is being blackmailed by a crooked salesman who framed Judy. Through various subterfuges and shenanigans, Saint Louis and Dan save Steve, after which they only too willingly return to their comfortable existence behind bars in order to play in a riotous prison baseball game and appear in a prison vaudeville performance, during which Saint Louis does a knife-throwing act with Dan as his assistant (and target). Happily ensconced in the "big house" where they belong, Saint-Louis and Dan are satisfied to serve as matchmakers and protectors of Judy and Steve.

The romance of Judy and Steve is little more than an excuse for the comedy of Tracy and Hymer, who Ford obviously exploits to boost a weak script (by Maurine Dallas Watkins, who wrote the popular play *Chicago*, with uncredited assistance from Ford and William Collier, Sr.). Their comic interludes have an air of improvisation, although it should be stressed that Tracy's characteristic naturalness typically create such an improvisatory air in all of his films, a naturalness which many co-stars and directors frequently noted came from painstaking preparation. Tracy's performance scores in several key scenes, not least in Saint Louis's arrival at prison in dapper dress, wearing a derby and carrying a cane. Making himself comfortable in the warden's office, he genially presents a list of demands for creature comforts equivalent to those in the best four-star hotel. Wisecracks fly, although by contemporary standards this scene and others in the film move too slowly for what is essentially a farce. *Up the River* also shows its age in racial attitudes, most notably in a minstrel show scene in the prison vaudeville show. However, major comic set pieces, most particularly the climactic baseball game, exude the rambunctious slapstick typical of similar sequences in many of Ford's lighter films. The knife-throwing sequence required Ford himself to stand-in for Hymer during rehearsals to prove that the expert knife-thrower brought in to double for Tracy had the necessary expertise to ensure safety. Ford's finger received a minor cut in the process, but Hymer was finally persuaded to play the scene.

Up the River was subsequently remade by 20th Century-Fox (20th Century Films and Fox had merged in 1935 shortly before Tracy left the studio) in 1938 featuring Preston Foster and Tony Martin, but with little success. The Ford-Tracy version was undeniably a modest effort and little more than a "programmer." It emerges as an extended comedy sketch satirizing the cinematic clichés of M-G-M's *The Big House* and a spate of prison films that filled screens in the early "talkie" period. Bogart's debut went largely unnoticed, but *Variety* pointed out that the film was "Spencer Tracy's first talker, and he easily makes the screen grade" ("Review: *Up the River*"). Some critics felt the film's highlight was the comic byplay of Tracy and Hymer, noting that they "make an excellent comedy team in this picture and perhaps they might be seen to even greater advantage if one did not have to think of the characters they impersonate as jailbirds" (Hall 117). However, Fox had no intention of further teamings of Tracy and Hymer, who had a brief career in leading roles before slipping down to bit roles by the time he appeared in *San Francisco* (1936), the M-G-M film which brought Tracy his first Academy Award nomination. One of Tracy's gifts was his skill at creating chemistry with his fellow actors and he frequently worked with co-stars in more than one film. He is most remembered for his teaming with Katharine Hepburn, but he also appeared in several films with Claire Trevor, Jean Harlow, and Joan Bennett, most of which were made in his early Fox years, and as mentioned earlier, with Clark Gable. He also worked with directors he admired on more than one occasion, including Ford. Twenty-eight years after *Up the River*, Tracy announced his retirement while filming *The Last Hurrah* (1958) under Ford's direction, but it was only one of several retirement announcements that fell by the wayside when another good role appeared. In 1964, Tracy hoped to appear in Ford's *Cheyenne Autumn*, but illness forced him to relinquish the role. *Up the River* is one of only a very few of Tracy's Fox films released on a commercial DVD as part of a lavish collection of Ford's output at Fox in late 2007. Even in restored condition, *Up the River* is in poor condition and choppily edited; it is not clear whether the problems with the editing are original or have occurred as a result of neglect.

The pleasant diversion of *Up the River*, and Tracy's effective comedic performance in it, encouraged Fox to sign him to a long-term contract and the studio began to search for appropriate vehicles. It was at this particular time that two of the aforementioned screen gangsters, namely Cagney and

Robinson, among other lesser stars, were attracting attention playing, or preparing to play, mobsters in a more realistic style than had previously been seen on screens. Cagney's "Tom Powers" in *The Public Enemy* (1931) and Robinson's "Enrico 'Little Rico' Bandello," based on Al Capone, in *Little Caesar* (1932), became critical and commercial hits of such magnitude that many studios tested leading players in hopes of finding those most suited to hoodlum roles. Tracy was an obvious choice for Fox since he exuded many of the requisite characteristics—he was virile, ruggedly handsome, spoke the language of the street, and could be convincingly menacing and, at the same time, expose the humanity behind the tough guy persona.

By the time Tracy went before the cameras in director/screenwriter Rowland Brown's *Quick Millions*, the problem he and Brown faced was to find an approach to a gangster character that had not already been exploited by other actors working in the genre. Various ethnic approaches—Irish, Italian, and Jewish—had already been tried, but Brown and Tracy (with uncredited assists from Ben Hecht and Charles MacArthur) found their hook in approaching Daniel J. "Bugs" Raymond as a social climber, driven to crime by a desire to escape his life as a trucker and for the love of a society woman, Dorothy Stone (played by Marguerite Churchill), whom he believes will not accept him without wealth and power. Bugs aspires to the "class" he believes Dorothy and her set exude, but despite gaining wealth and power through a protection racket exploiting fellow truckers, Bugs is still rejected by Dorothy, who plans to marry another man. This sends Bugs into despair and compulsion—and his henchmen (including a young George Raft) become convinced that he is not tending to their nefarious operations. When Bugs decides to kidnap Dorothy on her wedding day, the gang decides to take him for the proverbial "ride," a cleverly staged scene in which the blinds of a limo are pulled down to obscure the final fatal shot.

One particular innovation in *Quick Millions* is that the film does not depend on violence. Except for the final moment, there are no shocking "rub-outs"; instead, the film aims higher than the fast thrills of violent encounters to focus on the slow degeneration of Bugs Raymond's moral center and his relationships with other characters in the film are there to reveal his descent. Not unlike a Greek tragedy, *Quick Millions* emphasizes the hubris that slowly destroys its protagonist, causing him to fall from the heights, in this case as a "King of the Underworld." Without question, there is a continual undercurrent suggesting the potential for mayhem, but Brown draws attention away from violence that we know has occurred, as when Bugs slaps his girlfriend or when he is killed at the movie's end. One particularly meritorious element of the film is that it does not append a miraculous redemption for Bugs, nor does it sensationalize his death by showing it in any

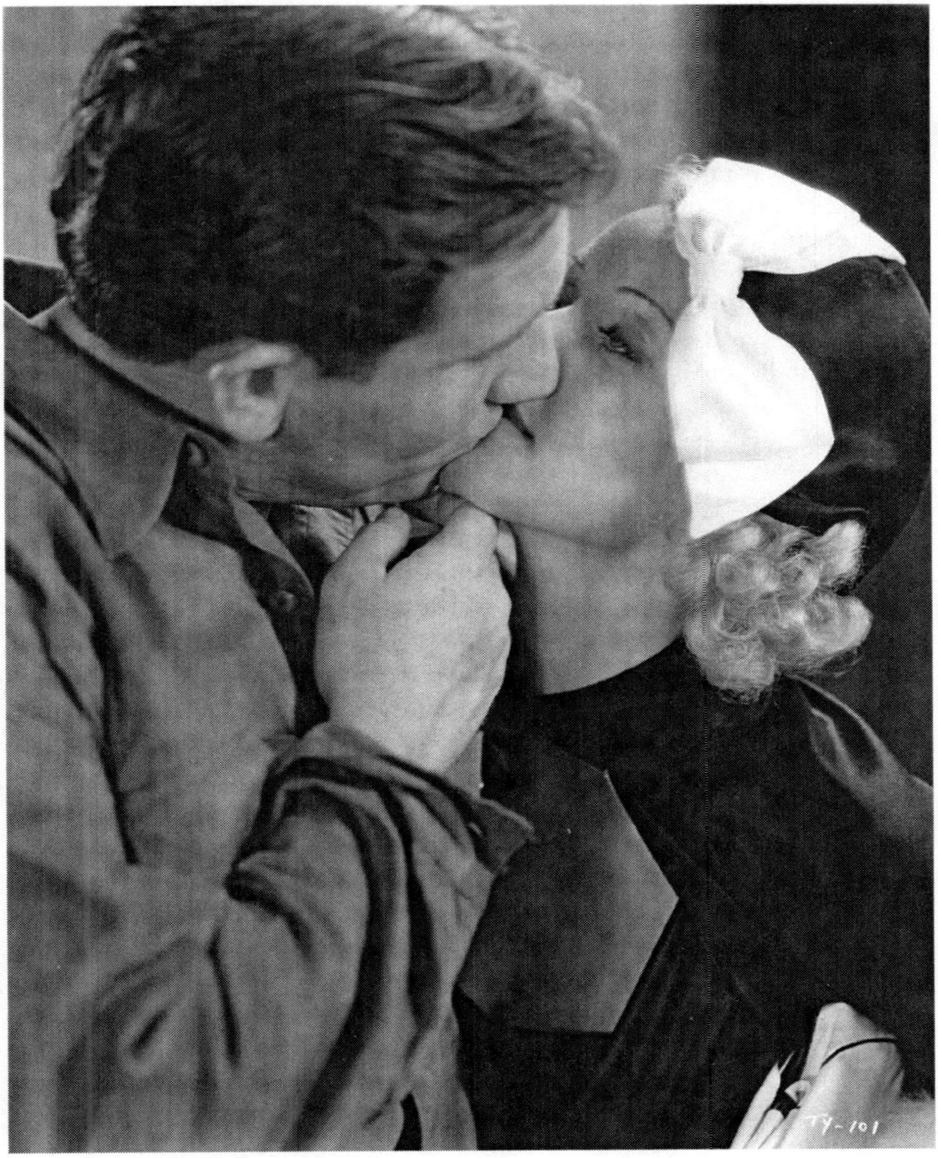
TY-101

sympathetic light. This may explain why Tracy's Bugs has not entered the ranks of the greatest screen hoods, including Cagney's Tom Powers, Muni's "Scarface," or Robinson's "Little Rico" (and, later, Bogart's "Duke Mantee" in *The Petrified Forest* [1935]) despite a well-crafted plot and dialogue, strongly developed characters, and evocative moments, as when George Raft, in an early screen appearance as one of Bugs' henchmen, does an erotic dance during a tension-filled party that clearly inspired the sinister meeting of hoods in Francis Ford Coppola's *The Cotton Club* (1984), when "Dutch" Schultz murders a rival gangster with a knife meant to carve a roast.

The pithy and often amusing dialogue in *Quick Millions* set a tone for other gangster movies—and the later *film noir*—as an effective means of off-setting darker aspects. Sexual undercurrents are also implanted humorously through the dialogue, as when one of the characters flirts with a secretary. He asks, "Say, baby, what do you do with your spare moments?", to which she replies with a glint, "I like to go to wrestling matches." Aspects of Tracy's character are also revealed through the film's language, as when Bugs announces to his colleagues, "I wish to report that we are making satisfactory progress. Of course, it must be born in mind that this project is still in its infancy. I mean, we ain't got a cent yet." This speech evokes humor by presenting both Bugs' pretension to the status of a legitimate businessman and his gutter roots. The idea of playing Bugs as an aspiring sophisticate offered a different approach to the gangster archetype, but it also allowed Tracy to play against the lower class "mugs" image he would perfect during the Fox years. Even in this case, however, Bugs is first seen as a small-time trucker and those Fox films in which he played wealthy or powerful men typically first show the character at the bottom of the socio-economic ladder aspiring through either legal or, in the case of *Quick Millions*, illegal means of rising out of poverty.

This is particularly true of what is arguably the finest of Tracy's Fox films, *The Power and the Glory* (1933), in which he plays Tom Garner, a railroad tycoon. Written by Preston Sturges, the movie is novel in its use of the device of breaking away from a linear, chronological unfolding of the plot (a device that inspired a similar approach in Orson Welles' *Citizen Kane*) by switching back and forth from "past" to "present," showing Tracy both as a powerful middle-aged railroad tycoon and also as a puppyish track walker driven to undesired success by an ambitious wife (played by Colleen Moore). On his Fox contract, both at the studio and on the occasional loan-out, Tracy plays cops, blue-collar workers, sailors, newspaper reporters, unemployed directionless young men, and so forth—even later, at M-G-M, Tracy almost never played an upper-cruster, and when he did the character was either corrupt (as in *Edward, My Son*) or a decent man of the people who had risen above his roots (*Cass Timberlane*, *State of the Union*). So, in essence, *Up the River* and more especially *Quick Millions*, established a template for Tracy's range of characters through the years.

Quick Millions also marks the first of three important gangster characterizations Tracy delivered during his Fox years—and these performances are individually unique. In the case of *Quick Millions*, critics wrote that Tracy "does his job perfectly" ("Review: *Quick Millions*" 216) and as early as five years after the film's release in May 1931 (only to be obscured by the huge popularity of *The Public Enemy* released by Warner Bros. a few weeks earlier), the *New York Times* viewed *Quick Millions* in 1936 as an overlooked landmark among gangster films, most particularly in its diminished use of dialogue, noting that "continuity was built up from short scenes; the dialogue was correspondingly laconic. Each scene quietly thrust home a point of character or plot—and stopped" (Graves X4). This almost certainly springs from Brown's recognition that as an actor Tracy required little dialogue to achieve a richly varied character and expressive individual moments. More importantly, it also makes clear that even at the beginning of his film career, Tracy instinctively understood the visual nature of cinema—that the image is at least as important as the word and that action and reaction could be most effective in revealing character.

This was never more evident than in Tracy's intricate performance in *20,000 Years in Sing Sing*, which he made on a rare loan-out to Warner Bros. There, Tracy found himself in the central gathering place of screen hoodlums and adapted well to the fast-paced, street-wise qualities of a typical Warner programmer. *20,000 Years in Sing Sing*, based on episodes inspired by the best-selling memoirs of Sing Sing's longtime warden, Lewis E. Lawes, is a briskly-paced, well-plotted (if improbable) movie, enhanced by realistic environments, a strong cast of supporting players and character actors (including a young Bette Davis in her only on-screen teaming with Tracy, as well as Louis Calhern overplaying as a crooked lawyer).

In *20,000 Years in Sing Sing*, Tracy is permitted to make his character, a small-time hood named Tommy Connors (was Warner Bros. hoping a little too hard for success by giving the character a name so similar to Cagney's Tom Powers in *The Public Enemy?*), more sympathetic than the amoral Bugs Raymond of *Quick Millions*. Tommy, a street tough, is framed and sent to prison where he adopts the attitude of a hardened criminal, refusing to conform to prison requirements. The swift dialogue establishes Tommy's pose:

Tom: "What are you guys trying to do? Make a monkey out of me?"
Policeman: "Go on and sit down."
Tom: "Say, I guess you don't know who I am. Maybe the warden didn't tell ya. I'm Tommy Connors."

Policeman: "Oh yeah? What of it?" [Tommy punches him]
Policeman: "Why, you!"
Tommy: "Come on and I'll show ya how tough I am."

    Locked in a battle of wills with Warden Long (played by Arthur Byron), Tommy angrily resists regulations and indulges in fights with other inmates. The warden has no choice but to send him to solitary confinement, although Tommy is cocky enough to believe he can withstand its isolation. Over time, he eventually relents and through the compassionate guidance of the warden he becomes a model prisoner. Tommy's lawyer, Finn (Calhern), is supposedly working to get Tommy released, but in fact he is conspiring to keep Tommy in jail for several reasons, not least because he lusts after Tommy's girlfriend, Fay (Davis). Attempting to escape Finn's advances, Fay is seriously injured in a car crash and when the heartbroken Tommy hears that she may not survive, he turns to the warden and begs for a twenty-four hour release so he can see Fay. The warden decides to trust Tommy, who arrives at Fay's bedside in time to overhear Finn's machinations:

Fay: "I don't want anything. Get out."
Finn: "So you changed your mind, huh? Just a trouble-making broad. And you're not gonna get a chance to squawk."
Tommy: "She ain't gonna squawk. And neither am I."
Finn: "Connors!"
Tommy: "Yeah, yeah, it's me. And I got here just in time to rub you out, you dirty . . . " [punches Finn]
Fay: "Tommy!"

    Finn and Tommy engage in a fierce fight and Fay, attempting to protect Tommy, shoots Finn. Tommy initially considers taking it "on the lam," but finally returns to prison and takes the rap for killing Finn to protect Fay, who recovers from her injuries. Sentenced to execution, Tommy is allowed an eleventh-hour death house visit from Fay through the intervention of the compassionate Warden Long, who is convinced of Tom's innocence. However, Tommy continues to insist that he is guilty for Fay's sake, so Long has no choice but to allow Tommy to face the sentence.
    Although the scene of Finn's shooting—and the fisticuffs between Tom and Finn—is overwrought, the somewhat sentimentalized film is otherwise sensitively directed by Michael Curtiz from a screenplay by Courtney Territt, Robert Lord, Wilson Mizner, and Brown Holmes from Lawes' memoirs. Not surprisingly, the scenes between Tracy and Davis, particularly their reunion after Fay's accident and their final scene on death row, are expertly acted,

revealing both the vitality of their screen presences and the delicacy of their emoting (those expecting the more florid acting typical of Davis' acting at her height, will be surprised at the naturalness of her approach here). Some Tracy and Davis biographers have suggested that the two had an affair during the making of the film (and others conversely posit that the two stars did not get along at all), which might explain their strong chemistry together and the emotional intimacy they achieve in the key scenes. The dialogue skirts cliché, but Tracy and Davis enlivened it on-screen, as when Fay comes to the prison on visitor's day:

Tommy: "I'd give a million bucks to be alone with you for a little while honey. Do you love me?"
Fay: "Yeah."
Tommy: "Well don't come up here dolled up like that anymore."
Fay: "Oh, Tommy."
Tommy: "What's the matter with you? Do you want me to go crazy? You have me foaming at the mouth like a cream puff."

In her memoirs, Davis lamented that she and Tracy never again worked together on screen (although they performed in a 1940 "Lux Radio Theatre" adaptation of Davis' classic *Dark Victory*, which is only one of several films Davis had hoped might co-star Tracy)—and in a better film—although *20,000 Years in Sing Sing* is a solid vehicle for the two stars, with a tightly-constructed script, generally inventive direction, and realistic production values typical of Warner Bros. in this era. Although *20,000 Years in Sing Sing* was released three years after *Up the River*, critics noted the presence of Warren Hymer in the comparatively small role of a jailbird named Hype, with *Variety's* critic calling for another teaming so that they could "dig for laughs" ("Review: *20,000 Years in Sing Sing*" 26). Critics uniformly praised Tracy for "a clever and convincing portrayal" (Hall, "Spencer Tracy in a Pictorial Conception" 26), with the *Motion Picture Herald* critic enthusing that "If you have seen *I Am a Fugitive from a Chain Gang*, you can appreciate the quality of Spencer Tracy's acting, inasmuch as it is fully on a par with Paul Muni's for effectiveness and pulling his auditors along with him" (*Motion Picture Herald* 44).

20,000 Years in Sing Sing includes considerable humor mixed with its inherent tragedy and is enhanced by the romantic underpinnings brought out by Tracy and Davis in their scenes. Laced with social commentary and, at times, a near-documentary quality in its prison segments, *20,000 Years in Sing Sing* presents a haunting examination of the problems of the penal system in the United States circa the 1930s and although it could be argued that the film's grittier elements are undermined by Tommy's final redemption through his heroic self-sacrifice to save Fay, it is an artful film thanks to Tracy's central performance, with a strong assist from Davis and, to a lesser degree, Calhern, and Curtiz's expert visual sense and tempo, as when in the opening sequence, prison conditions are briskly depicted as the camera pans across a row of prisoners each identified by a number. Even implausible moments, such as when the heavily-bandaged, bed-ridden Fay manages to draw a gun and shoot Finn or when Warden Long allows Tommy to leave prison to see Fay, are handled with a restraint that does not permit these scenes to become too preposterous. Curtiz enhances Tracy's performance in several instances, as when Tommy is in solitary and his grim, hardened face is superimposed over scenes of routine prison life to indicate a passage of time and the steady breaking down of Tommy's resistance.

20,000 Years in Sing Sing, which Warner Bros. had originally intended as a vehicle for James Cagney (and which would later be remade as *Castle on the Hudson* by director Anatole Litvak starring John Garfield, Pat O'Brien, and Ann Sheridan), provides in its initial scenes a hard-boiled performance by Tracy which must surely contain vestiges of his "Killer" Mears from his Broadway triumph in *The Last Mile*. The fierce intensity of Tracy's early scenes give way to gentleness in his encounters with Davis' Fay, which provide him the opportunity of humanizing the character in ways that Mears could not be softened. Of his performance in *The Last Mile*, Richard Dana Skinner felt that Tracy "puts the final seal on his qualifications as one of our most versatile young actors" (Skinner 25) in a performance offering the "haunting dejection of the condemned man" and "relentless fury and drive" as the play proceeds to the "sheer terror" of its tragic conclusion" (Hutchens 278). A completely ruthless character driven to lead a desperate revolt of death row prisoners, Tracy's Mears was provided no opportunity for humanizing—as the character's nickname implies. None of Tracy's screen gangsters were as completely ruthless as Mears (although Bugs Raymond, despite his genteel exterior, is not particularly redeemable), but little more than a year after the release of *20,000 Years in Sing Sing*, Tracy played his final mobster, a fictionalized treatment of gambler Arnold Rothstein, renamed Murray Golden in Fox's *Now I'll Tell*, based on the memoirs of Rothstein's widow. Here Tracy would merge elements of the ruthless Mears with the society pretensions of Bugs Raymond and a whiff of the self-sacrifice of Tom Connors.

Like *20,000 Years in Sing Sing, Now I'll Tell* (called *When New York Sleeps* in its English release) was also drawn from reality—and a topical source. Rothstein, the central figure of the "Black Sox" baseball scandal, in which he essentially "fixed" the outcome of the 1919 World Series, had been murdered in 1928 and his wife remarried and penned a book, also called *Now I'll Tell*, in collaboration with Donald Henderson Clarke. The role was originally considered for Warner Bros. character actor Allen Jenkins, who bore an uncanny likeness to the real-life Rothstein, but Fox, expending significant resources on *Now I'll Tell*, including on-location shots in New York City (most particularly Lindy's Restaurant—a favorite Rothstein haunt), opted to cast Tracy, one of their most bankable stars. Rothstein became a household name, inspiring several literary characters, including "Meyer Wolfsheim" in F. Scott Fitzgerald's *The Great Gatsby* and, in a lighter vein, "Nathan Detroit" in the Damon Runyon story, "The Idyll of Miss Sarah Brown," which morphed into the classic Broadway and screen musical, *Guys and Dolls*. Prior films, including *Street of Chance* (1930), starring William Powell, and a later B-picture *The King of the Roaring Twenties* (1961) featuring David Janssen, were also inspired by Rothstein's life, and like *Now I'll Tell*, these films added sensationalizing elements to Rothstein's admittedly sensational life story.

In *Now I'll Tell*, Tracy's characterization of the suave, charming scoundrel Murray Golden (despite the character's name, Tracy wisely eschews any attempt at indicating Golden's ethnic origins), begins with the character as a small-time hustler, once again allowing Tracy an opportunity of revealing the economically deprived roots of a character that would evolve into a "King of the Underworld." Golden runs several bunko operations targeting names from high society's Blue Book. Golden's genteel wife, Virginia (played by Helen Twelvetrees), hates his scheming ways and insists that he give up the rackets and he promises to do so once he has amassed $200,000. When Golden fixes a fight, he is at cross-purposes with a ruthless gangster, Mossiter (played by Robert Glecker), and is forced to pawn Virginia's jewelry. Virginia learns that Golden is romantically involved with a tough nightclub singer, Peggy (Alice Faye in an early screen appearance singing the aptly named Lew Brown/Harry Akst song, "Foolin' with the Other Woman's Man," in makeup, hairdo, and costume to make her look like Jean Harlow). Peggy is ultimately killed in an auto accident in which Golden is injured, leading Virginia to depart for Europe with intentions to divorce Golden, who finally loses all of his money to Mossiter. After taking out a large insurance policy, Golden kills himself so that Virginia will benefit from the proceeds. The somewhat convoluted plot, which also featured other secondary characters, including toddler Shirley Temple as Mary Doran, was constructed by the film's director, Edwin Burke, from Mrs. Rothstein's memoirs, and won praise for the briskly-paced, well-acted film. As usual, Tracy won particular kudos, with the reviewer for the *Literary Digest* noticing that he kept "the central character both credible and in a measure sympathetic" ("Review: *Now I'll Tell*" 50). *New York Times* critic Mordaunt Hall applauded Tracy's "vivid" performance, which he viewed "as thorough a characterization as has been seen on the screen" (Hall, "Spencer Tracy, Helen Twelvetress, Alice Faye" 12).

Tracy's quartet of cinematic gangsters essentially ends with *Now I'll Tell*. Once established at M-G-M, a studio given to glossier entertainments, Tracy no longer had the opportunity to assay such roles, although an early film at M-G-M, *Fury* (1936), directed by Fritz Lang, provided Tracy with the opportunity to demonstrate the menace of the hoodlum actor he might have been. Playing Joe Wilson, an innocent young man falsely arrested as a killer, Tracy had to make a total transition after Joe is trapped in a jail beset by a mob intending to lynch him. The prison is burned and it is assumed that Joe has died in the fire. However, he escapes the flames and is transformed into a desperate man hell-bent to avenge the wrong done to him. Only through the ultimate intercession of the girl he loves, played by Sylvia Sidney, in a somewhat unconvincing redemption scene, does Joe regain his original persona. Tracy gives a scalding performance, suggesting that M-G-M might have been wise to develop some mobster characters for him. However, it was not to be. The cinema fantasist could spend endless hours wondering how such later-day screen hoods as Don Vito Corleone of *The Godfather* (1972) or Francis "Frank" Costello, the Jack Nicholson character of *The Departed* (2006), might have evolved had they been played by Tracy. What dark characteristics evident in Tracy's early character films might have found their way into these gangster epics? He nearly played a gambler in *The Cincinnati Kid* in 1965, but illness cost him the role, which ironically went to cinema gangster Edward G. Robinson. But, of course, Tracy had already proven he could be as tough as the toughest tough guy, so any additional gangster roles would only have allowed him a chance to add new flavors to a dish he had already served.

Works Cited

Andersen, Christopher. *An Affair to Remember: The Remarkable Love Story of Katharine Hepburn and Spencer Tracy.* New York: William Morrow, 1997.
Barton, Ralph, "Theatre," *Life* 95 (6 June 1930).
Chandler, Charlotte. *The Girl Who Walked Home Alone: Bette Davis, A Personal Biography.* New York: Applause, 2006.
Davidson, Bill. *Spencer Tracy: Tragic Idol.* New York: Dutton, 1987.
Davis, Bette. *The Lonely Life: An Autobiography.* New York: G. P. Putnam's Sons, 1962.
—, with Michael Herskowitz. *This 'N That.* New York: Putnam's, 1987.
Deschner, Donald. *The Complete Films of Spencer Tracy.* Secaucus, NJ: Carol Books, 1993.
Eyman, Scott and Paul Duncan. *John Ford: The Complete Films.* New York: Taschen, 2004.

Fisher, James, "A Cinemactor's Forgotten Theatrical Resume: Spencer Tracy on Stage," *New England Theatre Journal* 6 (1995): 91-112.

—, "Pre-MGM Spencer Tracy," *Films in Review* XLVI.9/10 (November/December 1995): 2-23.

—, *Spencer Tracy: A Bio-Bibliography*. Westport, CT: Greenwood Press, 1994.

Graves, Janet, "Joining Sight and Sound; An Observer Sketches the Progress of Synchronization for the Screen," *New York Times* (29 November 1936): X4.

Hall, Mordaunt, "Fun in Various Forms," *New York Times* (19 October 1930): 117.

—, "Spencer Tracy, Helen Twelvetrees, Alice Faye, and Others in the Current Picture at the Roxy," *New York Times* (26 May 1934).

—, "Spencer Tracy in a Pictorial Conception of Warden Lawes's Book '20,000 Years in Sing Sing'," *New York Times* (10 January 1933): 26.

Hutchens, John, "Review," *Theatre Arts Monthly* 14 (April 1930).

Kanin, Garson. *Tracy and Hepburn*. New York: Viking, 1971.

McBride, Joseph. *Searching for John Ford: A Life*. New York: St. Martin's Press, 2001.

Motion Picture Herald (5 November 1932).

Newquist, Roy. *A Special Kind of Magic: Spencer Tracy and Katharine Hepburn*. Chicago, IL: Rand McNally, 1967.

"Review: *Now I'll Tell*," *Literary Digest* (9 June 1934).

"Review: *Quick Millions*," *Photoplay* (June 1931).

"Review: *20,000 Years in Sing Sing*," *Variety* (17 January 1933).

"Review: *Up the River*," *Variety* (22 October 1930).

Sikov, Ed. *Dark Victory: The Life of Bette Davis*. New York: Henry Holt, 2007.

Skinner, Richard Dana, "Review: *The Last Mile*," *Commonweal* 85 (9 April 1930).

Stine, Whitney. *I'd Love to Kiss You: Conversations with Bette Davis*. New York: Pocket Books, 1990.

—, *Mother Goddam: The Story of the Career of Bette Davis*. New York: Hawthorn, 1974.

Swindell, Larry. *Spencer Tracy: A Biography*. New York: World Publishing Co., 1969.

Waly., "Review," *Variety* (11 June 1930).

HE WOOED HER WITH WISECRACKS

You'll roar at the merry adventures of this jaunty smart aleck and his breezy blonde...

It's a high-speed comedy-melodrama

MARION BURNS
GEORGE WALSH
Directed by
RAOUL WALSH
Fox Picture

Spencer Tracy ... Comedian?!?

Charles Morrow

When I was in grade school there was a movie theater near my home that used to offer Saturday afternoon Kiddie Matinees, usually comedies of then-recent vintage chosen for their appeal to viewers between, say, third grade and junior high school level. These shows usually consisted of lightweight fare starring the likes of Jerry Lewis or Bob Hope (in their 1960s incarnations), animated features, or Robert Youngson's old-time silent movie compilations. One Saturday I went to this theater with a friend to see a wide-screen extravaganza that had been released a few years earlier. According to the newspaper ad the movie we were to see that day, *It's a Mad Mad Mad Mad World*, was the most stupendous chuckle-fest ever concocted, a huge production featuring the proverbial cast of thousands, with the twist being that the roster was made up entirely of comedians. Indeed, throughout its lengthy running time practically every inch of the movie's Ultra Panavision frame was filled with well-known comics, everyone from TV personalities such as Sid Caesar and Jonathan Winters to Hollywood old-timers like Jimmy Durante and ZaSu Pitts. The title proved to be an apt one, for this turned out to be a movie filled with fistfights, car crashes, and explosions, and at the center of all the mayhem was a flustered white-haired man who seemed quite out of place in such a farrago, and who functioned as the unlikely emotional core of an otherwise cartoon-y film that didn't have much use for any emotions more subtle than wild-eyed fury. The old man was Spencer

Tracy, of course. What was he doing here, in the midst of all this lunacy, and with these raffish co-stars?

The plot concerned a scavenger hunt of sorts, as a ragtag group of travelers crisscross the country in pursuit of a suitcase full of stolen money. It was apparently intended as a satirical jab at our greedy society, but the point seems to have been lost somewhere along the way, overwhelmed by the sheer bloated scale of the project. Viewing the movie again recently I was dismayed at how much of the humor consists of painful-looking slapstick violence and shouted insults. That wasn't a problem when I was a kid, however, in fact that's what I *liked* about it: my friend and I enjoyed the show enormously. Still, even at the time I found the presence of Spencer Tracy in the central role kind of weird, for I already knew who he was. I recognized him from a couple of movies I'd seen on TV, *Inherit the Wind* and *Judgment at Nuremburg*, courtroom sagas which dramatized momentous real-world cases. Serious stuff, the sort of movies our teachers would urge us to watch so we'd learn something. No slapstick there, and no car crashes. (I certainly would've been surprised to learn that the producer-director of *Mad Mad World*, Stanley Kramer, was also responsible for those films.) Whether he was defending a man for teaching evolution or condemning a fellow judge for knuckling under to the Nazis, Spencer Tracy, I thought, played tough-talking guys who meant business. He impressed me as an actor of gravitas who looked like he'd been through hell, but the one thing he didn't resemble was a comedian. Since then I've seen a lot more of Tracy's work, and while it's true that he was a dramatic actor first and foremost it's also true that he was adept with comedy and was frequently granted the opportunity to demonstrate this facility onscreen, not only in brief sequences within otherwise serious dramas but in outright comic roles as well. He appeared in a surprising number of comedies, especially in early years before the basic perimeters of his familiar screen persona were established. As I've researched his career further it has become clear to me that, however I may feel today about *It's a Mad Mad Mad Mad World*, the casting of Spencer Tracy in the central role was no mistake: he was making audiences laugh before some of his co-stars in Kramer's epic were born.

Even prior to his film debut in 1930 Tracy was honing his comic skills during his stage apprenticeship, appearing in everything from knockabout farce (e.g. *Getting Gertie's Garter*) to the more refined drawing room humor of Oscar Wilde's *Importance of Being Earnest*. On Broadway Tracy appeared in George M. Cohan's 1927 farce *The Baby Cyclone* in a part specially tailored by the playwright to fit him. This play concerned two married couples who quarrel over a pet Pekinese owned by one of the wives, with much of the humor stemming from the escalating verbal combat between the husbands. When *The Baby Cyclone* received a ho-hum critical response Tracy's wife Louise became concerned that Spencer was too strongly associated in the public mind with lightweight fare, and urged him to eschew comedy for heavier subject matter. He followed her advice, and began to turn down comedy parts in favor of serious roles in such dramas as *Conflict* and *The Big Shot*, a play initially known as *Nigger Rich*. When film director John Ford came to New York early in 1930, scouting Broadway shows for new actors and material, he got his first look at Tracy in a role that was anything but comical. After some hesitation, Tracy had accepted the role of doomed convict "Killer" Mears in John Wexley's prison drama *The Last Mile*. The play proved to be an immediate success when it opened in February 1930 and Tracy was a sensation. Ford came back to see the play repeatedly, then met with Tracy for drinks and all-night conversation. It was at Ford's urging, and despite an unpromising screen test, that the actor was signed to a one-picture deal with the Fox Film Corporation. Tracy, who had appeared in three one-reel Vitaphone shorts produced in Brooklyn, would make his Hollywood feature film debut on the Fox lot, under Ford's direction, in a prison saga to be called *Up the River*. Tracy took a temporary sabbatical from his stage work and left New York for Hollywood in June of 1930.

As originally conceived *Up the River* was to be a hard-hitting prison drama, from a story suggested by the 1929 riot at the Auburn Correctional Facility in upstate New York. The script was assigned to playwright Maurine Watkins, best known for her 1926 Broadway hit *Chicago*, later filmed with Ginger Rogers as *Roxie Hart* and, later still, transformed into a Kander-Ebb musical under its original title. Ford considered Watkins' first draft of the script unacceptable, and she was still revising it when the leading man arrived from New York. Spencer Tracy would make his Hollywood debut opposite another Broadway veteran appearing in his first feature, 31 year-old Humphrey Bogart. Production was delayed by administrative upheaval at the studio, however, and by the time the cameras were ready to roll the smash success of MGM's prison drama *The Big House*—also inspired by the Auburn riot—had dampened enthusiasm in Fox's front office for a carbon copy. Studio chief Winfield Sheehan was ready to cancel the picture, but Ford fought to make it. Eventually it was decided to revamp the project as a comedy, and *Up the River* was demoted to B-picture status. According to one account Ford chose to ignore Watkins' script entirely and urged his actors to improvise their parts. While this is surely overstated, the finished film does have a loose, spontaneous feel which suggests at least some scenes were casually blocked-out moments before the cameras rolled. Although Watkins received sole writing credit it's said that Ford revised the script himself in collaboration with stage veteran William Collier Sr., who had many years' experience as a playwright, director and screenwriter; Collier also played the aging, baseball-obsessed convict known as "Pop."

Up the River set the pattern for a number of comedies that would feature Spencer Tracy in the early 1930s. In this film, as in *Goldie*, *Face in the Sky*, and others, Spence plays a highly self-confident, know-it-all sharpster teamed with a loyal, dim-witted companion. Whether they're servicemen, laborers, or even criminals Spence and his partner are always average-joe working class types. Viewers struggling with the Depression could relate to these guys and perhaps share some of their aspirations but feel a bit superior to them as well. Seen today, these "buddy" movies suggest an early model for the popular wartime comedies of Abbott & Costello a decade later, at least where the level of humor and the nature of the central relationship are concerned. Spence, of course, is always the Bud Abbott figure, the alpha dog of the team, sharp-tongued, aggressive, and a wise guy. He's the one who makes the decisions, sometimes pulls rank on his subordinate, or metes out punishment. His partner in *Up the River* is Warren Hymer, a grinning lug whose Hollywood career would consist mostly of supporting roles as dumb but good-natured thugs, boxers, and harmless crooks. The version of *Up the River* that finally went before the cameras tells the story of St. Louis (Tracy) and Dannemora Dan (Hymer). When the film opens the two are in the process of escaping from an unidentified state prison in the South. They dash across a wall under cover of darkness, jump down, and find a parked, unoccupied car waiting for them. From their first exchange it's clear that we're meant to regard these cons as non-threatening and funny: St. Louis quips that the gang promised him a limo with a chauffeur, Dan remarks with plaintive sincerity that he hates prison life because the food is bad. They appear to be a team, but inexplicably St. Louis reveals a mean streak and tricks Dan into staying behind, then takes off without him. We pick up the story later in Kansas City, where an ostensibly reformed Dan beats a drum for the Salvation Army and testifies that he was led into sin by "bad company." As if on cue, St. Louis arrives on the scene, dressed to the nines and accompanied by a couple of flappers. The men wind up in a fistfight that draws the attention of the police, and thus leads to their re-incarceration at Bensonatta, a prison in the Midwest. Although it looks like an old-fashioned, grey-walled maximum security facility, Bensonatta is presented as a remarkably cheerful, informal sort of place—some might say *ridiculously* informal. It's a co-ed prison where the warden's young daughter plays casually on the grounds among the inmates (who amuse her with riddles), security is lax, and the major concerns are staging the prison talent show and winning the big baseball game. Prison comes off like the Hollywood version of collegiate life: Boola-Boola at ol' Bensonatta State U.

Once they take up residence at this friendly haven Tracy and Hymer resume their status as a team. It is apparent that they are already well-known here, though we never learn the nature of the activities that landed them in jail in the first place. It is clear, however, that St. Louis has more social prestige and is permitted privileges granted no one else: on his arrival at Bensonatta, decked out in a double-breasted suit and a derby, St. Louis is greeted as a celebrity, and not rebuked for sassing a guard or addressing the warden with high-handed grandeur. Dan, for his part, acts the cheery dunce, passing time in his cell tearing paper into a doily, opening it, and remarking brightly: "Ya never know how they're gonna turn out!" Meanwhile, young Humphrey Bogart, scarcely recognizable with locks of curly hair dangling before his eyes, struggles with a thankless role, playing an earnest young fellow named Steve who was jailed after accidentally killing another man in a fight. In a highly dubious bit of exposition Steve admits to another convict that members of his respectable upper-crust family back in small town New England don't know he was convicted of manslaughter or that he's in prison. How could this be? Steve says he changed his name, told his folks he's in China, and arranged for friends to cable them from there on his behalf. (Wait a second, he was convicted under a false name? Or if he changed his name after he was convicted, how did his family miss the news?) Despite his vague history Steve's friendship is valued by both St. Louis and Dan, who will go to great lengths to help him conceal his past from his family and friends. Soon Steve is paroled, and returns to his hometown hoping to go straight and keep his mother and sister ignorant of his recent experiences. (The film's funniest moment was perhaps unintentional: when a friend asks "How was China?" Steve replies *"Fine!"* then quickly drops the subject.) Steve also hopes to marry a fellow convict named Judy he met at Bensonatta—naturally, another good-hearted young person whose involvement in crime was more or less accidental. But when word reaches St. Louis & Dan that Steve is being blackmailed by the man who led Judy astray, and that his hope of straightening out his life could be ruined, they decide to break out of Bensonatta and head for Steve's hometown to set matters right.

Our heroes escape during the prison's vaudeville-style "annual entertainment," but instead of a suspense sequence the breakout is depicted as an absurdly easy feat, passed off as a quick sight gag. The talent show is produced under the auspices of a Mrs. Massey, who is present with a number of fellow social workers, all of whom are older ladies. After a blackface comedy act, a kazoo solo, and a sentimental "mother" song, St. Louis steps out wearing a silk tunic and announces that since he can neither sing nor dance (which, as it happens, was also true of the actor playing him) he will instead perform a knife-throwing act with "his old friend and partner" Dannemora Dan serving as human target. First, however, he inquires whether all the lights in the hall are controlled from a single source, and is told that they are. The act follows. St. Louis flings his knives and Dan narrowly survives intact, though it's clear to even the most unsophisticated viewer that the throws are faked. Afterward, as all the revue's performers take the stage for the finale (including several men in drag we haven't seen previously), the auditorium is suddenly plunged into darkness. The warden takes the stage, calls for calm, and instructs Mrs. Massey and her party to leave through the nearest exit. A close shot of the departing ladies reveals St. Louis & Dan in their midst, now in drag, leaving with them; Dan even smokes a cigar. Next thing we know, a cross-fade reveals that St. Louis & Dan have hopped a train to Steve's hometown.

As should be clear by now, the makers of *Up the River* were not concerned with realism. The movie suggests the kind of shaggy dog yarn that is meant to be diverting but not the least bit credible. Ironically, Tracy made his feature film debut in the sort of frivolous entertainment his wife urged him to avoid, though he certainly appears to be enjoying himself. Tracy & Hymer are cheerfully attuned to the spirit of their material, and develop an amiable rapport that jollies their scenes along even when nothing especially funny is happening, while poor Bogie appears to be out of the loop, stuck with the ludicrous passages that had to be played straight. It looks like the uncredited authors most responsible for the finished product, John Ford and William Collier, were engaged in a spirited competition to see who could pile the blarney highest.

(In 1967 when Spencer Tracy was interviewed on the set of what proved to be his last film, *Guess Who's Coming to Dinner*, he mentioned his movie debut but remarked, curiously, "Bogie was the hero and I was the villain." It would be more accurate to say that Bogart was the juvenile while Tracy was the comic anti-hero. A career criminal who breaks out of prison to keep his pal out of trouble is no villain.)

The film's best moments are in its later sequences, set in Steve's unnamed hometown. By this point in the narrative the actors have settled into a relaxed, easy-going groove which allows for some lightweight humor. Steve's mother is presented as a pleasant woman who still treats her adult son as a boy. Tracy's funniest moment comes during a dinner table scene when the old lady starts to quote from the New Testament and Dan solemnly finishes the verse; St. Louis stares at him in pop-eyed surprise as he drops his cutlery onto his plate with a sudden crash. But the most memorable scene in *Up the River*, and the one which most strongly suggests the Spencer Tracy we know from his later work, comes just after dinner. Once Steve's mother and sister say goodnight and go upstairs to bed, the mood changes. Steve has learned that his mother is being swindled by Frosby, the crook who is trying to force him into a life of crime. He intends to go find Frosby and shoot him, consequences be damned. St. Louis decides to have a little talk with the lad and cool him down, and begins with a friendly offer of a cigarette, which he lights himself. When Steve declines St. Louis forces the cigarette into his hand and barks *"Smoke it!"* Steve grudgingly does so. (In this, their only film together, Spence "out-toughs" Bogie.) St. Louis tells the younger man that he's a good kid, but with one bullet from that gun he'll ruin his whole life, and that only chumps settle arguments with guns. St. Louis reveals that he spent eight months on death row himself—although why this was, or how he got out, is not revealed—and then describes how he felt as he watched one pal after another go to the chair. His voice rises in intensity as he says "Let me tell you that's no picnic, kid! Listening to the drone of that lousy motor, and watchin' those lights go dim!" By the time he's finished, Steve has relented and agreed to let his pals handle the matter. They do so with their customary ease, then return to Dannemora in time to rejoin the baseball team and take part in a big game against a rival prison!

Tracy's speech to Bogart is played with an earnestness that is strikingly different from the rest of his performance. For just this moment Tracy seems to be channeling *The Last Mile*'s Killer Mears (a performance which, unfortunately, was not captured on film), lending this silly movie a rare somber note and giving a hint of the first, aborted version of the story. Otherwise, Tracy's primary contribution to the success of *Up the River*—and the film was indeed a box office success—is the air of breezy irreverence he lends the proceedings. He knows it's all a lot of hooey, and he knows we know it too. Hymer delivers most of the punchlines, though William Collier has some amusing bits as baseball fan "Pop." In the last sequence, as the convicts prepare to play ball, Collier takes part in a routine that will feel familiar to those of us who grew up watching Bugs Bunny cartoons: when representatives of the two teams meet for a pre-game parley they demonstrate precisely which maneuvers are off-limits ("there'll be none o' *that*, none o' *this*, none o' *that*" etc.) as they punch and kick each other. Perhaps this shtick originated here, but something tells me it was already familiar in 1930, one of those ever-popular comic devices that's a sure laugh-getter. Viewers who seek out this film today, conscious of the stature attained by Tracy, Bogart, and Ford in later years, may find *Up the River* disappointing, but it suited its first-run audiences as a pleasant diversion and, more importantly, secured a long-term contract for its leading man.

After this successful debut Tracy was assigned a serious role in a prestige picture, a gangster drama called *Quick Millions*; and after that, several more comedies. The first of these was a minor film called *Six Cylinder Love*, based on a hit play of 1921 which ran on Broadway for almost a year. Whatever the material's pedigree Tracy was unhappy with the assignment, a supporting role in a B-level project; according to co-star Edward Everett Horton he was grouchy and uncommunicative on the set. Next, Tracy was re-teamed with his erstwhile partner Warren Hymer in a talkie remake of Howard Hawks' 1928 silent comedy *A Girl in Every Port*. This time Tracy & Hymer played a pair of sailors at odds over women, boozing and brawling their way through a series of port cities which all bear a suspicious resemblance to sets on the Fox back-lot. The template for this kind of entertainment was established by the Broadway smash of 1924 *What Price Glory*, the army drama that introduced those famous feuding buddies Sergeant Quirt & Captain Flagg. The play spawned a hit film adaptation, sequels, and, in turn, a slew of imitations. These imitations always featured a pair of two-fisted servicemen who spend a lot of their time double-crossing each other and fighting—usually over "dames"—but whose loyalty to each other invariably survives the tumult, ultimately proving more durable than passing fancies for the women they meet along the way. The silent *A Girl in Every Port* was very much in this tradition, and even featured Victor McLaglen, the movies' perennial Captain Flagg, repeating the role in all but name. The talkie remake had the potential to be at least passably entertaining, but was sunk by a poor script and uninspired direction. When the film begins sailors Spike (Hymer) and Bill (Tracy) haven't yet met. Spike encounters attractive young women in successive ports of call, but is troubled to find that all have been tattooed in identical fashion, indicating that they have already been "claimed" sexually by the mysterious and obviously well-traveled Bill. When they finally meet Spike views Bill as a rival and is hostile toward him, but after the ritual brawling they become pals. Eventually in Calais the buddies encounter a sexy blonde known as Goldie who works as a carnival high-diver, and their competition resumes. Tomcat Bill makes his accustomed conquest, but soon he and Spike realize that Goldie is a no-good tramp, reject her, and leave together. That's it, and it's just as unpleasant as it sounds without the redeeming quality of wit. Tracy & Hymer's first teaming was no masterwork, but at least it was bolstered by the players' offhand charm; this time, no amount of charisma can overcome the tawdriness of the material. Tracy, cast in the unfamiliar role of ultra-macho horndog, is reduced to serving as a rather sour straight man for Hymer, who overplays his now-familiar dimwit persona. The best thing to come from this project for Tracy was his relationship with the leading lady, 20 year-old Jean Harlow, whose meteoric career was on the ascent with the release of her two most recent films, *The Secret Six* and *Public Enemy*. Tracy and Harlow struck up a fast friendship behind the scenes, and Spence reportedly gave his leading lady some valuable acting tips. Although her role is a fairly minor one—Harlow doesn't appear onscreen until the movie is almost half over—the studio touted her presence in the publicity campaign and even chose to re-title the film after her character. Seen today, *Goldie* is an unappealing dud (except perhaps for Warren Hymer enthusiasts) but five years after it was made Tracy and Harlow were re-teamed more happily at MGM, first in a melodrama called *Riff Raff*, and then in a most stylish comedy, *Libeled Lady*, which was written by the very same Maurine Watkins whose script for *Up the River* was rejected by John Ford.

After *Goldie* there were no more team-ups with Hymer; instead, over the months that followed Tracy's employers hustled him into a procession of generally routine dramas and action flicks. This proved to be the most prolific period of Tracy's film career: from the beginning of 1931 to the end of 1932 he appeared in eleven movies. He had a low opinion of most of the material he was getting at Fox and made no secret of it, but hoped for better when his home studio loaned his services to United Artists; the result, however, was another mediocre military comedy, *Sky Devils*. This one paired Tracy with a character actor named George Cooper and was set during the First World War, but the antihero cynicism of Tracy's character, Pvt. Wilkie, reflected the attitudes of the '30s, when a growing number of Americans looked back at U.S. involvement in the war as a costly mistake. Wilkie has no interest in fighting, no desire to be a hero and no intention of getting killed. In an attempt to desert he steals a military plane and takes off, but en route to Switzerland accidentally bombs the Germans' largest ammunition dump and becomes, yes, a hero. This storyline would have been unthinkable in 1918 and flirted with bad taste even so, but perhaps contemporary viewers were mollified by the lack of combat scenes and the emphasis on pompous officers and absurd regulations. Real war, like prison life, doesn't readily lend itself to comedy, but *Sky Devils* firmly maintained its distance from anything authentic. The anonymous critic of the London *Times* noted that Tracy's personality dominated every scene, and assured readers that "he keeps the whole film safe in a perfectly unreal world."

The trick, it seemed, was to make a comedy that was not only amusing but also grounded to some extent in life as we know it, and such a project finally came Tracy's way late in '32, when he landed the lead role in Raoul Walsh's *Me and My Gal*, arguably the most enjoyable movie he made at Fox and easily one of the best comedies he ever appeared in. Strictly speaking *Me and My Gal* isn't an outright comedy but something of a hybrid: a romantic comedy with proto-screwball elements and a dramatic subplot played straight. However one may categorize it, and despite a flawed opening section, it's a smoothly handled charmer with a number of strong scenes and several genuinely funny moments, a B-movie that packs as much entertainment into its tight 79 minute running time as many a prestige picture with a bigger budget. For modern viewers the movie captures the mood of its historical moment with time capsule precision, as the characters exchange wisecracks about the Depression, Prohibition, the duplicity of bankers and politicians, and current sexual mores. Spence plays Danny Dolan, a good-natured and somewhat dim patrolman newly assigned to Pier 13, a tough New York precinct on the waterfront. From the opening scene director Walsh establishes a rich tapestry of personalities, colorful, cranky and broadly drawn but recognizably real: denizens of the neighborhood include hard-partying Irish, sharp-dressed crooks, a paralyzed veteran, obnoxious drunks, a tough guy with an unexpected interest in opera, and a sad old man who attempts to drown a dog he can no longer feed. As Officer Dolan makes the rounds he stops in at Ed's Chowder House and encounters a cashier named Helen (Joan Bennett), a sassy, gum-chewing blonde who, we soon learn, relishes verbal sparring. He's fresh with her but she more than holds her own, and the courtship is under way. As for police work Danny seems like the kind of cop who busies himself swiping fruit from local vendors (which he does, openly and repeatedly), shooting the breeze, and seldom, if ever, catching any criminals. Even when he's promoted to detective and visits a hat shop to purchase a new derby, Danny demonstrates his keen cognitive ability when he buys his own hat back from the milliner.

The film's tone varies from light-hearted to serious, but the developing relationship between Dan and Helen unifies the disparate plot threads and provides a sympathetic hook while the supporting characters' doings drive the story forward. Still, it's the romance that lends *Me and My Gal* its special charm. The dialogue is especially refreshing, for when Dan and Helen exchange flirtatious quips they sound like everyday people, not like actors quoting a script:

DAN

Didn't I meet you somewhere once?

HELEN

I've been somewhere, once.

DAN

That's where I met you.

HELEN

Well, once was enough.

And etc. Perhaps everyday people couldn't keep up the pace Dan and Helen maintain in scene after scene, but their dialog sounds true to life, saucy and funny. It's a pleasure to see Spence paired with a leading lady who can match him quip-for-quip, and a relief to note that he's evolved from the cocky machismo of his *Up the River* and *Goldie* characterizations to a more secure, nuanced masculinity. Danny is decidedly sure of himself, but sensitive to Helen's feelings and not too egotistical to apologize when he realizes he's gone too far. Gradually the Dan-Helen relationship evolves from aggressive sparring to softer, more playful gamesmanship, building up to a delightful proposal scene, just the two of them alone in the restaurant late at night, climaxing when their excited embrace upsets a glass jar of doughnuts. But the movie's comic highlight occurs earlier, when the two of them snuggle on a sofa at her place and Dan mentions that he's recently seen an interesting picture, one where the characters say one thing and then, a moment later, reveal what they're *really* thinking: "Strange something—Strange Innertube." Helen, as it happens, saw the picture too. And then, in a single take lasting almost three minutes, Tracy and Bennett play the scene in the style of Eugene O'Neill's *Strange Interlude*, exchanging friendly but guarded remarks with each other while voice-overs reveal their actual thoughts to the viewer. For instance, Danny says aloud "I feel as though I'd known you for a long, long time" as he muses: "I think I'd better slip this dame a kiss before the old man gets here." It's an unexpected, hilarious sequence, well written and beautifully played by both actors, and one has to wonder if it inspired the similar scene in Woody Allen's *Annie Hall*.

Not all the comic devices in *Me and My Gal* are as offbeat or effective as this one. When a detective named Al is ordered by his boss to follow Dan around and do what he does, the result is a rather tiresome running gag in which Al doggedly mimics Dolan and repeats everything he says. More damaging than this, however, is the deeply irritating contribution of actor Will Stanton, who plays an unnamed drunk in the opening scenes. In Hollywood films of this era there were several comic actors such as Arthur Housman and Jack Norton who specialized in playing "comic relief" drunks, but their bits were usually brief and at least moderately diverting. Stanton is aggressively unfunny and outstays his welcome almost immediately; moreover, his "relief" is entirely unnecessary, for the other performers are considerably more amusing than he is. Tracy scores his first big laugh of the film with a quip aimed at Stanton: on his way out of the diner, Officer Dolan turns to the drunk and offers regards to his wife. When he replies he's not married Dolan retorts: "What a lucky woman." The overuse of Stanton's character in the early scenes weighs down the film, but once he departs—happily, Dolan literally kicks him out of the picture—*Me and My Gal* regains audience goodwill and finds its rhythm.

Several of the major characters are present at the raucous wedding of Helen's sister Kate. The plot proper concerns Kate's extra-marital involvement with a dangerous criminal named Duke (played by George Walsh, the director's brother) who escapes from prison and uses the attic above her apartment as a hideout. When he and his gang break into the bank where Kate works and steal safe deposit boxes—using inside information she supplied—the sequence is played with eerie intensity. Detective Dolan is lamentably slow on the uptake regarding these activities, but belatedly pieces things together when he receives a crucial coded message from Kate's father-in-law, a paralyzed soldier named Sarge (played by pioneering silent film actor Henry B. Walthall). Helen decodes the message and attempts to conceal it from Dan in order to protect her sister, but he figures out what's happening and rushes to Kate's apartment. There he's shot and injured by Duke, but manages to return fire and kill him. In the film's somewhat rushed finale we learn that Dan will recover, that he will collect the bounty on Duke and generously split it with Sarge, and that (less credibly) he will succeed in protecting Kate's reputation. *Me and My Gal* concludes with a cheery coda at Pier 13 as newlyweds Danny and Helen embark for their honeymoon in Bermuda. There's time for a few more quips although gaping holes in the plot are left unresolved, and given the film's basically lightweight nature and the pleasure it has offered we're content to let the heavier matters go. As Dan takes his leave of Sarge and confidently tells him that everything is going to be okay, the line seems to pack a larger meaning, perhaps aimed at contemporary audiences during a deeply troubled time in America. Spence says everything's going to be okay, and we want to believe him.

Where the crime story is concerned it's plain that *Me and My Gal* is only slightly more credible than *Up the River*, but while Ford's spoof of prison flicks seemed to revel in its unreality Walsh created a gritty and strangely appealing milieu that looks lived-in and sounds right. A major share of the credit for the film's success belongs to Tracy and Joan Bennett, a credible screen team who look like they belong together. The two were first paired a year earlier in a forgettable picture called *She Wanted a Millionaire* and hit it off. This time they found a vehicle more worthy of their talent (as they would again in the '50s, as the middle-aged bourgeois parents in *Father of the Bride* and its sequel). Bennett's respect for Tracy lasted a lifetime. In an interview conducted in the mid-1980s she observed that her co-star had a remarkable ability to deliver a line as if he'd just thought of it. This, of course, is a concise definition of what a good actor is supposed to do, and pinpoints one of Tracy's major gifts. She also recalled that although he was willing to walk through a scene to allow the crew to test the lights and practice camera movements he didn't like to rehearse the material itself. He wanted to keep things fresh, and if he was forced to do multiple takes of the same scene he'd grumble: "Bore, bore, bore." By this point in his film career Tracy knew what worked best for him. Under Walsh's direction, with the right script and the right leading lady, he proved that he could play a funny, irascible, even halfway-sexy romantic lead opposite one of Hollywood's most beautiful actresses, and furthermore that he could be amusing without any assistance from a dim-witted male sidekick.

After a one-picture loan-out to Warner Brothers Tracy was back at Fox for another comedy. In an ostensible step backward he was once more teamed with a dim-witted male sidekick—this time sleepy-eyed, mush-mouthed Stuart Erwin—but based on the finished product it appears that the filmmakers in charge may have learned something from Tracy's work with Walsh. Released early in 1933, the little-known *Face in the Sky* is an oddball comedy-drama built around a romance. In most respects it's quite different from *Me and My Gal*, yet, like that film, it's a difficult-to-categorize hybrid, populated with colorful supporting characters and perked by offbeat directorial touches that occasionally border on the bizarre. It's certainly no routine buddy comedy, for Tracy's byplay with Erwin is secondary to the development of his romance with the leading lady, the lovely Marian Nixon.

Spence was cast as a self-confident working man, blessed with a character name that latter-day viewers familiar with *Midnight Cowboy* may find amusing: Tracy (decades ahead of Jon Voight) plays Joe Buck, only this Joe Buck is a commercial artist who paints billboards. Right away we're in unusual territory, outside the realm of Tracy's typical blue collar types. This time he's an *artist*. Lest there be any doubt, it's quickly made clear that Joe is no sissy, nor is he one of those rogues who maintains a garret studio and lures young women in to pose. The film begins with a pair of silent movie-style title cards, written in archly ironic, mock heroic prose: "All over America go brave men—facing fatigue and farmers' daughters—making swamps sweeter—barns brighter—persuading Navajo squaws to wear girdles around their pueblos—and what not—" And then, the punchline: "—the traveling sign painters!" This intro establishes a self-mocking tone while also undercutting any suspicions a viewer might harbor about the red-blooded manhood of our protagonist. Joe is no smoothie who works in a garret, he's a man's man who drives across the unpaved dirt roads of America's rural heartland in his appealingly beat-up truck, with his loyal, simple-minded sidekick Lucky (Erwin). The wording suggests that our hero has had sexual encounters with women he's met along the way, but not sophisticated city girls: he's known farmers' daughters and Indian "squaws," which places Joe squarely in the time-honored company of traveling salesmen, medicine show hawkers, and, of course, actors.

In the opening scene Joe and Lucky are bumping along in their truck, heading to the next job. Lucky expresses doubts that they're advancing professionally, but Joe insists that with hard work and persistence they can reach the top like Napoleon and Julius Caesar, both of whom, he asserts, started out as sign-painters. In any case, he has his own future all planned: he sees himself marching to the altar someday with "a beautiful delicate dame with lots of culture" whose father happens to own a railroad. Their next assignment is to paint a billboard advertising Beauty Magic cosmetics on the side of a large barn owned by the Brown family, a site visible for miles around. Despite Joe's show of bonhomie he and his partner are met with sour hostility from old Nathan Brown and his son Jim. When Joe's fast-talking salesmanship leaves the men unmoved a bribe wins the day, and the guys settle in to work. Soon we learn that old Nathan has a beautiful young "ward," Madge (Marian Nixon). She is sweet and naïve, and resistant to old Brown's intention to marry her off to his horrible son. Perhaps it goes without saying that Madge quickly falls for Joe, who takes a break from his work to talk to her, flirt with her, and deliver inspirational speeches for her benefit, telling her she can be whatever she sets her mind to be. (Fortunately, these speeches were written in tongue-in-cheek mode and delivered accordingly.) It may also go without saying that trouble soon erupts on the farm. Fighting breaks out between the menfolk, and Joe, Madge and Lucky are compelled to flee in their truck with the Browns in hot pursuit across the countryside. After the fugitive threesome enjoy an interlude at a small-town carnival the Browns catch up with them, recapture Madge and haul her back for a forced marriage to Jim. A downhearted Joe and his sidekick return to their employer's headquarters in New York City—high up in the newly completed Empire State Building, no less. Now Joe must paint a "the most beautiful face in the world" to advertise Beauty Magic from the top of a skyscraper. Madge, after some misadventures of her own, makes her way to the big city just in time to witness the unveiling of the billboard featuring her own face in the sky, which brings about her reunion with Joe.

There's no logical reason a film as hokey as this one should be so entertaining; its flaws are certainly easier to identify than its merits. *Face in the Sky* 's allure lies in its earnest approach to material which in other hands might have come off as insufferably old-fashioned and sentimental. The screenwriters knowingly adopted some of the hoariest elements of 19th century stage melodrama and presented them naturalistically. As in those old stage shows the characters are simple, quickly recognizable types playing their parts in a story which serves as little more than a framework for easily predictable events. When Joe announces in his first scene that he has his future all laid out the viewer knows perfectly well that he's in for a surprise that will upset his plans, just as we soon figure out that old man Brown is a mean guy; that Madge will fall for Joe; that Lucky will mess things up; and that ultimately the bad guys will be thwarted and the lovers reunited. If the viewer is familiar with Stu Erwin's work a lamentable level of wit in the verbal repartee can also be expected:

JOE

You're so dumb you don't even know the Civil War is over.

LUCKY

Yeah? Well how would you like to know I knew it two years ago!

But the hokum is redeemed, to an extent, by the sincerity Tracy brings to his scenes with leading lady Marian Nixon, and the surprising tenderness of their relationship. This is a far cry from the urban wise-cracking of *Me and My Gal*, and the chemistry between the leads, while similarly relaxed and natural, differs in virtually every other respect. Madge is an under-age girl from the sticks with a childlike understanding of the world, easily impressed by a confident and seemingly smart guy like Joe. As her affection for him grows Madge nurtures a desperate hope that Joe might be her ticket to a better life. Joe, for his part, tries to suppress his growing attraction to the girl and cling to his plan for the future, i.e. to marry money. Even after Madge flees the Browns' farm and takes up residence in the back of his truck, Joe struggles to maintain a brotherly façade toward her. It crumbles, of course, in a sweet scene between the two of them after they've attended the Centerville carnival. Joe and Madge sit before a campfire by his truck. Joe munches on a popcorn ball and feigns indifference to Madge, which isn't easy since she looks quite fetching, wearing his pajamas. ("You're safe with me," Joe tells her, "But you wouldn't be with a lot of guys, you know." She replies: "I wouldn't wear 'em with a lot of guys.") He tries to be brusque, and orders her to go to bed. She tests him, asking if he'd be upset if she got married. Naaah, he says, that wouldn't upset his plans none. Finally Madge goes for broke. She asks if he's afraid, and puckers up. He kisses her, then pours out his feelings for her in an excited rush of words. The scene builds beautifully, and gives us a look at Tracy's comic technique in action. It isn't a punchline or a sight gag that's laugh-provoking when he plays comedy, it's his readability, the fact that we can tell what he's thinking regardless of what he's saying. We laugh at the sight of this lovesick man trying to act stern and dismissive, maintain his dignity and conceal his feelings, all while munching on a *popcorn ball*.

On paper his dialogue isn't funny, but Tracy's delivery is both funny and real. We're amused by Joe Buck because he's such a lousy liar, but we never get the sense that the man playing him is straining for a laugh. As film critic Charles Champlin noted, Tracy in comic roles or scenes was always an actor acting, never a comedian.

For modern viewers *Face in the Sky* (which was photographed by the great Lee Garmes) is enhanced by elements that would have appeared prosaic and ordinary to 1933 audiences but lend it a rich period flavor to our eyes: the look of rural America in the location shots, a small town store, the carnival, and even the stark, stylized Manhattan of the Fox back-lot. Director Harry Lachman, himself a former painter and magazine illustrator, was apparently inspired by the subject matter to experiment with some artsy effects which, depending on individual taste, may come off as clever and amusing or a tad precious. The most memorable of these touches comes in the New York sequence, when Madge is roaming the streets trying to find Joe. Frightened by the chaos of Times Square, she wanders into a seemingly deserted alley where there are five billboards, each featuring the sort of graphic design Joe paints. As she watches the people in the ads come to life, each offering her food, shelter, or love—except for the last one, which depicts a caped and bearded Satan in a liquor ad. He greets her with mocking laughter, scaring her away in a panic. Ultimately, however, it's neither period charm nor directorial gimmicks but the emotional pull of the central relationship that makes *Face in the Sky* so watchable today. Tracy's rapport with his leading lady overrides his self-consciously windy speechmaking and provides more genuine amusement than any of Stu Erwin's shtick. The "buddy" byplay is mildly funny at best, but the scenes with Miss Nixon demonstrate that by this time Tracy had become as adept as any of his peers at playing a love scene with a comic undercurrent. It reminds us too that his later expert turns in *Woman of the Year* (1942) and *Adam's Rib* (1949) were not conjured up on the spot, but were instead the result of a long and ultimately fruitful apprenticeship.

Released at the low-point of the Depression in January of 1933, *Face in the Sky* did not score a hit with the critics. Some spoke well of the film's early scenes, but it was generally agreed that the urban finale did not live up to the promise of the rural opening. The London *Times*' reviewer praised director Lachman's experimental touches but lamented that this particular vehicle didn't allow him more opportunities to apply them. The dated elements of the story were widely noted, usually with disdain: the New York *Sun*'s John Cohen scornfully compared the film to an old Mary Pickford silent short, implicitly equating "old" with wheezy and tired. Richard Watts of the New York *Herald Tribune* roundly panned the film for its whimsical tone and, in reference to the lead actors, said "it is all just a trifle distressing to find such excellent and otherwise sane performers forced into orgies of proud and unashamed coyness." Watts concluded that the acting was better than the movie deserved, "particularly on the part of the invariably excellent Mr. Tracy."

During the year that followed Tracy appeared in four more dramas, including two of his most memorable movies of the period, William K. Howard's *The Power and the Glory* (from a script by Preston Sturges) and Frank Borzage's *Man's Castle*. His next comedy—or rather, his next film to incorporate comic elements—would be made for Darryl F. Zanuck's newly formed Twentieth Century Pictures, an independent company which released its product through United Artists and would soon merge with Fox, shortly after Tracy's departure from the studio in 1935. Filmed under the working title *Trouble Shooter* and directed by the estimable William Wellman, *Looking for Trouble* was in some respects a retread. Once again, Tracy is a blue-collar worker paired with a dum-dum sidekick (Jack Oakie) driving from job to job in a weathered truck and running afoul of crooks. This time the love story is conventional, and there is no trace of eccentricities such as talking billboards. But in other respects this film is unusual, starting with our heroes' profession: Joe Graham (Tracy) and his partner Casey (Oakie) are telephone linemen, "trouble shooters" whose work thrusts them into a series of surprisingly colorful, exciting situations; more such situations, one suspects, than the average AT&T employee could expect to encounter in a lifetime. Early on, when Graham is offered a promotion to a desk job, he turns it down with the explanation that he prefers "the constant hurry, the ever-lasting change [sic], the unexpected adventures" of being a trouble shooter. He's not kidding about his career: this guy leads an exciting life. Almost immediately, he and his new partner literally stumble into a home where they discover a corpse on the floor. (When Oakie tries to touch it Tracy smacks his hand away, in a very Bud Abbott-like moment.) Joe calls the police and off-handedly reports the discovery of the "stiff," and when the cops arrive it's clear that he and the captain have long since established a joshing acquaintance. Soon the guys are fixing a phone at a swanky nightclub where Joe sees fit to punch someone out; and later still they're sent to investigate a possible wire-tapping scheme. As depicted here a job with the phone company looks like a specialized, action-packed branch of law enforcement.

Although Tracy is once more playing Abbott to a stand-in Costello, a distinct evolution in his screen persona is apparent by this point. Joe Graham is the dominant guy in this partnership and at his company, but he's not a braggart or a tomcat; those traits are now assigned to his clueless sidekick. Jack Oakie's Casey is introduced as an obnoxious, self-infatuated practical joker from Azuza (a town he mentions repeatedly, apparently because it's got a funny name) who claims to be catnip to the ladies, despite ample evidence to the contrary. In his early scenes Casey's foibles are heavily emphasized, and Oakie, never one to downplay, is almost unendurable, but fortunately his character's more unappealing traits are soft-pedaled as the plot kicks in. *Looking for Trouble* is primarily a crime story with the emphasis on action and suspense, and for the most part our hero plays it straight, though he takes advantage of several comic moments opposite his co-star, reacting with exasperation to Casey's irritating pranks. No one could glare like Spencer Tracy, and when he shoots Oakie an angry look we half-expect it to hurt.

Tracy's love interest is Constance Cummings, playing a colleague named Ethel who works as an operator staffing the information switchboard. Joe and Ethel spend much of their time together bickering about his over-investment in his job. In frustration she gets involved with an obvious sleazeball named Dan, who hires her to work as his secretary in a phony real estate office, located next to an investment firm. (Ethel seems almost as clueless as Casey, both in her dealings with the opposite sex and in her naivete concerning Dan's activities.) Dan and his hoodlum cohorts have tapped the adjacent firm's phone line in order to use overheard information to make money on the stock market. But when the crooks learn that $2 million worth of negotiable securities will be kept in the firm's safe for the weekend they put aside their investment scam and plan to break in and take the money. Joe and Casey become involved when the suspected wire-tap is reported, and when they arrive to investigate they are captured and tied-up by the gang. They escape, but through a dubious twist of fate Ethel is accused of murder and, despite flimsy evidence, seems headed for conviction. And so, our heroes Joe and Casey dutifully rush to Long Beach to track down the real culprit and force a confession.

There are several more twists and turns in the plot, topped with a genuinely surprising finale involving a timely earthquake, no doubt suggested by the Long Beach earthquake of March 1933 which killed over a hundred people. So much incident is packed into the tight 77-minute running time it feels like the screenwriters could have easily stretched their tale into fourteen 20-minute chapters and made a serial instead. *Looking for Trouble* is a real popcorn movie, a smoothly handled B-picture that combined all the elements considered necessary to keep the customers satisfied and score a decent success at the box office of its day. Modern viewers may be a little surprised by the occasional risqué quips which were still permissible when this film was released in March of '34, just prior to the imposition of the motion picture industry's stringent Production Code. Tracy, at one point, nearly refers to Dan the crook as a "son of a bitch" and catches the last word just in time;

moments later he salutes this same character with a startling middle-finger gesture. Later still, Casey and Joe are riding in their truck when the topic of Dan's real estate business comes up, and Joe exclaims: "Real estate my ass!" An abrupt car-honk covers the last word, but the line is easily lip-read.

Speaking of lip-reading, an odd footnote to this project can be found in a biography of Tracy by a man named Bill Davidson published in 1987. Jack Oakie told Davidson he was uncomfortable working with Tracy on *Looking for Trouble*. Oakie confided to the author that he was deaf, and had been throughout his prime years in Hollywood, but that he would get through his scenes by carefully reading the lip movements of the other actors. According to Oakie, Tracy mumbled and was difficult to lip-read, which is why he never agreed to work with him again. The story seems hard to credit, especially considering that Spencer Tracy's only son John was deaf from birth, but a 1960 profile of Oakie in *Screen Stories* also mentions that he was deaf in one ear. In any event, the team of Tracy & Oakie played no encores.

Reviewers were generally kind to this film, and some seized the opportunity to concoct phone-related jokes for their critiques. *Looking for Trouble* was "live wire entertainment," a "rampant adaptation of the telephone book" whose producers "certainly turned on the current," etc. etc. Reading the reviews it's surprising to learn that this film was in direct competition with a similar flick about telephone trouble shooters called *I've Got Your Number*, which starred Pat O'Brien and Joan Blondell, released just weeks earlier by Warner Brothers. Who knew there were *two* of these?

1934 proved to be Spencer Tracy's most comedy-packed year. After *Looking for Trouble* he was loaned to MGM to play the leading role of braggart Aubrey Piper in the second movie adaptation of George Kelly's hit play *The Show-Off*. In the 1926 silent version Piper had been portrayed by Ford Sterling, one-time Chief of the Keystone Cops, while in the 1946 Technicolor remake the role was taken by Red Skelton; finally, a 1955 television adaptation would feature Jackie Gleason. The succession of remakes over the decades in each of the newly emerging entertainment media (i.e. from Broadway to silent cinema, talkies, Technicolor, and then TV) places the Aubrey Piper role firmly in the century's popular comic tradition, though it's strictly a matter of personal taste whether seeing the part go from Tracy to Red Skelton represents a move in the right direction. In any event, the loan-out proved to be a significant turning point in Tracy's career, for while he was working on the MGM lot he came to the attention of legendary producer Irving Thalberg, who became interested in luring the actor to MGM on a more permanent basis.

Back at Fox Tracy was assigned to a new comedy, this time one with songs. Tracy himself couldn't carry a tune (as he warned his fellow convicts and other spectators in *Up the River*), but in *Bottoms Up* he is never required to sing or dance, simply to play a fast-talking sharpster who fires off wisecracks between the numbers. Musical films were very much in vogue at this time. After wearing out their welcome with audiences during the first wave of talking pictures, musicals returned to favor in a big way in 1933-4 with the spectacular success of Busby Berkeley's kaleidoscopic extravaganzas for Warner Brothers and the concurrent success of the Fred Astaire/Ginger Rogers series at RKO. Fox would jump into the market with lightweight, escapist musicals featuring Janet Gaynor, Lilian Harvey, and—soon—Shirley Temple and Alice Faye. *Bottoms Up* is a Hollywood satire primarily intended as a showcase for 24 year-old Pat Paterson, a pretty singer from Yorkshire, England who married actor Charles Boyer shortly after filming wrapped. The story owes more than a little to *Once in a Lifetime*, the hit play by Kaufman & Hart that set the pattern for most comedies about moviemaking. Like a lot of the others, this film features an insecure producer who surrounds himself with Yes-men, a matinee idol with a drinking problem, a pretentious, bitchy leading lady who kowtows to foreign nobility, a comic figure who accidentally invades sets and ruins takes, etc. And like a lot of those other films, *Bottoms Up* is an enjoyable exercise in self-parody which is a particular treat for '30s movie buffs.

Tracy plays an egotistical con man known as "Smoothie" King, a down-at-the-heels but unflappable schemer who hangs out with a sidekick, an English crook called Limey Brook (Herbert Mundin). The guys arrive in Hollywood with no place to stay, but plan to invade the lodgings of their old pal Spud Mosco (Sid Silvers), a sheet music peddler. In a bit typical of the film's slightly naughty pre-Code humor Spud is first seen standing on a street corner hawking songs, unaware that the titles he's rattling off combine to form double entendres. Smoothie is determined to take on Hollywood, confident that he'll be running things in the movie capital soon. The trio is sitting at a counter in an all-night diner when they first encounter Wanda (Paterson), a beauty contest winner from Canada rewarded with a couple of bit roles but then cut loose by her studio. Smoothie takes pity on her and offers her a place to stay—Spud's place, that is, which he hasn't yet seen. Spud, as it happens, is staying rent-free in a shack located on an abandoned miniature golf course. It is there that Smoothie and his buddies first hear Wanda sing, and the Big Idea is born: Limey will assume the identity of Lord Brocklehurst, Wanda will pretend to be his daughter, they will stage a grand arrival in the movie capital, and Smoothie will promote his client to stardom. Wanda, for her part, is keen to meet leading man Hal Reed (John Boles), a handsome but hard-drinking star she has long admired. The plan works, to a point: Hollywood's elite fawn over the bogus aristocrats and Wanda is promptly signed by the 4-Star Studio, landing a role opposite Reed in a picture. Unexpectedly, however, Smoothie falls for Wanda and observes in growing dismay as she and Reed become romantically involved. In the end, convinced that Reed has reformed and genuinely loves the girl, Smoothie gallantly steps aside for the lovers.

Enjoyable as it is, *Bottoms Up* certainly never posed any threat to Busby Berkeley or Fred & Ginger. This is a musical that is primarily song-oriented with very little dancing, and although Pat Paterson and John Boles sing well even devotees of the period's music will be hard pressed to recall the tunes introduced here, i.e. "Turn on the Moon," "I'm Throwing My Love Away," "Little Did I Dream," and "Waiting at the Gate for Katie." The last-named song is given the most elaborate showcase, a Berkeley-esque number with a Gay '90s setting featuring dozens of performers, including young Lucille Ball (who is also visible during a party sequence, sitting with Boles). Faithfully following the Berkeley pattern the sequence is supposedly staged for the cameras in a single uninterrupted take despite the physical impossibility of doing so. The number involves several changes of set and costume, creative use of such cinematic devices as rear-projection and freeze-frame, and several amusing sight gags. By an amazing coincidence one of these gags involves models on a billboard who come to life and join in the number, thus making an unintended satirical comment on the limits of creativity in the movie business, specifically at the Fox Studio: if it worked once, hey, why not do it again?

As incongruous as it may be to imagine Tracy in a musical comedy it must be said that he fits in surprisingly well. Perhaps he relished the opportunity to poke fun at Hollywood pretensions, for he delivers his quips with zest and seems to be enjoying himself. Moreover, it's refreshing to find Tracy at the center of a comic trio rather than paired off once again with a single, simple-minded partner. Neither sidekick plays dumb: Herbert Mundin, a pint-sized character actor with a Dickensian face, plays 'Limey' as an eloquent rogue, while Sid 'Spud' Silvers is a streetwise, energetic Bowery Boy type who is usually the butt of the humor but never as dense as Warren Hymer or Stuart Erwin. (Spud also performs a high-speed version of Boles' love song "Turn on the Moon" that turns out to be a highlight; when he's finished, Smoothie remarks: "Isn't he cute?") Limey and Spud are often at odds with each other and require Smoothie to act as referee. Tracy, for his part, easily slips into a nicer version of his wise guy persona, abundantly sure of himself but also gallant towards a young lady down on her luck. When they meet he warns Wanda not to fall in love with him ("They all do") adding firmly that he "ain't the marryin' kind." Coming from almost anyone else this attitude would be insufferably smug, but Tracy manages to make Smoothie endearing. Besides, having seen *Face in the Sky* we're fully expecting an ironic fillip, prepared to see Smoothie eventually march down the aisle with Wanda, but that's where the screenwriters of *Bottoms Up* pulled an unexpected twist, ending this lightweight confection on a surprisingly downbeat note. In the final scene Smoothie, Limey and Spud are back at Spud's rundown quarters at the miniature golf course, listening to radio coverage of the gala premiere of Wanda's debut as a star. The radio announcer invites Hal and Wanda to the microphone and she sends Smoothie a special thank-you, but our trio looks downcast as Smoothie sadly intones: "They make a swell couple. Good thing I wasn't the marryin' kind." Fade out as the music swells...

Fast forward almost thirty years to the final scene of Stanley Kramer's gargantuan comedy *It's a Mad, Mad, Mad, Mad World*. For more than two hours a motley assortment of character types has engaged in an increasingly desperate, greed-crazed scramble after a suitcase full of money. Police Captain C. G. Culpeper, the white-haired gent played by Spencer Tracy, and the man we initially believed represented sanity and reason in this mad-mad world, has turned crooked, grabbed the suitcase away from the others, and fled with the gang nipping at his heels. The chase winds up on a rickety fire escape dangling from a condemned building, as one by one the guys (or, to be more precise, their stunt doubles) are flung every which way: onto treetops, through awnings, into ponds, onto electrified telephone wires, and elsewhere. Culpeper, the last to be flung, is hurled through the roof of a pet store, lands in the corner and is discovered having his face licked by a Great Dane. (It's difficult, but not impossible, to imagine *Me and My Gal*'s Danny Dolan winding up like this.) Fade out, and fade in on the final scene: the setting is a hospital intensive care unit. As in animated cartoons, none of the mayhem we've just witnessed has resulted in actual death or dismemberment, merely in comic-looking *discomfort*. Sid Caesar, Buddy Hackett, Eddie "Rochester" Anderson, and the rest of the gang are all in traction, wrapped in swaths of bandages like mummies, hoisted into comically undignified positions. And squarely in their midst is Culpeper. Rather startlingly, the old man has been put in a crucifixion-like posture, arms outstretched. He looks miserable. The character played by Phil Silvers says that, whatever may happen to them, he hopes that what happens to Culpeper is *worse*. The latter replies that he needn't worry about that: his pension has been revoked, his wife is divorcing him, their daughter is having her name changed, etc., and furthermore, when they're all tried for their crimes the judge is likely to single him out for especially severe punishment. He adds:

CULPEPER

I'd like to think that sometime, maybe ten or twenty years from now, there'll be something I can laugh at. Anything...

As if on cue, Mrs. Marcus (played by Ethel Merman) strides into the ward. From her first scene this woman has been firmly, unmistakably established as the Mother-in-Law from Hell, an angry harpy who hectors the males whether they are her in-laws or not, and generally makes a nuisance of herself. As she launches into another tirade aimed at male stupidity, Mrs. Marcus (or, rather, a stuntman in drag) slips on a banana peel and lands squarely on her butt. The ward erupts in raucous laughter. Culpeper looks on, unsmiling at first, but then he grins and joins in with the others, laughing heartily, as Kramer's long and exhausting marathon comes to a close.

And here too, Spencer Tracy's career in comedy came to a close. His final speech is poignant, given his character's dire circumstances, and doubly poignant in a larger sense if the viewer is aware that he died less than four years after shooting this scene. He would make one more film at the very end of his life, but although *Guess Who's Coming to Dinner* has its comic moments it was primarily a drama which addressed the serious social issue of interracial marriage. *It's a Mad, Mad, Mad, Mad World* marked Tracy's last full-fledged comedy role, and while it's unfortunate he didn't have wittier material to work with my reaction at that long-ago matinee was misplaced: Tracy did indeed belong in comedy, had extensive experience with it, and was adept at playing it. That he was a difficult, troubled man off-screen is widely known, but not inconsistent with the fact that he possessed a sharp sense of humor. In conversation he often expressed amusement at life's incongruities and absurdities. As an actor he was able to draw from a well-honed repertoire of comic devices dating back to his earliest stage appearances, when it was noted that his delivery of such simple lines as "The hell it is!" could bring the house down. "He was never trying to be funny," observed actor Robert Wagner, who appeared in two movies with Tracy and became a sort of surrogate son to the older man. "He was always in character, it was always inside—this interior kind of life that he had. He was able to let it out, and that film just drank it up."

The strenuous machismo of his earliest appearances doesn't wear well, but in his better comic turns Tracy imbued his performances with a likeable Regular Guy quality, self-satisfied without being too smug, though he sometimes has to be taken down a peg or two. Like Cagney, we enjoy him most when he's a bit cocky and kind of a wiseacre, and when the elements come together the result is a well observed, recognizably human characterization. Tracy could deliver a wisecrack with the best of 'em, but more importantly he could breathe life into his (sometimes two-dimensional) roles, find humor in a script's situations and achieve a warm rapport with his co-stars, even when the trappings of a particular project were patently unreal or downright silly, as they occasionally were. Spencer Tracy earned his place in Stanley Kramer's super-duper comedy extravaganza, whether or not one believes the final product was worthy of him. He may not have been a comedian per se, but when Tracy played comedy he did so with élan and usually made the material he was given sound more crisp and funny than it actually was. In the course of his career he may well have scored more big laughs than any "serious" actor of his era.

Sources

Books

Davidson, Bill. *Spencer Tracy: Tragic Idol*. New York: E. P. Dutton, 1987.
Deschner, Donald. *The Films of Spencer Tracy*. New York: Citadel Press, 1968.
Newquist, Roy. *A Special Kind of Magic*. Rand McNally & Company, 1967.
Swindell, Larry. *Spencer Tracy: A Biography*. New York: World Publishing Company, 1969.
Tozzi, Romano. *Spencer Tracy*. New York: Pyramid Books, 1973.

Video

The Spencer Tracy Legacy: A Tribute by Katharine Hepburn. Directed by David Heeley. MGM/UA Television, 1986.

UP THE RIVER

with
SPENCER TRACY   CLAIRE LUCE
Warren Hymer   Humphrey Bogart
William Collier, Sr.   Joan ("Cherie") Lawes

Story by Maurine Watkins

Directed by
JOHN FORD

A FLOCK of birds in an ungilded cage — having more fun than the law allows. That's "UP THE RIVER."

Just a bunch of irregular fellows — getting their comedy degrees in the College of Hard Locks. For rowdy, rough and ready wit, for quick getaway and quick come-back, this is the season's best.

"Up the River" is unique. It sets its own standards and laughs up to them.

The story's a riot. The acting's a panic. The effect is devastating. You'll laugh inside and out!

Joan ("Cherie") Lawes, the little daughter of Warden Lawes of Sing Sing makes her screen debut in "Up the River". She can't keep a straight face — and who can blame her? Take a trip "Up the River" yourself. You'll laugh all the way.

Contributors

Jeremy Bond knew he had to write about movies when he found himself wading through titles of obscure silents from the 1910s and memorizing eight decades of Academy Award winners. His favorites range from avant-garde shorts to the European New Wave, but he has a soft spot for classic Hollywood, particularly the pre-Code era. In his other life, Bond has a master's degree in journalism from the University of Maryland and has covered the federal government from inside the Beltway. He is a freelance writer and book editor in southern New England, where parenthood has given him a newfound appreciation for Disney movies.

Shelly Brisbin has worked as a technology journalist for 20 years, and has been a fan of Spencer Tracy's work for nearly 30 years. She is currently editor-in-chief of *Blogger & Podcaster Magazine,* and is the author of 12 books, and hundreds of articles on computer technology and applications. Her specialties include the Macintosh and networking technology. She hosts several podcasts, including *The Tracy-Hepburn Podcast* (tracyhepburnpodcast.com), a free audio program for fans of Spencer Tracy and Katharine Hepburn. She lives in Austin, Texas with her husband and assorted cats.

A freelance writer, editor, and amateur film buff, *Sean Connell* has been writing almost as long as he's been watching movies. A fan of all genres, he has a special fondness for old black and white noir films and the novels that inspired them. As a published writer, he's written on diverse topics ranging from social commentary to comparative studies. He currently lives and works in the New England area.

Thomas Doherty is a professor of American Studies at Brandeis University and the author of *Hollywood's Censor: Joseph. I. Breen and the Production Code Administration* (Columbia University Press, 2007).

James Fisher, Professor and Head of the Theatre Department at the University of North Carolina at Greensboro, is the author of *Spencer Tracy: A Bio-Bibliography* (Greenwood Press, 1994). He has also authored the forthcoming *Understanding Tony Kushner* (University of South Carolina Press, 2008), *The Historical Dictionary of the American Theater: Modernism, 1880-1930* (with Felicia Hardison Londré; Scarecrow Press, 2007), *The Theater of Tony Kushner: Living Past Hope* (Routledge, 2001), *The Theatre of Yesterday and Tomorrow: Commedia dell'arte on the Modern Stage* (Mellen, 1992), and bio-bibliographies of Al Jolson and Eddie Cantor, both for Greenwood Press. He has edited several volumes, including the forthcoming *"We Will Be Citizens": Gay and Lesbian Theatre and Drama: New Essays* (McFarland, 2008), *Tony Kushner: New Essays on the Art and Politics of the Plays* (McFarland, 2006), and six volumes of *The Puppetry Yearbook* (Mellen). Along with numerous publications, he is also a director and actor, has held several research fellowships, and is book review editor for *Broadside*, the publication of the Theatre Library Association. In 2007, Fisher received the Betty Jean Jones Award for Excellence in the Teaching of American Theatre from the American Theatre and Drama Society.

Cinzi Lavin is a humor columnist and essayist whose works have appeared in *The Danbury News-Times*, *The Agenda*, *IQ Magazine*, *The Soundview News*, and *The Scene Journal*. Born in Manhattan and educated in Texas, her postgraduate study focused on dramatic theory and criticism. After college, she ran off and joined a comedy troupe and later worked as an actress in Dallas. An accomplished musician, she has performed at Madison Square Garden and taught at several private music schools across the U.S. She lives in Hull, Massachusetts with three spoiled houseplants who prefer to remain anonymous.

Brenda Loew's love affair with the silver screen dates back to her great uncle who captivated her with stories of Hollywood royalty (Loew owned the Loew's chain of movie theaters as well as Bay State Raceway in Foxboro, MA and the famous Latin Quarter nightclubs in NYC, Boston and Palm Island.) While maintaining the family connection to show business as President of the New England Vintage Film Society, Inc, Brenda is a writer, lecturer, public access TV producer and entrepreneur in Newton, MA.

Charlie Morrow spent the '80s writing and directing radio plays for WBAI in New York City. He later developed some of these works into stage pieces, and one, *The Ministry of Progress*, was turned into an Off-Broadway musical and produced at the Jane Street Theatre in 2004. Charlie's one-act version of that play has been staged in Indiana, Kentucky, and Florida. Meanwhile, he has been a longtime staff member with the Theatre on Film and Tape Archive, located at the Performing Arts Library at Lincoln Center, and has written articles on theater and cinema. He submits mini-essays on classic films to the Internet Movie Database under the Nom de Internet wmorrow59.

William Russo, Professor of Film Studies and Literature at Curry College in Milton, Massachusetts, has written several books on movie subjects. With film star and Emmy-winning writer, Jan Merlin, Russo wrote *MGM Makes Boys Town* with a focus on Spencer Tracy. His other books include *Troubles in a Golden Eye*, a look at Marlon Brando, and *Riding James Kirkwood's Pony*, an examination of how Pulitzer Prize author Kirkwood turned his boyhood in Hollywood memoir into a movie, play, and novel.

Paul Sherman is the author of *Big Screen Boston: From Mystery Street to The Departed and Beyond*. He is a past president of the Boston Society of Film Critics.

Eric Shoag, a Boston-based freelance writer, received his Bachelor's Degree in Communications and Film from Boston University. He attended the Art Institute of Boston, has been a teacher and independent bookstore manager and currently serves on the Board of the New England Vintage Film Society. Eric is working on a book analyzing the Woody Allen films of the 1990s.

Sparkling with Laughs and Songs and
Three smart flim-flammers help a homeless little girl to love and happiness by making monkeys out of Hollywood's big movie moguls!... A love story to make life worth living, bristling with roaring laughter and rhythmic with singable, lovable song hits!
Made by the producers of "Sunny Side Up"—and surpassing it in everything!
BOTTOMS UP
A FOX PICTURE
with
SPENCER TRACY
"PAT" PATERSON
JOHN BOLES
HERBERT MUNDIN
SID SILVERS
HARRY GREEN
THELMA TODD
PRODUCED BY B. G. DESYLVA
DIRECTED BY DAVID BUTLER
Copyright MCMXXXIV Fox Film Corp. Made in U.S.A.

Printed in the United States
142642LV00002B/7/P